Praise for Dr. David
and *Living Beyond*

"Written by an outstanding and compassionate physician, this remarkable book is destined to become a classic in the field of behavioral medicine and expand the frontiers of knowledge about mind/body interactions and the healing effects of linking our lives with others. *Living Beyond Limits* is an enormous source of help and hope for better lives to the millions of Americans and their families who are facing a life-threatening illness."

—Susan J. Blumenthal, M.D., M.P.A., Chief
Behavioral Medicine Research Branch,
National Institute of Health
Clinical Professor of Psychiatry
Georgetown University of Medicine

"A lucid, inspiring vision of how to live, endure, and triumph beyond limits. This book is not just for the sick who are facing the limitations of their illness but for all of us who must face the reality of our own mortality."

—Irvin Yalom, M.D.
Author of *Love's Executioner*
and *When Nietzsche Wept*

"Dr. Spiegel's book is going to be of enormous benefit to many people with cancer and other life-threatening illnesses to help them better adapt and cope with that challenge in their life."

—Fawzy I. Fawzy, M.D.
Department of Psychiatry
and Biobehavioral Sciences
University of California at Los Angeles

David Spiegel, M.D.

Living Beyond Limits

Fawcett Columbine • New York

A Fawcett Columbine Book
Published by Ballantine Books

Copyright © 1993 by David Spiegel, M.D.

All rights reserved under International and Pan-American Copyright Conventions.
Published in the United States by Ballantine Books, a division of Random House,
Inc., New York, and simultaneously in Canada by Random House of Canada
Limited, Toronto.

This edition published by arrangement with Times Books, a division of Random
House, Inc.

Grateful acknowledgment is made to Universal Press Syndicate for permission to
reprint one HERMAN cartoon. Copyright © 1977 by Jim Unger. All rights
reserved. Reprinted by permission of Universal Press Syndicate.

Library of Congress Catalog Card Number: 94-94253

ISBN: 0-449-90940-9

Cover design by Georgia Morrissey
Cover photo © Kazuhiko Nakano/Photonica

Manufactured in the United States of America

First Ballantine Books Edition: October 1994

10 9 8 7 6 5 4 3 2 1

Contents

Preface

eauty and tragedy are inextricably interwoven in people with serious illness. Those with diseases such as cancer can be both heroic and frightened, generous and selfish; they can transcend death and be conquered by it. They can indeed "live beyond limits." Cancer and other serious illnesses impose limits that are undeniable, but that challenge us to live better in the face of those limits. I have become convinced through twenty years of clinical work and research that the best way to face the threat of serious illness is to look it right in the eye, to face the worst rather than simply to hope for the best. Modern medicine has largely focused on the physical side of the problem, aggressively attacking the illness, often ignoring the person who has it. On the other hand, "alternative medicine" has focused on the person rather than the disease, insisting that it is simply "mind over matter": Fix it in your mind and the physical problem will take care of itself. This approach is equally wrong. It is the *interaction* of mind and body that matters. Coping with illness is both a mental and a physical process. We live better not by denying or avoiding illness, but by bringing our full resources to bear in facing the situation and living beyond it. Serious illness is a threat to life. A diagnosis of disease such as cancer seems at first to bring an end to life, but what it really does is change it. There is life after cancer and heart disease. What we think and feel is relevant to the course of disease, but it does not provide us with straightforward control over it either. In this book I describe what I have learned from cancer patients about how one can live fully in the face of illness, how mind and body can work together, how facing dying can intensify living.

I was trained as a psychiatrist, a physician specializing in disorders of the mind and brain. How did I get beyond my own limits and wander into this distressing but rewarding line of work? I have always been fascinated by the "mind/body problem"—how our thoughts, emotional states, and intentions get translated into physical actions.

As a college student at Yale in 1963, I began reading philosophy, intent on understanding how we know things at all. A series of patient but argumentative teachers convinced me that there is no "pure" knowledge. We can perceive things only through the apparatus we are given, which has quirks that inevitably color what we can know. I also became convinced through reading existential philosophers such as Kierkegaard and Husserl that the power to make relationships—among ideas, perceptions, people—is uniquely and fundamentally human. I was tempted to become a philosopher, which seemed like one of life's highest callings. However, teaching freshmen Plato seemed far less exciting, and I was drawn to the body half of the mind/body problem. I felt that to really understand how we think, I had to know something about the body in which we do it. So I became a physician instead of a metaphysician.

In college I had enjoyed dancing with theories; in medical school at Harvard I swam in facts. The many interacting systems of the body —neurological, circulatory, endocrine, etc.—were extraordinarily complex, yet elegant. They regulated themselves and one another. There were intricate feedback systems that assured just the right production of hormones, neurotransmitters, and proteins. And yet what distinguished people from other animals was the massive nervous system sitting at the top of the body, allowing for prodigious memory, planning, and intentional activity. I found myself drawn to the study of how that system as a whole functioned—and malfunctioned.

I had the good fortune to take a course on hypnosis in medical school with Dr. Thomas Hackett, then chief of psychiatry at Massachusetts General Hospital. We explored this fascinating phenomenon, discovering that it seemed to provide unusual control over physical processes. Hypnosis was not a new subject to me, since my father has been a pioneer of the field of medical hypnosis since World War II, when he used it to help soldiers in combat. But I couldn't pursue something in depth because my father liked it, of course. I had to find out for myself, so I did.

I will never forget Caroline. I was a medical student on rotation at Children's Hospital in Boston in 1969. I was told at the nursing station that my next patient had come to the ward in status asthmaticus—that is, she was having an acute asthma attack that would not respond to medication. This information made me so nervous that I forgot her room number as I set out to examine her, but located her by following the sound of her wheezing down the hall. I found the sixteen-year-old redhead sitting bolt upright in her bed, struggling for breath. Her knuckles were white and she was unable to lie back. Her mother stood near the bed wringing her hands. Caroline had been hospitalized during each of the past three months. I wondered what to do. Since she had been unresponsive to medication, the only other treatment available at the time was the induction of general anesthesia, which carried risks of its own. Not knowing what else to do, and fresh from my hypnosis course, I blurted out: "Would you like to learn an exercise to help with your breathing?" "Yes," Caroline gasped. I quickly taught her how to enter a hypnotic state and then told her, "Each breath you take will be a little bit easier and deeper." I do not know who was more surprised, she or I, when after a few minutes she was indeed breathing more easily. Her knuckles were no longer white, she was able to lie back in bed, and her mother stopped wringing her hands.

Considerable turmoil ensued. The nursing supervisor was informed that I had hypnotized a patient, and she filed a complaint to the effect that I had violated a (nonexistent) Massachusetts law by hypnotizing a minor without parental consent (although her mother had been in the room). I was told to stop using hypnosis, because when I went off the rotation, I would not be able to continue its use with the patient. This order came down despite the fact that Caroline was learning to use it on her own and was practicing regularly, to good effect. I said that I would not imply to my patient that the hypnosis was harmful by stopping its use, but accepted that my supervisors were free to take me off the case. Finally, the intern on my rotation had a brilliant idea: "Let's ask the patient," she suggested. We did, and we all agreed to continue practicing hypnosis. Caroline had one subsequent hospitalization a month later, but none for years afterward, during which time she studied to become a respiratory therapist and help other asthmatics. I figured that any technique that could help a patient to that extent, shake up the health care staff, and violate a nonexistent Massachusetts law had to be worth looking into.

The ability to use this altered state of concentration so quickly to show a patient how to better control a serious physical problem seemed to me a precious resource. I also found that I could make a difference to many patients through the use of hypnosis to control the symptoms of their illness. No one else was likely to think of it. Many of my classmates were better versed in new drug and surgical interventions; I seemed to be of most help by introducing this complementary approach.

After medical school in 1971, both because of (and despite) the fact that both of my parents are psychiatrists, I entered the same field. We would joke that they told me I could be any kind of psychiatrist I wanted to be. In spite of the fact that it seemed like destiny—and I believe in self-determination—I identified with my parents' fascination with emotional problems and how to treat them through psychotherapy. I sought motive and meaning everywhere, having inherited a cock-eyed optimism that people could negotiate even the deepest problems if they talk, think, and feel enough about them. In my psychiatric residency at the Massachusetts Mental Health Center I learned to tolerate uncomfortable feelings, to let people talk and to listen. This meant mastering my own internal discomfort, my desire to "do something" when a patient cried or got angry. I learned from supervisors like Dr. Elvin Semrad and Dr. Nick Avery that there is something therapeutic about giving vent to such strong feelings and that doing so could help people develop and consolidate new points of view about their problems. It appeared to me that being able to express how upset you were freed you to create a new relationship to the issue, to look at it differently, and to see yourself standing beside it, allowing for a different way of acting on it.

I then did a fellowship at the Laboratory of Community Psychiatry at Harvard with Professor Gerald Caplan. He emphasized the concept of healing factors in the community: networks of "kith and kin" that helped people cope with mental and physical illness. I began to study self-help groups, noting that there was something therapeutic about "going public" with a problem. Many people seemed to start the process of recovery by revealing their problem in a group with others who had a similar problem (the classic example is Alcoholics Anonymous, but there are many others). I studied a group called Action for Prevention of Burn Injuries to Children, founded by Andrew McGuire, a man who himself had been burned as a child. He, and many in his group, had at first been reticent to talk about their injuries. However, they felt better and got closer to others as they did so. Later, the participants turned outward and became involved in public and political action, eventually inspiring laws requiring that children's sleepwear be flame retardant. They went from denying that there was a problem, to admitting it, to insisting that something good come of it. Being burned is a tragedy, but if as a result of it you can help others who have been burned and prevent others from being burned, you have injected enormous meaning into that personal tragedy. And this allows you to feel better in large part *because you can deepen your relationships with other people, by using your tragic experience to help others*. The therapeutic aspect of this has been called the "Helper-Therapy Principle" by sociologist Frank Riessman. Using your own experience to help other people not only gives them a needed resource, but allows you to feel better about yourself.

When I began my academic career at Stanford after my training, I had the good fortune to begin working with Professor Irvin Yalom, a noted psychiatrist and expert on group psychotherapy. He had written the standard textbook in that field and was developing an interest in existential psychiatry. This approach to psychotherapy emphasizes the importance of cutting through falseness and our own tendency to see other people as objects to be manipulated rather than as beings free to make choices and to change. The task of authentically being with other people, getting beyond two-dimensional views of one another, is an important part of existential psychotherapy. The therapist and patient work on examining and removing obstacles to greater intimacy in their doctor/patient relationship, as well as in the patient's other relationships. However, these obstacles are not analyzed, as they are in traditional psychoanalysis, in terms of past patterns acquired at mother's or father's knee. Rather they are interpreted in terms of the future—concerns about death, isolation, freedom, and meaning in the world—as Dr. Yalom defined it in his textbook, *Existential Psychotherapy*.

Professor Yalom had decided to study these themes by working with women who in a very real sense faced their own mortality, since they had advanced breast cancer that had spread to other parts of their bodies. The question these women faced was less *whether* the illness would kill them but *when*. Dr. Yalom kindly invited me to become involved with the project, and I had the exciting opportunity to colead a support group with him and other therapists. This gave me a chance to put my ideas about relating, venting feelings, and controlling physical symptoms into action.

I had to face some tough questions: Could I be of help to these women who were so physically ill? Could I tolerate my own feelings of helplessness and sadness when they died? Could I face my own vulnerabilities and fears of dying? In fact, these women asked me quite directly whether I was afraid of dying, and I had to answer, in truth, "yes." But this set me on a path to examining the boundaries of mind and body at the most difficult time, when the mind is struggling to accept the failure of the body.

Dr. Yalom also invited me to participate in a research project involving these women in addition to coleading some of the groups with him, and I jumped at the chance. We spent three years in the late seventies recruiting eighty-six women with advanced breast cancer, assigning them randomly either to our experimental support group or to routine cancer care, conducting the treatment, and evaluating the results. We met weekly with those in the experimental group. The group therapy consisted of sharing their fears, planning means of coping with the threat of death, grieving the losses of members, teaching the women self-hypnosis to control their pain, and learning to savor the preciousness of life. We did not deny the threat of death, but rather faced it openly and together. This direct approach to the worst somehow freed us to enjoy the best as well, and there was as much laughter as crying in the groups. (I discuss this study in more detail in chapters 5 and 6.)

After the study ended (at least we thought it had ended), we evaluated our patients' moods, styles of coping, family interactions, and levels of pain. As we had hoped, our experimental treatment had been of help. Despite the fact that one quarter of the women in our sample had died, the mood of the patients in our support group had improved. They were demonstrably less anxious and depressed than the patients who had received only routine care. In addition, our treatment patients had only half as much pain by the end of the year as the control group. Buoyed by these positive if not entirely surprising results, we published them in psychiatric journals in the early 1980s and went on to other studies.

I had been troubled for some time by the wish-away-your-illness approaches of many workers in so-called alternative medicine, since the presumed and illusory power to control illness in your mind carries with it the inevitable responsibility for its progression. I believed that these approaches made people with cancer feel unnecessarily guilty if their disease got worse after their efforts at "positive thinking." If they got sicker, it implied not the simple physical advance of a disease, but a failure of the will. As disappointed as I was with the reticence of the medical profession to pay sufficient attention to the emotional aspects of cancer, I was equally concerned about the tendency of those in alternative medicine to claim too much for their approach, thereby blaming the victim for its inevitable failure. I was also wary of the lack of scientifically controlled experiments to test more claims. In the mid-1980s it occurred to me that I could easily disprove the idea. All I needed to do was find out what had happened to the women in our earlier study—how many had died and when. If I could show that despite the positive emotional help we gave them there was no difference in the progression of their disease, the issue of "mind over body" would be put to rest. I could publish a useful paper with a negative result.

As I describe later in this book, the results were surprising to everyone: to me, to traditional physicians, and to the alternative medicine community. My colleagues and I found that there was indeed a difference between the survival time of the women who had been in our support groups and those who had not. The women in the experimental group lived on average twice as long from the time they entered the study as the other women. The group therapy seemed to have extended the lives of the women in the experimental group by eighteen months—an amount that was both statistically and clinically significant. That a psychotherapeutic treatment could seem to have such a powerful medical effect was astonishing to me, and surprising to many physicians, although some commented that there are many "intangibles" that seem to affect the way different people with cancer manage their illness. It was also surprising to the alternative cancer treatment community, since our approach was radically different. Rather than focusing on wishing away cancer, we urged patients to face it. Rather than denying dying, we confronted its inevitability and used that fact to help women reorder their life priorities. Rather than focusing on living longer, we helped these women focus on living better. Nonetheless, many of these women wound up living longer as well.

Since the study was published in 1989 in *The Lancet,* a highly regarded medical journal, I have been invited to lecture in many corners of the world, and research groups in the United States, Canada, and Europe are conducting similar research. In our own laboratory we have begun new experiments to attempt to confirm our results and to learn more about how the mind and body interact during what we call Supportive/Expressive group therapy. The women in our studies have taught us something very valuable about living and dying, which they wanted me to share with you. I am grateful to these remarkable women, who dealt with their lives and deaths with tremendous dignity, grace, and wit, and I hope that their wisdom will help you to live beyond limits.

Acknowledgments

I thank the remarkable group of women and men who allowed us to study and share their living and dying with cancer. I am deeply grateful to the many patients, their families, and physicians, including those in our current research projects, who are woven into the pages of this book. In the midst of their own personal crisis they have given generously of their time, feelings, and concern in the hopes that they will be of help to others. It would make them very happy to know that they had helped readers in some way.

I received invaluable advice about the writing of this book from a number of people: Frank Conroy, John Freund, M.D., M.B.A., and Irvin Yalom, M.D. I am also grateful to many individuals who read and critiqued earlier drafts of this manuscript: Helen M. Blau, Ph.D., George and Gertrude Blau, Ann Spiegel Clark, M.D., Marcia Greenleaf, Ph.D., Herbert Spiegel, M.D., Natalie Shainess, M.D., Sandra D. Allen, Lorna Barati, Judy Christiansen, Ramona Jenrick, Sheila Moore, Lucy Swatt, Marianne Pomeroy, Bette R. Ritchey, Jean Martin-Vegue, Ann Arvin, M.D., Barbara Ballinger, M.D., Robert Carlson, M.D., Catherine Classen, Ph.D., Susan Diamond, M.S.W., Pat Fobair, M.S.W., Jessie Gruman, Ph.D., Kaye Hermanson, Ph.D., Cheryl Koopman, Ph.D., Elaine Miller, R.N., and James Spira, M.P.H., Ph.D. I thank Daniel Goleman, Ph.D., for invaluable editorial encouragement. Betsy Rapoport provided outstanding editorial support: the perfect blend of enthusiasm and criticism. I would like to thank Esther Newberg for her expertise and support in transforming this book from an idea to a reality.

I also thank my collaborators in this research: Irvin Yalom, M.D., who started the original support groups reported on here and first invited me to join him in the research; together with Joan Bloom, Ph.D., at the University of California at Berkeley; Helena Kraemer, Ph.D., a superb biostatistician at Stanford who guided our statistical analyses; Ellen Gottheil, M.D., a postdoctoral fellow and psychiatrist, Laiani Kuspa, and Corky Rey, M.D., all of whom assisted in the data analysis.

I am fortunate to have a dedicated, bright, compassionate and highly skilled team of researchers working on our current projects. Elaine Miller, R.N., has been in charge of recruiting and testing new patients entering our studies, along with Jane Benson and Leslie Smithline. Postdoctoral fellows Barbara Ballinger, M.D., Catherine Classen, Ph.D., Kaye Hermanson, Ph.D., Abdoline Soleman, M.D., and Jim Spira, M.P.H., Ph.D., have worked long hours and been thoughtful and sensitive to our patients' needs as well as to the quality of the research. Cheryl Koopman, Ph.D., has supervised research in the lab, and Stanford medical students Lisa Bernard, Dierdre Pearl, and Amitava Biswas, along with Bita Nouriami and Catherine Byers-White, have worked for many years on our videotape recordings, physiological measures, and evaluation of the therapy program. Helen Abrahamson, M.A., provided devoted administrative support. Reggie Kriss, Ph.D., was research coordinator and a cotherapist in the original study, along with Susan Weissberg, M.S.W. Pat Fobair, M.S.W., has been a collaborator in this line of research for many years, and is a superb therapist. All are sensitive and thoughtful therapists and collaborators, devoted to their patients and to the development of ways to help them.

The patients, families, and research staff in our current research program are grateful to Bill Moyers and the team of David Grubin

Productions, including especially Pamela Mason-Wagner and Kate Tapley, for their thoughtful, emotionally sensitive, and caring work with us in producing their excellent "Healing and the Mind" series. Many of the issues in this book are beautifully portrayed in the program and discussed in the accompanying book by Bill Moyers.

Generous and welcome financial support has made this research possible. I am indebted to the Alan and Laraine Fisher Foundation, The American Cancer Research Fund, the John D. and Catherine T. MacArthur Foundation, the Linda S. Pollin Foundation, the Nathan S. Cummings Foundation, the Fetzer Institute, the Institute for Noetic Sciences, the American Cancer Society, the National Institute of Mental Health and the National Cancer Institute for their support. I thank them for their concrete expression of belief in the importance of this line of research and our approach to studying it. I also thank the Rockefeller Foundation and the Bellagio Study Center for providing a beautiful setting in which I wrote the initial draft of this book.

Finally, I want to thank my family for putting up with my absorption in this book: my beautiful and brilliant wife, Helen Blau, my toughest critic and best friend, and my wonderful children, Daniel and Julia, who remind me constantly of the joy and meaning in life, and who encouraged me to "go for it." My parents, Drs. Natalie Shainess and Herbert Spiegel, both psychiatrists and psychoanalysts, have inspired me with a fascination for the field and imbued me with the sense of caring which is the foundation of good doctoring.

LIVING BEYOND LIMITS

Introduction

Death is so interwoven with life that we often fail to notice it when it is staring us in the face. We think of life as an infinite force interrupted by occasional, unwanted intrusions. We treat death as though it were a defect in the organism, rather than a fundamental part of its life cycle. Yet no matter how intuitive and brilliant our advances in medical treatment become, the death rate is and always will be one per person.

I was staring at an idyllic, life-enhancing scene. The gentle swells in the Monterey Bay were framed by graceful sculptured cypress trees. Three pelicans flew in a line barely inches above the water. The scene was peaceful and quiet, and yet somehow I found my thoughts veering toward death. What were these pelicans doing, after all? They were searching for fish that they could kill and eat to sustain their own lives. Indeed, the huge, gentle ocean was filled with creatures who were killing and eating one another. I was reminded of one of my breast cancer patients, who likened herself to a swan. On the surface, she appeared to be calmly gliding through life; beneath the water she was paddling furiously. Similarly, under the gently rolling surface of the ocean lay an ongoing struggle between life and death.

I began to realize why viewing scenes like this is so peaceful. The sense of serenity we feel when we watch the waves roll in comes not just from an appreciation of how something can change subtly and yet remain the same—like a fire in a fireplace—but, like the fire, that ocean is a form of destructiveness tamed, and so this scene represents a transient victory over death. Surveying this silent battleground, I could feel even more alive because the deadly forces that struggle beneath it had not yet consumed me. I came to feel that the comfort I took in the scene was not so much from my watching the ocean, but from the ocean watching me: I stood alone in the face of the overwhelming fact that life and death are intertwined, but I had not yet been sucked beneath the surface. Sometimes I think that life is a never-ending struggle against gravity: an ultimately vain attempt to keep our body above the ground. Sometimes we fail in pieces; sometimes all at once. Nonetheless, there are times when facing all of this lifts one up, rather than pulls one down.

My goal in working with people who are dying is not to help them wish away death, trivialize it, or turn its conquest into a project like building a house or taking a long journey. On the other hand, turning one's face away from death or quietly succumbing in despair is no solution either. The aim is to help people tolerate their anxiety, fear, sadness, and grief enough that they can make the most out of whatever remains of their lives. I want to help them enjoy the view rather than be overwhelmed and demoralized by it. Patricia, a woman in our support group, told of driving along and suddenly hearing Bach's "Toccata and Fugue" come on the radio, and thinking, "how lucky I am to be alive and able to enjoy this beautiful music."

Cancer is, sadly, a major and growing problem. In any given year, 5 million Americans have cancer. And at one time or another during our lifetime, 30 percent of us will struggle with the disease. Cancer is the second leading killer of Americans, after heart and vascular disease. Furthermore, it is not just a problem of the developed world. Worldwide, as birthrates fall, infectious diseases and malnutrition are reduced, and economies develop, life expectancy is increasing, especially in developing countries. This means that more of us are living long enough to fall prey to chronic illnesses such as cancer and heart disease. The longer we live, the more likely we are to experience the diseases common to old age, including cancer.

I've written this book not only to help you take control of your cancer or other serious illness, but to help you enhance the quality of life by living beyond limits. Of course, we all have a limit—but we don't have to abandon ourselves to hopelessness. Yet if we ignore that limit, we lose in another way, forgoing the chance to take what control we can of the lives we live before we die. Even in those turbulent moments when illness forces us to face our limitations, the fact that we do not control death does not mean we cannot control how we live in the face of dying. As psychiatrist Irvin Yalom said, "The fact of death destroys life; the thought of death gives us life."

"Basically, there's nothing wrong with you that what's right with you can't cure."

Drawing by D. Reilly; © 1993 The New Yorker Magazine, Inc.

Helplessness is often the lot of people with serious illness and their families. When you are that sick, you desperately want and need control. This means controlling what you can in your personal life as well as managing your disease. You can enhance your control to the extent that it is possible in three domains: mental, physical, and social.

Controlling the mental aspect of your illness means delving into the psychological and emotional domain: for example, learning to face and deal with your deepest fears in such a way that you go from feeling like a victim of intrusive fears to becoming someone who can master and direct your own thoughts, feelings, and activities. As you take control, you shift from a passive to an active perspective.

Managing the physical domain of your illness means taking control of your body. Using techniques such as self-hypnosis can enhance your control over pain and the sense of physical tension that often accompanies mental anxiety. It can speed your recovery after surgery —e.g., it can aid your ability to rehabilitate sore arms or move despite incisions. In addition, hypnosis can help you learn to control the side effects of chemotherapy such as nausea and vomiting.

The third domain in which you can take more control is the social: intensifying and improving those relationships with family and friends that can be improved. By the same token, distancing yourself from relationships that cannot be deepened is important, as is learning to say "no" to social obligations that you don't want, while investing yourself fully in those that are rewarding. You can bring the same sense of control to the doctor/patient relationship; learning to work collaboratively with your physicians helps you and your family feel more in control of the process of treatment.

How can you navigate the two extremes of the mind/body dilemma? On the one hand, there is the cut-and-dried, no-nonsense, mindless, materialist notion that a life-threatening illness will take its inevitable course, regardless of what you do mentally to cope better with it. This point of view tends to reinforce hopelessness, your sense of being victimized by a disease that has invaded your body. You might feel almost as though your body has betrayed itself, one set of cells turning on another in a relentless march. Many people with cancer have nightmare images of tarantulas biting at their feet, attacking them, or snakes wrapping themselves around their head. The term *cancer* actually means "crab." The idea of a crablike organism attacking your body is extremely frightening, especially when you feel like a helpless victim of the attack.

The other extreme point of view is a disembodied spiritualism: the idea that if you fix a problem in your mind, it will simply disappear in your body. Thus, visualizing your white blood cells as "Pac-Men" that gobble up your cancer cells is supposed to magically transform your immune cells so that they actually attack and kill cancer cells with greater vigor and success. The problem with this approach is that there is not a shred of scientific evidence that this actually happens. And it leaves a legacy of guilt. If your mind has the power to "cure" the disease, it had the power to cause it, and any failure to get well is your responsibility. Thus, not only are you frightened and disappointed when the disease spreads, but your belief that visualization can slow or eliminate the spread of the disease now becomes a source of guilt: "The cancer spread because I was not imaging well enough or hard enough."

But how do you find a middle course? The answer I propose is to make the most of your personal and social resources in the service of living while fighting the disease.

UP THE RIVER WITHOUT A PADDLE

This approach to coping with the tragedy of having a life-threatening illness may be likened to a lesson my wife and I learned on a rafting trip on the Salmon River in Idaho some years ago. River rafting is exciting precisely because it has a certain threat of danger to it. We were duly life-jacketed and led by experienced rafters. It happened, in addition, that we were triply protected. Then–President Carter was also enjoying a rafting trip and we were flanked by the orange tents of the "Secret" Service everywhere amidst the wilderness up and down

the river. The exhilaration of negotiating our way around the rocks
made us acutely interested in the skills of our guides in steering the
rafts. They pointed out that the most common mistake novices make
is to waste energy pulling against the current of the river. The force of
the water leaves little doubt about which direction you will take. It is
futile to pull upstream: Your energy becomes quickly depleted. It is
similarly gratuitous to row downstream; the river will take care of
that. The way a good guide steers is by moving the boat *perpendicular*
to the flow of the stream. This means that you accept the direction,
but the quality of your trip is influenced enormously by which portion
of the onrushing flow you ride. Moving a mere five feet to the left can
allow you to avoid disastrous collision with a rock. Indeed, we learned
that there are portions of most streams along the banks that actually
flow slightly in the opposite direction so that you can move upstream
a bit simply by getting near the edge.

It struck me that there was a lesson in life in that river. Coping
with cancer or another serious illness can benefit from this rafter's
wisdom. The ultimate direction has been determined and opposing it
is exhausting and futile. However, the nature of the trip and how safe
and pleasant it is can be enormously influenced by maneuvering within
this fundamental direction. It is even possible to slow the trip down.
Some illnesses are curable, some are chronic afflictions that one lives
with for many years, and some may lead to death fairly rapidly. Many
medical treatments can make a difference in the odds, but sooner or
later the outcome for all of us will be death. Where we have enormous
control is in how we live whatever life we *have*. It is sad to waste that
precious time and ability in the futile exercise of rowing upstream. On
the other hand, simply giving in to the loss can make the rest of life
far more unpleasant than it need be. Illness is both a danger and an
opportunity. Certain inevitable biological processes are set in motion,
but the nature of the journey, and even how long you take to travel it,
may be influenced by the path you choose.

It is not uncommon for people to cling desperately to the appearance of a normal life after being confronted with a diagnosis of cancer or its spread. Often coupled with this is the absolute determination not to "give in" to the disease. One sad example of this is actor Michael Landon's courageous but futile pronouncements that he would not give in to pancreatic cancer. Sadly, we are not offered that choice, and he died shortly after announcing on television that his illness would not get him. Trying to maintain such a pretense is draining. It can deprive dying persons of the power they have to compel attention, elicit love and caring, do what needs to be done in a hurry. Some waste this precious time in a vain search for fringe cures that are ineffective and sometimes risky. Not only does death find them regardless, but they lose much of the quality of what was left of their lives.

Ironically, it seems to be the people who more fully accept the threat who also make the most productive use of the time they have left, rather than abandoning family and life goals in a vain search for a magical rescue from their illness. One particularly striking example is Belinda Mason, who tragically contracted the human immunodeficiency virus (HIV), the virus that causes AIDS, from a contaminated blood transfusion during an emergency cesarean section. A reporter for a Kentucky newspaper and a writer of short stories, she sent then-President George Bush a letter asking him to protect people with AIDS from being stigmatized. Below is an excerpt from her impassioned letter to the president. Even as she was dying she seemed to be remarkably serene about what had happened to her (*The New York Times,* August 4, 1991, p. 1):

In these days, which will be my last, my family has become my respite from the storm. . . . I'm not bitter and never have been. I've encountered hardships. I sometimes think of the people who screwed up and did this to my life, those who released the infected blood without checking it. But the bitterness puzzles me. It seems to me that it is based on an assumption that things are supposed to be easy in life, that what happened is not fair and shouldn't have happened to me. This occurs to people, particularly to people like me who got AIDS from a blood transfusion and Kimberly Bergalis, who got it from an unfortunate contact with her dentist.

But the question is, why should it happen to anybody? I never felt I was a member of an exclusive club that should go through life unscathed. I suppose that as I say this it sounds hokey, like "Polyanna gets AIDS," but I have always had wonderful things in life.

There is no time for me to do much more about any of this. But there is time for you, Mr. President. Doctors don't give people AIDS—they actually care for people with it. The blanket screening (mandatory blood tests) of healthcare workers will create the false illusion that people with AIDS are a threat to others.

In the waning days of her life, Belinda Mason took the trouble to oppose mandatory testing of health care workers. She was clearly facing the tragedy that had befallen her and her family and yet had risen above it by addressing the broader issues that it represents and its effect on other people like her. One can only admire her wisdom, serenity, clarity of thought and expression, and her willingness to share some of her remaining energy with all of us.

But if positive thinking doesn't conquer disease, what does? Every person with cancer needs help coping with his or her illness. Everyone who has cancer fears that it will kill him or her. Although statistics show that only half of those people diagnosed with cancer will die of it, every one of them fears the worst. More than a million people in the United States will be diagnosed with cancer each year, beginning a lonely and frightening journey, and half a million will eventually die from the disease. Even so, many people emerge from the threat stronger, emotionally and even physically, from their own personal struggle with their fears of death. Knowing in a very personal sense that your life may end sooner than you expected forces you to take stock of where you have been in life's journey and where you are going. It is something like preparing for a trip. The impending departure forces you to assess the resources you have and what you will need to take with you. When you learn you have a terrible illness, suddenly you discover that your life is finite. You have to think hard about how to spend the precious time you have left. You don't want to waste it acquiring what you don't need, seeing those you don't want to be with, and doing what you want to avoid.

> Susan, who had advanced cancer of the cervix, had endless arguments with her husband about how to raise the children. She came into her support group one day and said, "I finally figured something out. I'm never going to convince him that I'm right about how to raise the kids, and he's never going to convince me that he's right. I've been wasting all this time arguing with him. What I should do instead is to spend that time with my children, teaching them how I think they should live life."

Other problems face people with cancer, especially those whose disease is worsening. They worry about money. Medical treatment is expensive, and often their ability to work is reduced. Their families are worried about their own vulnerability to cancer, perhaps even resentful of their loved one's illness. The disease is impinging on all of their lives.

People with cancer must also face new challenges: how to communicate with doctors, sort through the options available for treatment, and live as well as they can while undergoing treatments that may leave them feeling weak, sick, or disfigured. Many have to cope with pain. This may reinforce their sense that something is terribly wrong with their body, and thus the pain makes them anxious and even sleepless as well as uncomfortable.

This all sounds so depressing that you might think that the only thing to do is give up. Yet many people with cancer find in this struggle that they are able to clarify both life's limitations and what truly matters to them. Looking death right in the eye can be invigorating as well as frightening. Sharing one's deepest fears—of death, of being alone—

with others in the same boat can help you feel intensely connected and no longer alone.

This book is intended to help people coping with cancer and their families and friends. I hope it will also be meaningful for people with other serious illnesses who carry with them similar burdens of fear, pain, and loss of control. Although my research has focused on cancer, I believe the lessons I have learned from my work apply to other chronic illnesses as well. I do not seek to give advice about the latest medical and surgical treatments—your doctor is the best source of information about chemotherapy, radiation, and surgery. Instead, I want to provide guidance about the personal side of living with life-threatening illness—the fears, joys, sorrows, pains, choices, and opportunities that come with the territory. The ideas and information presented here derive from fifteen years of experience at Stanford University School of Medicine, where my colleagues and I talked, listened, cried, and laughed with women and men who were dying of cancer. We grieved their deaths, rejoiced at their successes. And we found that the unflagging caring that the people in our Supportive/Expressive groups showed to one another helped them emotionally and, much to my surprise, even physically.

At this point, we know that the women who participated in our support groups lived longer, but we do not know why. That is the subject of our current research. We have received several grants from the National Institute of Mental Health, the National Cancer Institute, the John D. and Catherine T. MacArthur Foundation, and the Fetzer Institute to study more women with metastatic breast cancer. We have also received support from the National Cancer Institute and the Nathan S. Cummings Foundation to team up with the University of Rochester to do a multicenter trial at twelve sites around the country to study the effect of support groups on women with primary breast cancer.

Meanwhile, other researchers are getting similar results. As we discuss later, investigators of the effects of psychotherapeutic support for people with other kinds of cancer, such as lymphoma and malignant melanoma, and also those with heart disease, are finding that disease progression can be slowed and death delayed with such techniques. None of this proves that the mind cures serious disease. However, there is a small but growing body of evidence that our ability to deal with disease is influenced by psychological and social, as well as medical, interventions. This does not mean that we can wish away cancer or heart disease, but it does mean that our bodies seem to be able to fight off the disease better with a little help from our friends. This approach is not in place of, but rather in concert with, aggressive medical treatment of the illness. It is not simply that mind can triumph over matter, but that mind matters.

I hope to conduct you on a tour of the experience of living with serious illness, from the time of first diagnosis, through the anxieties that occur after the initial treatment is over, to the problems and opportunities that come with living with the threat of dying. I will review research from our and other laboratories exploring the relationships among attitude, social support, and your body's ability to fight disease. Our experience working with seriously ill individuals has shown that certain themes are especially important to coping successfully: finding and nourishing new networks of support, dealing directly with fears of dying, reviewing and reordering life priorities, strengthening family relationships, improving communication with doctors, and controlling pain and other symptoms. I will review these important aspects of living your life fully while dealing effectively with serious illness.

What follows is what my colleagues and I have learned from our patients. The voices in this book are those of the women and men in our first study, begun in 1976, and also those of women and men in our current support groups and individual therapy. The identities of many are disguised; other people wanted me to use their real names. We are grateful to all of them for their courage and wisdom, for how they faced their illness and took hold of their lives, for how they helped one another and helped us. It would give them great pleasure to know that some of what they learned about coping with cancer and living life might be of help to you.

1. Weathering the Diagnosis

It was just a minor ache or lump that crept into the edge of your awareness, an unwelcome intruder. At first you ignored or minimized it—it couldn't be anything important; there are many things you have to do. But, finally, you went to your doctor, and with just a glance and a few words, your life was changed. You learned that you have a life-threatening illness. Suddenly, everything else seems unimportant. You feel removed from the pleasant everydayness of life. It feels as though your life is over, that you will never be able to enjoy anything again. You find yourself sailing on uncharted waters in a storm. How can you weather the diagnosis, let alone the illness?

While there is no inevitable course that people follow in reacting to the diagnosis of a life-threatening illness, there are some common responses. These are not so much stages as stopping points in the course of making sense of living with serious illness. Renowned cancer psychiatrists Jimmie Holland and Mary Jane Massie, who work at Memorial Sloan-Kettering Cancer Center in New York, divide the initial response to cancer into three phases: disbelief, dysphoria, and adaptation. Their approach can be applied to any serious illness.

The first phase, lasting about a week or less, is characterized by three *D*'s: disbelief, denial, or despair. The diagnosis of cancer produces a sudden break in the rhythm of our lives, and at first it is hard to believe. The common response is, "It cannot be true. There must be some mistake. Maybe they mixed up the lab tests. I haven't been sick a day in my life. I don't even feel sick."

Drs. Holland and Massie describe the second phase as "dysphoria"—that is, a state of feeling unhappy and unwell. It usually lasts one to two weeks, sometimes more. Feelings of anxiety and depression are common. The news is beginning to sink in as the initial disbelief fades. You go from insisting that it cannot be true to feeling that life is over, nothing is left, the bad news is the only news. During this period you may lose interest in eating, sleep poorly, have great trouble concentrating, and find it difficult to carry out your routine. More important, it seems at this time as though the mood you are in now will never change and the misery will continue indefinitely, which makes it far worse. If the cancer will not go away, how can this anxiety and sadness leave? The answer is, it does. Most people learn to live with cancer.

"I was so excited when I realized that I had gone an entire day without even thinking of cancer," said Sandy. "A while ago, I would never have thought that possible."

The third phase is described as "adaptation." This usually begins by about two weeks after the diagnosis has been made, and it is a time when you absorb the new information about the disease, confront problems involving treatment decisions and their effects on day-to-day life, and adjust your plans for the future. At this time many people find reasons for optimism: "At least they were able to get it all." "They can save my breast." "Many people are cured of this type of cancer." This is a time when you resume your everyday activities and become involved in your medical treatment. It is an important time, because it signals the resolution of the initial dilemma. You convert your emotional distress into action, your depression into determination.

Each of these three phases is discussed in detail below.

DEALING WITH THE DIAGNOSIS

Anyone would react to the initial diagnosis of a life-threatening illness with shock and disbelief. You are sure that there must be some mistake, that the laboratory tests are in error, that the doctor has given the bad news to the wrong patient. As the reality of it sinks in, you come to feel isolated, removed from the happy day-to-day world everyone else seems to inhabit.

> Frank, a patient with cancer of the tongue who underwent a laryngectomy in November of 1990, said he understood how the soldiers going to the Persian Gulf during the war felt. "The possibility of my death, not someone else's, suddenly became real."
>
> Another recently diagnosed cancer patient found a kind of black humor in the Loma Prieta earthquake of October 17, 1989. The "Baysball" World Series was just starting between the San Francisco Giants and the Oakland Athletics. The 7.9 quake hit as fans were pouring into the windy San Francisco ballpark. The huge escalator became a roller coaster. She said: "For a few minutes, everybody at Candlestick Park felt what it was like to have cancer."

A BODY WITH AN ATTITUDE

Many cancer patients report a sense of betrayal by their bodies—the old familiar body starts to seem alien, hostile, and treacherous. A woman with breast cancer who developed a malignant melanoma (a cancer of the skin) reported noticing that something just did not feel right about the skin on her leg: "While it looked innocent enough—a little patch of white surrounded by a dark spot—it just felt like something was wrong." It turned out to be a malignancy, a cancerous growth that had to be removed surgically and that took quite a while to heal. Another woman in the group commented about her sense of betrayal: "You have a body with an attitude." It is not simply that a part of your body fails to function properly, as with heart disease or a stroke. It is not that a part of your body still functions, but only at the price of pain, as in arthritis. Rather, in cancer, a part of your body betrays the rest, indeed turns on it and becomes an enemy, invading other parts of the body. This sense of betrayal by your own body is a uniquely threatening aspect of cancer. As the Nobel-prize-winning cancer researcher Peyton Rous put it, "Cancer destroys man in a unique and appalling way, as flesh of his flesh, which has somehow been rendered proliferative, rampant, predatory, and ungovernable."

Anyone who has the good fortune to reach that point in life when you stop wishing to be older and start wishing to be younger has had the experience of waking up to find a body that is not quite as eager to greet the world as you are. You notice that your previous and permanent sense of benign well-being can no longer be taken for granted. Lucy, a laconic widow in her sixties, described her relationship with her body in this way: "I would like to think of my body as if it were a dog: 'Sit, lie down, roll over.' If I want to stay up for twenty-four hours to do something, it should." When Lucy got cancer, she told us that she felt as though her body had gone from being an obedient servant to a needy, greedy predator. It was not merely that her body had let her down. Rather, it had attacked her. It had not merely failed to do what it should; it was causing damage. She and Sandy talked in the group about how conflicted their feelings were toward their bodies. On the one hand, they were angry at their bodies for letting them down and, even worse, for imposing limitations on their lives for the first time. Lack of energy erects a permanent barrier between you and everything you want to do. Radiation and chemotherapy appointments steal time from something else. The body demands more and gives less. At the same time, Sandy noted that she found herself investing a new kind of feeling and hope in her body: She perceived it as fighting the disease and helping her live with it. At the very moment when the body threatens to "go on strike," to cease performing its daily service, you become angry with it while at the same time you value it all the more. You experience something akin to that moment of panic you feel when your young child becomes lost: You are angry with the child for wandering away and making you so worried, and at the same time, you are acutely aware of how much that child means to you, how deeply it would hurt to lose him or her. The moment of potential loss can be one of reevaluation as well.

Denial or Death

After your first reaction of numbing denial—"It can't be true. There must be some mistake"—you will probably be seized by a desperate need to search for facts, to gather information about the diagnosis. This is as it should be. "What does it mean? What do I have?" You'll question those who gave you the diagnosis: "Who are they? How qualified are they? Do they know what they are talking about? Can there be a mistake?" Then you'll worry about the implications of the diagnosis: "Is my life over? What treatments are available? Will it shorten my life or not? Will I suffer pain, disfigurement, loss of function?" This information gathering is part of an important process of coming to terms with the illness, of making sense of it, of putting it into perspective. It does not happen all at once. Such things are so overwhelming that you and your family simply can't take it all in with a single bite. Don't be too hard on yourself and don't expect to comprehend it all right away. You will need to reorient yourself and take stock of your new situation again and again as you learn an entirely new skill: dealing with a grave illness.

Adaptation: The Middle Way

In a sense, the next task is getting from "It's not true" to "It's not new." The doctor says, "I'm sorry, but this lump looks serious. We're going to have to do a biopsy and take it out." These few words unleash a torrent of worry. *Cancer* and *death* are both terrifying terms, and they seem synonymous. There is no cancer patient who does not immediately fear the worst. At the same time, there is no one who does not believe desperately that it must be some kind of mistake. The doctor is wrong, the pathologist was wrong, they read somebody else's slide— we cling to the momentum from our life before the diagnosis. "I must carry on as before." The only alternative seems the worst—that life is over. Yet, in most cases, the real truth is somewhere in between. Life will never be the same again, but it is not over. So the task becomes one of staking out the middle ground. The challenge is to absorb the new information and put it into perspective so that it fits in with your life rather than taking it over.

A friend suffered a badly fractured leg in a skiing accident. It required surgery and months of recuperation. As she reflected on it, she said: "I became my leg." For a period of time it seemed that there was nothing else in her life except the pain, procedures, and immobility caused by the broken leg.

At first, it seems that your whole life has been taken over, if not taken, by cancer. But it is important to adhere to a middle ground, because the overall news about cancer is good and getting better. Half of all people diagnosed with cancer will live either free of it or long enough that it is not cancer that ends their lives. Thus, the plain fact is that cancer is not, in and of itself, a death sentence. That is true of many other serious illnesses as well. Yet people know, and there is no denying, that cancer is the second leading killer of people in the United States and thus the diagnosis is in fact a life threat. The more widespread the disease is in the body, and the later it is diagnosed, the more of a threat it is. Nonetheless, there is much that can be done about it.

Unwelcome news that comes early is a lot better than false reassurance, which only delays the correct diagnosis and potentially life-saving treatment. Better bad news now than worse news later.

Pam retains a kind of measured bitterness about her general surgeon's bland reassurance that a lump in her breast was benign and did not require further treatment. On his advice she did nothing about it for two years, while it continued to grow. By the time she got to a second surgeon and he told her that she had cancer and it had to come out at once, Pam knew that her odds of survival were far lower than they might have had the cancer been removed two years earlier. Pam was angry at herself for believing the first doctor and angry at him for missing the diagnosis. In addition, she found that every other specialist she went to seemed to treat her with "kid gloves," as though she had some kind of communicable disease. In fact, they were thinking that she had grounds for a lawsuit and were afraid that no matter what they did they would be caught up in legal complications as well.

She talked, with great feeling, about a turning point in her treatment, when a consulting surgeon, having heard the story and reviewed her records, looked her in the eye and said, "You must have felt terrible." "Those five little words meant more to me than anything else," said Pam. He simply acknowledged what a difficult and trying situation she had been through and in doing so communicated, powerfully, that he was on her side and that her feelings were normal and to be expected. She was not being "difficult"; she was simply being human.

THE NEED FOR ALLIES

When you are in a desperate situation, you need an ally. Think about how the hostages who returned from years of captivity in the Middle East described their fellow captives, how deeply they had come to know and care about one another. In a desperate situation the need for meaningful relationships deepens. At a time when you wonder whether you are still part of the world of the living or the dead, you become especially sensitive to the presence or absence of supportive friends, family, and professionals who can help you. Any sign of abandonment can trigger panic. It is as though you have been cut out of the world of the living. On the other hand, any sense of compassion and caring from others can go a long way toward reversing that sense of panic. Feeling in touch with another human being conveys a powerful message—"I'm still alive and worth being cared about"—which dra-

matically helps to counteract the panicky feeling that "my life is over."
I discuss this in more depth in chapters 5 and 6, but my point here is
that it's helpful to marshall support for yourself as soon as possible,
particularly in the information-gathering stage of your illness. Clear
communication is especially important at the point of diagnosis; having a friend or family member with you to listen and ask questions will
help ensure that you learn what you need to know.

OVERCOMING THE "PARALYSIS OF ANALYSIS"

As you come to know more about the diagnosis of your illness, you
find out that even a terrible truth is better than a vague lurking fear.
Knowing what is happening allows you to think clearly about what
you can do about it, whereas holding it at bay immobilizes you. There
is nothing worse than paralysis in the face of a threat. The Rev. Dr.
Martin Luther King, Jr., used to call this the "paralysis of analysis."
Notice how much better you feel about anything that worries you
when you come up with a plan for dealing with it. Long before you
have actually done something, you reduce your sense of discomfort by
planning what to do. But there is nothing you can do about a threat
that you don't confront. As you face the fact of your diagnosis you
come to see that life goes on, even with a grave disease. Usually you
find that things are not as good as you had hoped, but not as bad as
you had feared. There is life after your diagnosis, after all. Gradually
your illness becomes only one of your many concerns. It is almost with
relish that you find one morning that you are more worried about a
problem at work or with your child than about whether or not you
will survive your illness. Life is not the same, but it is not overrun by
your illness, and it is not over. Indeed, such a threat provides you with
an opportunity to reexamine the way you have spent your life and the
way you plan to spend the remainder of it, to redefine life goals and
values. I discuss this in Chapter 7. Serious illness is not a good thing,
but good things can come of it.

TALKING WITH YOUR DOCTOR

Putting your diagnosis into perspective is complicated by a number of factors, not the least of which is the difficulty of talking with your doctor about what is happening. Why should this be? Suddenly, you depend on your doctor for everything. We learn by experience, and your recent experience is a cruel teacher. You came into the doctor's office with what you had hoped and thought was a minor complaint. The physician's words suddenly transformed it into a major life disruption. The experience is something like stopping a stranger to ask for directions and having him pull a gun on you. You understandably hesitate to ask another stranger for information. In behavioral terms, the nature of the reinforcement shapes your subsequent behavior. Thus, whether you are aware of it or not, the bad news from your doctor will to some extent discourage you from asking for more information. The last thing you want from your doctor is another jolt like the one you just got. So you may feel even more inhibited, even more reluctant to bring up new complaints or problems, out of a dimly perceived fear that the next innocent question or comment will likewise yield devastating results. In a way, you're acting out the famous Greek myth of killing the messenger who brought the bad news. At the same time, your reluctance complicates your adjustment to your illness. To the extent that you become fearful of asking the very questions you need to ask to gain more perspective on what has happened, you hamper your ability to cope. Very often what doctors can say is comforting rather than frightening. So, although what you may hear could be hard to take in and comprehend, bite the bullet and ask.

This process requires patience on your part and on that of your doctors and others who are helping you and your family. You may have to ask doctors time and again the same questions. A single answer to an important question may not even seem real at first. It will be hard for you to hear it. Therefore, it is perfectly legitimate, indeed important, to ask the same question again just to be sure you have heard it right. "Does this mean that the cancer has spread to another part of my body, Doctor?" Recent studies show that patients go to the doctor's office with an average of four questions and leave with an average of one and a half answered. This is not enough. Most people would inquire more of an auto mechanic fixing their car than they would about the diagnosis and treatment of a life-threatening illness in their own bodies. This is no time for shyness or for worrying about trying the doctor's patience. It is your life that is on the line. Write down your questions in advance and carry the list with you when you go to see your doctor. Tell your doctor at the beginning rather than at the end of the interview that you have some questions that need attention. This way the doctor can allot enough time to answer them. Do not be afraid to appear "stupid." Medical jargon may not make sense to you, and it may require a statistics course to appreciate the meaning of a prediction of the odds for the return of your illness. Insist on plain English, and keep inquiring until you understand what your doctor is saying. You may not like it, but at least be clear about it. Write down the answers. Then you can decide what to do.

There is an important difference between anxiety and fear. Anxiety is a general sense that something is wrong, which can lead to discomfort, restlessness, and worry, but which is not specific enough to point the way to any resolution of the problem. Fear is something more specific—you know what you are afraid of, and this tends to make the possibility of effective action to control or reduce the fear more real. One of the best means of treating anxiety is to convert it to fear, to change a general sense of discomfort to a fear of something in particular. Thus, a general sense of anxiety in relation to cancer or other illness is best addressed by seeking to define exactly what it is you are anxious about: the discomfort associated with treatment, the possibility that the disease will spread, the threat of death. Each of these issues can be explored and addressed, which can reduce the discomfort they cause. The way to tame anxiety is to confront it directly. Ask rather than avoid.

Marilyn, a college teacher who made it a project to think about her situation as well as to live through it, talked about a way she had learned to manage her fear. "I think of the fear as a *feeling*. It is real, but the intensity of the feeling does not necessarily represent the severity of the *problem*. I recognize that I am afraid, but I feel less overwhelmed when I identify it as a feeling."

Although Franklin D. Roosevelt's famous dictum "The only thing we have to fear is fear itself" does not apply, since cancer is indeed something to fear, recognizing that anxiety is part of the problem can keep fears from escalating.

The flow of information can seem as overwhelming as its meaning. The new vocabulary of illness can obscure rather than enlighten. You must study for the role of patient as though you were learning a new job. Let doctors, nurses, social workers, and other patients be your teachers (more on this in Chapter 10). Ask everyone to explain words you do not understand. You may think you "should" know what they mean, but the fact is that there is no reason why. What may be routine for others, at this point is not for you. Even worse, you may think you understand something that sounds worse than it is. A notorious example is the prediction of your odds of survival. Your doctor may say that you have "a seventy percent chance of survival." What does this mean? It depends on the length of time being predicted (For one year? Five years?), your particular type of illness, and the treatments employed. Your particular circumstances may put you on the positive (or negative) side of those odds. They apply to large numbers of individuals with similar problems, but say little about your specific situation. In any case, such predictions are an inexact science at best. It's only natural to ask about the quantity of life, but ask your doctor also about its quality. What are you likely to be able to do? How taxing will the treatments be? You have a right to know, and you may well have to hear it more than once before it sinks in—good news as well as bad.

Indeed, no one could absorb all he or she needs to know about cancer and its treatment in one visit to a doctor; doctors themselves train for years to understand it. You can manage the overload by focusing on what you need to know *now*. If there is an immediate decision to be made—about a type of surgery or a course of chemo-therapy—make solving that problem your top priority. You can learn about other aspects of your illness later. At first it will seem that everything about your illness must be important. You will learn that there are many different cancers, for example, each with its own course and prognosis. Keep the focus on yours, but give yourself a break from time to time. Don't eat, sleep, and breathe your illness. It may be a new and unwelcome part of your life, but don't let it take over your life. Think of it as an unpleasant neighbor who will not leave you alone and who will not go away. You have to reach some sort of an accommodation, but you don't want to spend all of your time doing it.

BLAMING THE VICTIM

The danger of blaming people with cancer for their disease has grown along with theories that the wrong mental attitude may make you more likely to get cancer.

Marianne recalled being at a retreat with some "New Age" friends when she was diagnosed with breast cancer. To her surprise, she found her friends to be rather judgmental, with excessively clear ideas about what she should do, none of which involved traditional medicine. She was about to drive away from the retreat when one of her friends stuck his head in the window of her car, and said: "You caused your cancer; you can cure it." "I started rolling the window up on his head," she said, laughing. "Then, I went to the hospital. By contrast, the nurses and doctors were so nonjudgmental and sup-portive. 'Try your diets, use your medication,' they said. 'Do what you need to do.' "

You may feel a tremendous temptation to blame yourself for having cancer, even if you lack the kind of "friend" who would accuse you of it. Too much fat in your diet? Not enough fiber? The "wrong" attitude? We all want to be in control of ourselves, our world, and our bodies. We detest the sense of helplessness that comes with feeling out of control. Oddly, one way to pretend that you are in control when you are not is to blame yourself for what is happening. This is a common problem among victims of physical trauma, such as sexual assault or natural disasters. It is typical for a rape victim to blame herself, as though hindsight should be foresight: "I should have known that it would be dangerous to walk to the pharmacy" (at 6 P.M. on a summer evening on a busy street). The odd sense of comfort that comes from this irrational self-blame is a sense that the world is once again predictable. If it was your mistake in judgment, you can learn not to make the same mistake, and so regain control. You can almost convince yourself that you could replay the event and do it differently this time.

In the same way, it is not uncommon for people with cancer or another illness to blame themselves for the diagnosis. Sometimes they may have good reasons—perhaps they smoked or didn't have regular checkups. But however imperfect we are, no one chooses to become ill. Even if somehow we did, once the process has started in our bodies we are victims of it deserving of compassion, not perpetrators deserving of blame. (However, even compassion can make you uncomfortable—are you "feeling sorry for yourself" or "pulling for pity"? Does it reinforce the feeling that something terrible is happening to your body? It may, but it is part of the process of coming to terms with what is happening.)

Other people mistakenly blame their family, boss, or other source of stress for their cancer. I have known women who were certain that the stress of intervening between feuding husband and children, the loss of a job, or a blow to their breast during a fight gave them cancer. There is no evidence that any of these or related terrible stressors lead to cancer, yet we look for some way to explain what has happened to us. This only leads to recrimination and alienation. Imagine how it must feel to be accused of giving someone cancer. Think how you would feel if you were certain someone had done that to you—could you feel as close to him or her? Just at a time when you need more social support because you have cancer, such ideas can cut you off from it. We humans manage to inflict enough real harm on one another. It does no good at all to add the burden of coping with imagined and unproved harm. I discuss this further in chapters 3 and 4.

CONSTRUCTING THE SOCIAL REALITY OF YOUR ILLNESS

We have other ways of managing the reality of illness. One is choosing whom we tell. Understandably, you may first keep the diagnosis of serious illness within a tight inner circle of people, such as close family and friends. You don't want others to know. It seems too personal, too private. What business is it of the grocer to know about a lump growing in your breast or your need for surgery? Will the diagnosis affect your children or the way people talk to them? Will your boss think you're unable to do your job? Or are unsuitable for promotion? All of these are legitimate concerns. And you don't want pity from the idly curious. But in addition to your understandable reasons for keeping your diagnosis private, you may want to consider some subconscious motives. Somehow it doesn't quite seem real when other people don't know about the illness. One way of attempting to manage the reality of your illness is by managing how widely it is known. To tell other people is somehow to admit that terrible truth. Yet sooner or later you must come to terms with it, because it is a tremendous waste of energy to manage such information, to keep it from some people but not others.

Marilyn was desperate not to let anyone know that she had breast cancer that was spreading rapidly. She hadn't even told her son yet. As a single parent, the thought that she would not be able to raise him through his full childhood was extremely painful for her and she believed it would be terribly upsetting to him. She thus felt she had to make sure that no one would be in a position to let the secret slip. Yet Marilyn's son knew his mother was sick with something, that she was receiving treatments that made her feel bad, and he kept pressing her for information. "What did the doctor say, Mommy? How many people with an illness like yours will live for five years?" In other words, he knew that something serious was going on and he wanted to know more. His questions gradually convinced her that he, in fact, did know more than she had thought. The prospect of being closer to him, of not having a secret divide them, finally held sway over her desire to keep painful information from him— and in an odd way, from herself. She told him the truth, which brought them closer together, and she allowed him to comfort and nurture her.

The more things stay the same, the more they change. "Wait a minute," you may be wondering, "Didn't you get that old French phrase backwards?" (*"Plus ça change, plus c'est la même chose."*) I did, on purpose. Something strange happens when you try to keep everything just the same after being diagnosed with a life-threatening illness. Superficially, everything looks the same. And yet everything is different. You *feel* different. It's difficult to maintain the usual superficial banter. You, in fact, feel estranged from others. Your friends don't know what you are going through. And that sense of estrangement only reinforces the feeling a life-threatening illness gives you of being removed from the flow of normal life. The more you try to keep things as they were, the more your life feels changed. However, when you first start to tell others that you have cancer, you suddenly find that relationships heat up, become intense. People react, not always well, but they react. And that sense that people are hearing you, responding to you, can break down the barrier of isolation and make you feel more a part of the world of the living again.

ROLES AND LABELS

There is a sense in which becoming someone with cancer is a lesson in the power of discrimination. You learn quite suddenly what it is like to become part of a group that is feared and excluded. You become a second-class citizen in the minds of many. The word *cancer* itself is loaded with unpleasant meaning. It makes you an object of fear, as though you were contagious. The word often keeps company with the term *victim,* further emphasizing the expectation that you will be passive and helpless in the face of the disease. Even the label *cancer patient* carries additional freight—the idea that you are a permanent patient, twenty-four hours a day. The label is a constant reminder that you are "sick." The language itself implies the limited possibility of a meaningful response on your part to having the disease. It is not merely that you, a complex, interesting person, have an additional if unfortunate attribute—cancer. Rather, it begins to seem as though there is suddenly little else of importance about you other than being a cancer victim.

Becoming a cancer patient can be jolting in another sense. You suddenly enter a system in which you have far less recognition and control than in most other parts of your life. I remember the moment when I arrived, full of excitement, at medical school, and decided to visit the hospital next door to the student dormitory to watch a delivery as my first introduction to medicine. The smell of antiseptic in the hall was strange, and I felt alien and out of place. "What am I doing here?" I thought to myself. "I don't even *like* hospitals. Do I really want to spend my life in them?" Well, I did get used to hospitals as a doctor, but I had a similar experience eight years later that brought back the old alien feeling when I required an X ray for a troublesome shoulder. I sat in a large, totally empty room awaiting the procedure. A technician entered the room, looking at a list on her clipboard. "Spiegel," she announced to the empty room. Not "Dr. Spiegel," or "Mr. Spiegel," or "Sir, it is time for your X ray." Just "Spiegel." It is amazing how quickly you can feel reduced to the status of a thing.

Unfortunately, much about modern institutional health care is designed to treat the problem rather than the person, leaving you feeling worse, even before the treatment begins. Thus, in addition to the burden of the illness, you have to face dehumanizing institutions and onerous labels. It is best to face such problems head-on. When you hide your problem, you tacitly accept the idea that it is bad to be what you are. Rather, say, "Yes, I have cancer. Now, let's get on with whatever it is we need to do as people together."

WE HAVE COME a long way from the time when having cancer was a source of shame, a terrible secret, although the stigma persists for many. We find inner reasons to keep it to ourselves, to suffer in silence. Anyone needs a certain amount of time to process the reality of having the disease and to decide what to do. But when it is on your mind, it should also be on the minds of those who care about you. You can start taking charge of your cancer and its treatment by taking charge of what you know, getting the information you need, and letting others know as well.

The diagnosis of cancer and other serious illnesses threatens to end life, but what it really does is *change* life. You can get beyond the sense of doom and catastrophe that can paralyze you into inaction. You're ready to cope with the next phase of your illness.

2. The Lull After the Storm

Most people with a life-threatening illness expect to be relieved after surgery, chemotherapy, radiation, or other treatment is over. However, often when treatment ends, you may experience renewed anxiety and a sense of loneliness. You find yourself waiting for the other shoe to drop, no longer feeling that you are "doing something" to fight your illness. When you have to show up regularly for chemotherapy or radiotherapy, you enter a new social world, one peopled with others who have similar problems, as well as technicians, nurses, social workers, medical students, and doctors. While not all of the interactions are positive, many are. You are surrounded by people who know what you are going through, who chat with you, who inquire about how you are feeling. Suddenly, once treatment is completed, they are gone. Perhaps without realizing how much you have come to depend upon them, you find yourself without a ready replacement. Long-simmering family problems surface now that the "crisis" is past. This is a time of quiet and often painful reflection, during which a new recognition of the reality of your illness begins to sink in. The struggle seems lonelier, and this loneliness, in turn, reinforces your anxiety about death by making you feel that you are removed from the flow of life—in a sense, already a little bit dead.

You, your family, and friends need to be aware that the very moment when everything seems to be getting better may be the time when you can use extra support.

Several factors make the expected transition back to a semblance of life before illness harder than you might expect. They involve your expectations, your body's reaction to the illness and its treatment, and on top of those, life's usual problems.

THERE IS NO GOING BACK

While life can pretty much get back to normal, it will never be the same. You have been diagnosed with a life-threatening illness. You have come face-to-face with a vulnerability we would all like to ignore. You cannot feel quite as insulated from danger as you did before. In part this is because the actual nature of your dying has taken shape. You can visualize the unthinkable because its form has become all too real. When we're healthy, if we think about our deaths at all, it is usually in a vague and comforting form—in our sleep when we are in our eighties, or perhaps the way a parent or grandparent died. Nonetheless, such thoughts are comfortably diffuse and easily brushed aside. How different when a doctor tells you that you have a specific illness that is life threatening. Suddenly you can picture your death all too easily, and the image intrudes upon your consciousness. You can try to ignore death, but it will no longer ignore you. The comfortable sense of invulnerability is taken away. Life after such a realization can be rich, rewarding, even improved, but it will not be the same. It is laced with the knowledge that it can and will slip away.

LIVING WITH A TIMETABLE

Many people find themselves coping with predictions made by their doctors about the amount of time they are likely to have. In this sense, cancer is rather different from heart disease. After your first heart attack, you may live on happily for another forty years, or you could die the next day. Cancer is more plodding and predictable. Knowing your general health, history of other illnesses, and the type and stage of cancer, doctors have good awareness of the overall course of the disease for most patients. Nonetheless, there is a fundamental rule of statistics that gets in the way of predictions. Aggregate numbers tell you (and your doctor) very little about your specific case. If you toss a coin in the air enough times, it is certain that half the time heads will come out on top, and half the time tails. That tells you nothing about what the next toss will bring. If your doctor tells you that 80 percent of people with your illness live for more than five years after diagnosis, what does that tell you? *You* will be either 100 percent alive or 100 percent dead. People often want to know what their survival time will be so they can plan their lives, and not uncommonly, the predictions are wrong.

> Karen had started out irritated with her oncologist, since for five months her doctor had decided to observe rather than remove a lump she had felt because her mammogram had been normal. When she saw the oncologist, he said: "There is no chance—you have one and a half years." Her comment was: "He had a God complex. He would say upsetting things and walk out. I've already outlived his little prediction."

Thus both uncertainty and artificial certainty can be extremely stressful. What doctors know is an *average* or usual time course for a person with your type of cancer. This average time until recurrence or death is composed of a *range* of possible times, some much shorter, others much longer. Nobody can be sure which of these groups you will be in. These predictions are based upon probabilities, not certainties.

Ask your doctor to explain what he or she means by the numbers. No one can tell you with assurance, "You have two years to live." He or she can tell you that it is likely that you will die sooner rather than later. Just as the diagnosis of cancer becomes an important part of your life, but not the only thing that matters, so a prediction of survival time is significant but not absolute. Let it be a guideline for how to plan your life, rather than a countdown.

DOING NOTHING

It is easy to overlook how stressful it is to do nothing. As I mentioned earlier, at least during your treatment you had the feeling that you and your doctors were doing something to fight the illness, and something effective at that. Your anxiety about the disease was channeled into participating in vigorous treatment of it. All of a sudden when the treatment is over, you no longer have anything active to do to fight the disease. That makes you anxious—fearing but not doing.

After treatment ends, people often feel helpless. Researchers Gerald Koocher and John O'Malley at the Sidney Farber Cancer Center in Boston refer to this as the "Damocles Syndrome," in reference to the mythical sword of Damocles, which hung over potential victims who were never certain when it would drop. Cancer patients have been confronted with at least one terrible shock—the diagnosis. They must face each day wondering whether the disease will recur.

> Jane, a feisty, "take-charge" mother of four, found herself terrified by every new ache and pain. She was sure that each one was a sign that her cancer had returned. Initially she responded by insisting that her doctor, who practiced in a large health maintenance organization, order a new diagnostic test. That made her feel as if she was doing something to counter the cancer. She had learned that she could insist on having an initial report immediately after the scan had been conducted, reducing the waiting and uncertainty afterward. However, as time went on, she felt that she was running out of her "bag of tricks" in coping with new symptoms.

How can you live with that sword dangling over your head? Some choose not to look up, trying to ignore the threat or pretend it is not there. However, any small reminder of the threat of the illness then becomes catastrophic, and out of sight does not really mean out of mind. A better approach is to acknowledge the threat and the discomfort it causes. Gradually, you will learn to put it into perspective. Your challenge will be to grieve your "carefree" life before illness and acknowledge that a new, elevated level of risk is a part of your life. Paradoxically, this will help you see that the danger is real, but not absolute. You begin to appreciate the degree of risk: It could be higher, or lower. Also, facing danger helps you to feel more prepared. Think about what you would do if what you fear happens. Suppose the cancer does come back, what would you do? You would 1) tell your spouse; 2) make an appointment with your doctor; 3) get a second opinion about the treatment; etc. Thinking this through makes you feel less passive, allows you to focus on what you would do, rather than simply dwelling on what might happen to you. Use this time to take stock of what has happened, plan the next step, and move on.

THE SPIRIT IS WILLING, THE FLESH WEAK

You expect your body to go back to normal right away, yet it often does not comply. In our research, my coworkers and I found that the loss of energy associated with radiation therapy and chemotherapy can last as long as a year after the formal treatment is over. You (and your family) expect and hope that as soon as treatment is over, you will feel just fine. Similarly, many women coming to the hospital to give birth to their first child bring their old, prepregnancy clothes to change into when they go home and are dismayed when they find they don't fit. It takes their bodies a while to resume their old shape. Similarly, it will take your body time to readjust after intensive treatment.

When we studied patients with Hodgkin's disease, a cancer of the white blood cells, we found, to our initial surprise, that one of the worst times emotionally is just after radiation therapy is *over*. Hodgkin's disease used to be almost certainly fatal. However, due to pioneering research by Drs. Henry Kaplan and Saul Rosenberg at Stanford, vigorous chemotherapy and radiation therapy result in cure rates of better than 80 percent. However, the treatment regimen is intense and may last up to a year.

Hodgkin's patients often look forward to the end of treatment as a time to get back to their normal routine. In fact, our studies revealed that the end of treatment brought with it the second highest levels of anxiety and depression experienced during the entire course of the disease. The worst time was during the initial diagnosis and surgery, as you might expect. But patients and their families found the end of the intensive radiotherapy and chemotherapy, the lull after the storm, almost as difficult.

However, there was a steady improvement in mood over time. As part of a study of how people adjust to treatment, Stanford social worker Pat Fobair, radiation oncologist Richard Hoppe, and I compared questionnaires from forty-five patients who had been diagnosed and treated for Hodgkin's disease within the past two years with those from 350 patients who were more than two years postdiagnosis. By these measures, the more recently treated patients were, on average, 50 percent more depressed. Thus, depression does diminish with time —but it takes time. The period immediately after treatment ends (usually about a year after the illness is first diagnosed) is not one of joyful relief. Spirits improve, but slowly. Both the illness and its treatment are terrible insults to the body. You have to come to terms with the idea of having a life-threatening illness, along with the depletion of energy that comes with being ill and coping with treatment, and the time and effort that must be devoted to pursuing treatment. Even a good outcome comes at a price.

Loss of energy is a chronic and serious problem for people with cancer. There is the physical and emotional stress of the disease itself, the effects of the treatments, and the possible complication posed by depression. We all expect to bounce back physically almost as soon as the treatment is over. However, it took the people with Hodgkin's disease a long time to recover their energy. We found that they experienced a considerable drop in energy at the beginning of treatment, and energy levels did not return to normal until a year after the patients completed radiation therapy. Don't expect to be able to go back to your full routine right away. Be patient with yourself; your desires will outpace your abilities. Guard your energy reserves and allocate them with care. Knowing what to expect can help you avoid feelings of guilt and frustration.

RETURN OF THE REPRESSED

We often postpone stressful problems while we are immersed in treatment. The big decisions about the job, finances, old arguments with a spouse, concerns about the children are all put aside while we adjust to the idea of having a life-threatening illness and get on with its treatment. However, none of these problems will simply go away, and not uncommonly, the illness complicates them. They clamor for attention after the acute treatment is over.

For example, it is rare for couples to fight during the initial diagnosis and treatment. They are stunned, worried, and want to do everything they can to fight the illness together. But at some point, old resentments and new problems will emerge. The husband who has been wonderfully patient during the initial diagnosis and treatment starts to wonder whether he will ever get his "old wife" back. The hugs and tears are replaced with resentment that the chores are not getting done. "Don't cry anymore; you'll just make the cancer spread," one husband told his wife with breast cancer. That was his way of saying, "I don't want to hear any more about it. I want life as usual."

Sandy's twenty-two-year-old daughter, Jennifer, wanted her mother to be a "tower of strength." She had always counted on her mother for support when things in her life were not going well: "My mom is the one person I can count on to back me up no matter what," she said, fighting back tears.

"Maybe it would help her to hear that from you," I suggested.

"I just can't do it," Jennifer replied. She felt that her mother's illness was pulling the rug out from under her, and it added to her conflicted sense that she needed her mother more than she could admit. Instead of forcing her to grow up faster, Sandy's breast cancer had made Jennifer feel trapped in her dependency on her mother, frightened, and even resentful that she could not count on her forever. It was, in fact, time for the daughter to give more and take less, but admitting that seemed to her to mean that she accepted and even "permitted" her mother's cancer to exist. Indeed, Jennifer found herself provoking more of the same old fights, almost as though she could re-create the healthy precancer times by resurrecting the old arguments.

Often we are let down by old methods of coping, which had worked well in the past but seem strangely inappropriate now that we face this new and different challenge. We tend to bring to our struggle with serious illness the baggage we have carried with us throughout life. We develop coping styles and patterns of activity in life that may serve us well in one situation and yet prove quite unhelpful in another. Sometimes, in fact, it is the people who have been most effective in managing their lives in general who are hit the hardest by an illness that disrupts their usual patterns of coping, especially when they are facing something they cannot fully control.

A scientist in his late fifties found himself suffering increasing back pain. He assumed that he had simply overexerted himself and continued his relentless schedule of meetings, travel, lecturing, and writing. However, the pain progressed to the point where it was virtually immobilizing. After several diagnostic evaluations, his doctors discovered that he had a lymphoma, a cancer of the blood and lymphatic system, which weakens the bones and therefore caused a pathological fracture of portions of his spinal cord, resulting in his pain. He was hospitalized to undergo intensive chemotherapy and radiation. He went from being an outgoing, remarkably energetic, and productive man to a person who would have stayed in bed all day had his wife not lovingly insisted that he get up. He suddenly felt hopeless about his medical condition despite the vigorous treatment he was receiving. But worse than that, he blamed himself for being a failure and a "bad patient." He felt that he was letting down his doctors, his colleagues, his friends, his wife. He became convinced that his wife would be fed up with him and unwilling to stay with him through this, despite a long and good marriage.

While part of this man's reaction is attributable to depression itself—that is, the hopelessness and the tendency to blame oneself— another factor was at work in shaping his attitude. His style of dealing with problems had simply been to work at them incessantly, to throw all of his energy into completing the research project, the paper, the lecture. He often worked eighteen-hour days, traveled ceaselessly, and took on far too much. Nonetheless, he found it a rewarding and successful way of advancing his career and his personal life. He wanted the cancer to yield to the same kind of personal control. He berated himself for not having made the diagnosis (of a rare and unexpected cancer), and for not being able to do something that would make treatment go more rapidly, that would return him to his work sooner. Indeed, despite being a physician himself, he felt ashamed of having cancer and reluctant to let the word out among his colleagues that he had the illness. He acted as though he should be able to will himself out of the illness. He found it emotionally easier to blame himself for not having been able to work away or will away his cancer than to accept his helplessness and sense of limitation, to admit that his old coping strategies simply did not fully apply. (It should be noted that they applied to the extent that he was able to obtain for himself the best possible cancer treatment, but beyond that, he took every side effect and setback as a personal failure.)

My colleagues and I worked with this man to help him to bear the limitations that the illness imposed, to admit to his colleagues and friends that he was ill with cancer but expected to return to work in a few months, and to master self-hypnosis exercises so he could better control his pain and anxiety. That, coupled with some medication for his depression, gradually brought him out of his state of psychological collapse. Part of what was necessary was helping him realize that the skills that worked so well elsewhere not only did not work with his cancer, but were in some ways counterproductive because they led him to blame himself for events over which he had little or no control.

At times, serious illness interferes with the normal process of growing up, with the natural progression of developmental milestones.

> A brilliant young woman had been in the process of declaring independence from her loving but staid Southern family. This declaration took the form of the announcement of her engagement to a man whom she loved but whom her family considered socially unacceptable. Two weeks later, she was diagnosed with Hodgkin's disease. "I felt like I had just been so grown up—finally I had declared that I was an adult and would live my life the way I wanted to, and then I had to 'run home to Mommy with a boo-boo.' " She, of course, had to postpone her marriage plans, and accept, temporarily, more direct support and control from her parents than she otherwise would have.

MONEY PRESSURES

Financial problems are the last thing you need but often the first thing you have to deal with when someone in the family is ill. If the ill family member worked, you can no longer count on that income. The healthy breadwinner(s) must put off retirement or desperately cling to a job for fear of losing the health insurance that has become a lifeline.

> Mary's husband had been considering a career change for several years before her diagnosis with breast cancer. He was deeply resentful that, in addition to all the other changes the illness had brought about in their lives, he was no longer free to leave his job. If he did

so, his new job's health insurance plan would exclude preexisting conditions, meaning that Mary's illness would no longer be covered. He thus found himself doubly trapped: by her disease and by his job.

Even worse, more than 30 million Americans have no health insurance. They may work for small businesses that do not offer or cannot afford health insurance or are self-employed, but are not poor enough to qualify for state medicaid or federal medicare programs. Illness sometimes puts people in the awful position of assigning a "dollar value" to someone's life. Life savings are wasted on fringe treatments lest the family endure feelings of guilt for not "trying everything."

Increasingly, families have two wage earners to make ends meet, and the illness of one of them deprives the family of needed additional income. Costs are up; income is down. On top of not feeling good, now you have to worry about staying afloat financially. We face a health insurance system that is far more willing to collect your premiums when you are healthy and do not need services than to provide care when you are ill. This is one more way in which patients and their families feel isolated, even from those who are paid to help them when they become ill. We need a government mandate to insure all people; refusing coverage to those who need it most is a disgrace. In the meantime, you will have to learn to do battle with insurance companies and make tough choices about how to allocate your limited resources.

REENTRY

After the intital shock and treatment are over, you naturally want to resume life as it was. Often, that is more or less possible, but it's important to acknowledge that things will never be quite the same. It's more realistic to expect that the period of time following treatment will bring new sources of stress. In particular, having found yourself thrust into the unwelcome role of patient, you will need to find a way to reemerge from it. This is important not just for you but for your family. You cannot go back to life just as before. You may wish to reassess how you allocate your time and whom you spend it with (more on this in later chapters). Sometimes it's a relief to get back into the normal world of everyday problems, but at the same time you may feel less like dealing with it all. You face new uncertainties, and your old ways of handling things may not work as well. In addition, you have new financial burdens to think about. This means that your task is not simply to add the new worries and tasks to the old ones, but to change priorities. Someone else can be a den mother, coach the soccer team, or take on that new project at work. Recognize that your resources are finite, and allocate your energy where you need it most. Later on, as your recovery is more complete, you may be able to take on more again. You are more than simply a patient, but you cannot live as though you have not been through a serious illness.

However, being ill does not excuse you from life's responsibilities, and it is demoralizing to relinquish roles you can, in fact, fulfill. Your family and friends are counting on you to do what you can to help them. It will make you feel better to get back to doing what you used to do, but within realistic limits. If you have physical limitations, acknowledge them, but direct others in doing what you used to do yourself. No one knows better than you how to do it.

One woman wrote a detailed manual for running the household for her husband. In the short run, it aided them in keeping things going. In the long run, it was a gift to him to help him cope after her death. It may be hard at first to make such changes. It may seem as though you are preparing prematurely for your absence, and this is emotionally wrenching. Nonetheless, think of it as providing yourself and your family with options, ways of getting things done.

Life-threatening illness seems to have an all-or-none quality. Are you just an eternal "patient"? Or are you perfectly normal, cured, beyond it forever? Usually the answer lies somewhere in the middle. You can resume life, but with a new set of anxieties, tasks, and responsibilities to your body and to your family. You have a new role to learn, that of being a functioning patient, aware of your illness, treating it medically, but not yielding more of your life to it than is necessary. This takes thought, effort, and support. Use the period after active medical treatment is over to divert the time and energy you spent on treatment to taking charge of your newly revised life. Even if you must wait and see about the illness, you can take plenty of control over the time you have.

3. Illness, Personality, and Coping

Living well is the best revenge.

LIVING WITH YOUR ILLNESS

Jim is a handsome, intense, thirty-eight-year-old systems analyst who has been diagnosed with leukemia, a cancer of the white blood cells. He was undergoing a bone marrow transplant. Even with his head shorn of hair because of chemotherapy and his lips painted with Vaseline to keep them from cracking, he managed to look vigorous, engaging, and in command. He liked analyzing problems, seeing what needed doing, and fixing them. That was his job and that was the way he had run his life. Determination and logic had never failed to solve a problem before, but as he lay in his bed recovering from the effects of the bone marrow transplantation, he struggled with a system of coping that lay in tatters.

"I thought," he said, speaking crisply but sadly, "That all I had to do was get through this transplant, that it was a matter of enduring tough treatment for a few weeks or a few months, and then my life would be back to normal. I could work as hard as I did and be with my family. I selected the most aggressive treatment, found an outstanding place to give it to me, and thought I had solved the problem." The only alternative seemed to be giving up, letting the disease win rather than him.

"But now I'm having to rethink the problem. I realize that the illness is a factor in my life, even after the transplantation. I can't get rid of it that easily. I have to find a new way to think about this, because I don't want it in my life, but I can't seem to get it out of my life." Jim was used to identifying and solving problems. This problem had identified and changed *him*.

J im described clearly a mental process that many people with serious illness go through. His initial thought was that he would endure a temporary period of discomfort to restore the life he had had before. He then expected to wake up one morning and have life just as it was. In the service of this goal, he was willing to endure a great deal. For some illnesses, this is possible. Some cancers can be completely removed. Certain infections can be eliminated. Some blocked arteries can be opened. However, for many illnesses, the answer is not black or white. The progression of the illness can be slowed, the damage caused by it reduced, but the disease, or the threat of its return, cannot be entirely eliminated. This means giving up the fantasy that life will be just as it was before the illness became a part of your life. It also means that you are challenged to find ways to live well, perhaps even better, but differently, accepting but not yielding to the illness, which has become a part of your body and your life.

I believe Jim was caught on the horns of a dilemma because he conceived of his situation in one of two extreme, unrealistic ways: Either I am a cancer patient, in which case I am ill, dying, and have no hope of normal joy and pleasure in life, or I am no longer a cancer patient, in which case I have no fears or worries, and I am free to work and be happy. How do you get beyond this either/or dichotomy so you can live a happy, even invigorated life, savoring the good without ignoring or being overwhelmed by the bad?

Modern medical diagnosis and treatment have made an enormous difference in our ability to survive certain cancers, notably those of the blood and lymphatic systems (lymphomas and leukemias, especially Hodgkin's disease), testicular cancer, and certain childhood cancers, many of which can now be cured. Early detection and vigorous treatment of other more common cancers such as colon and breast are extending survival time and in a smaller number of cases leading to a cure. While the outlook is less optimistic with such cancers as those of the lungs and pancreas, treatment controls symptoms and may prolong life. What this means is that more people are living *with* cancer rather than just dying of it. Medically, cancer was once thought of as a terminal illness; it is now thought of as a chronic illness, similar to diabetes, arthritis, or heart disease.

Remember, approximately half of all cancer patients will get through their treatment and live to die of something else. The other half come to recognize that their lives will be deeply affected and eventually limited by cancer. In either case, cancer is a chronic disease, and adjusting to it requires living with cancer more than dying from it. People with cancer tend to think that life is either normal and happy or destroyed by the threat of death. The reality is that we all live under a death sentence. Living with a more pressing reminder of this fact, such as cancer, is really just a special case of the human condition. While it may induce fear, it can also enhance life. However, many make the mistake of pretending that the disease is not there, avoid talking about it, thinking about it, or even seeing doctors about it. This creates a kind of inner tension that is draining and pernicious. Energy goes toward keeping up the façade of normalcy, instead of fighting the disease and living life as fully as possible. Cancer is more a fact of life than a fact of death.

One of the odd things about cancer is that often the diagnosis seems worse than the disease. Frequently, in fact, there is little or no dis-ease associated with having cancer. You may notice a nonpainful lump, a dark spot on your skin, a little bleeding, and learn from your doctor that the tests indicate cancer. It seems unfair that you can feel quite good physically, and yet have your doctor tell you that you have a serious and potentially progressive illness. Many patients complain that it seems to be the treatments rather than the disease that make

"My feeling is that while we should have the deepest respect for reality, we should not let it control our lives."

Drawing by Richter; © 1986 The New Yorker Magazine, Inc.

them feel sick. (I describe how to cope with specific side effects of treatment later in the book, in Chapter 11.)

CANCER VERSUS HEART DISEASE: LEARNING BY COUNTEREXAMPLE

Each illness presents a unique set of problems, yet the threat posed by any serious illness is ultimately the same. What effects do personality and coping have on illness? It is instructive to compare what we know about these factors as they apply to cancer and heart disease. People with heart disease as well as cancer often employ considerable denial. At the time of a first heart attack, many conclude that the sudden chest pain is really an attack of indigestion. In rare cases, some even try to do exercises such as push-ups to "prove" that there is nothing wrong with their heart. This denial is quite dangerous; the first heart attack is often fatal. Similarly, many cancer patients ignore that first lump or sign of bleeding, putting off the visit to the doctor as if putting it out of mind would put it out of their body.

Yet in some ways, people with cancer seem to view their illness quite differently from those with heart disease. There is a common fantasy of control among those with heart disease. Survivors of heart disease often have as unrealistically optimistic a point of view as cancer patients have a fatalistic one. They believe that if they finally lose weight, cut down on cholesterol in their diet, stop smoking, and reduce stress, they can control what is happening in their body. After all, it makes sense. We can picture how our nervous system connects to the heart, regulating its rhythm. We can see how cholesterol in the diet could make its way into the coronary arteries, blocking them. The idea that the mind or changes in our behavior could somehow control the body makes more sense in the context of heart disease than it does in that of cancer. Because we can more easily visualize how we could control physical events in heart disease, we often feel that we do.

Indeed, such apparently unwarranted optimism can at times have a positive outcome. The belief that you are doing something to control your illness can have beneficial effects. A Yale University study published in *The Lancet* examined the efficacy of a type of drug called a beta blocker, which controls heart rhythm, in helping patients recover from a heart attack. Some 2,175 men were assigned to one of two courses of action. One group received the beta blocker; another group received a placebo, in essence a sugar pill with no specific activity. All patients were assigned randomly—that is, they could not choose which part of the study they were in, and patients who got a pill did not know whether they had received the active drug or the placebo. The likelihood of surviving the ensuing year was 2.6 times higher among those who took the pill as prescribed. This does not seem surprising, except that it did not matter whether they took the beta blocker or the sugar pill! While those men who suffered less stress and those with good social support were less likely to die, the effect of adherence to treatment on survival was independent of these factors. In other words, the act of taking a pill, regardless of what was in it, had a more powerful effect on subsequent heart disease than the pharmacologic effect of the pill itself. The study provides clear evidence that those who felt they were actively doing something to affect the course of the disease did better physically.

There have been no such similar findings for people with cancer, and this study does not prove that you can do or believe anything, regardless of how irrelevant, and your illness will improve. Rather, it shows that there are situations in which belief and action directed toward controlling a disease may well have physical as well as psychological effects.

Individuals who are prone to heart disease are thought to have a unique personality type, referred to as "Type A." This theory, put forward by cardiologists Ray Rosenman and Meyer Friedman, holds that such individuals are characterized as hard driving, impatient, and hostile. Indeed, Redford Williams at Duke University has shown that anger and hostility seem to be the crucial defining characteristics of such individuals. Many studies have shown that Type A individuals are at higher risk for getting heart disease, although recent research complicates the picture by showing that Type A individuals may also be more likely to survive a heart attack once they get one.

In this body of research, Type A individuals have been contrasted with so-called Type B's, who are relatively relaxed, patient, and not especially hostile. There are therapeutic implications in the findings. Stanford psychologist Carl Thoresen has shown that training Type A individuals in groups to be more Type B–like lowers their subsequent rates of heart disease. Again, this all seems rather plausible—you can picture the change in nerve signals from the brain to the heart and the body, reducing stress on the heart, changing heart rhythm, even relaxing the blood vessels supplying oxygen and nutrients to the heart.

Internist Dean Ornish at the University of California in San Francisco established a program for patients with heart disease. Everyone in his study had already suffered a heart attack. He randomly assigned half of the patients to a program that consisted of group support meetings several times a week, a strict vegetarian diet, moderate exercise, and training in meditation and relaxation. I had an occasion to visit Dr. Ornish's program in San Francisco. His patients demonstrated tremendous caring for one another. Many of them felt (and Dr. Ornish has come to feel as well) that the group support portions of the program have been the most important. In those groups they shared common fears and problems, and felt cared about, less alone with their anxieties.

Dr. Ornish's program had a surprising and impressive physical effect. Those patients who had gone through this treatment study group showed an actual *increase* in the size of their coronary arteries, as measured with sophisticated imaging techniques, while those in the control group, who received standard cardiac care, showed a similar *decrease* in the openness of their coronary arteries. Although the differences were small, about eight millimeters, the significance was not. The patients on Dr. Ornish's protocol demonstrated a *reversal* of the disease process that blocks the inside of coronary arteries, while in the control patients the disease worsened. The long-range health effects of these differences are now being followed.

What these studies show is that a number of factors may influence the *course* of heart disease beyond medication and surgery. These include social support, placebo pills, and various kinds of group therapy. What does this imply for people with cancer? It suggests that serious illness can be addressed from the top down as well as the bottom up —that is, using one's mental resources could produce positive physical results. These approaches produced no cures of heart disease, but they did influence the course of it. We are finding and describing in this book similar results with cancer patients.

CANCER AND PERSONALITY STYLES

Many people with cancer, in contrast to many of those with heart disease, frequently feel helpless. They and their doctors cannot conceive of what they can do to fight the illness, other than comply strictly with the regimen of chemotherapy and radiation, while perhaps maintaining a diet low in fat and high in fiber for good measure. Scientific studies on the effects of psychological interventions on the course of heart disease and cancer are few, but consistently encouraging and generally well conducted. By contrast, the literature on personality style and cancer, unlike that involving Type A behavior and heart disease, is less clear, and has provoked considerable controversy within the scientific community.

The theory presented is that the "typical" cancer patient's personality is thought to be the opposite of the "typical" heart disease patient. Instead of demonstrating the impatience and hostility typical of the Type A person, the person with cancer is described as patient, repressed, and strangely devoid of anger. The ancient Greek physician Galen described a "polite, almost apologetic" quality in cancer patients. Like any generalization, this one has its limitations, and there is considerable debate about the relationship between personality and cancer. The biggest problem was best described by the British philosopher David Hume, who said that "constant conjunction does not imply causation." Even if the relationship exists, there might be some common intervening factor, such as a poor energy level, for example, that makes it hard to get angry and reduces the body's defenses against cancer. Second, personality measures are notoriously complex. It is clear that we do not know enough to tell people that their personality gave them cancer.

Before we get into the details of the research, let me stress two points. (1) While there may be a statistical relationship between certain personality "types" and the occurrence of cancer, there is *no* evidence that having a personality of one type or another *causes* cancer; and (2) There is no evidence that changing personality traits affects the course of cancer.

AVOIDING ANGER

Researchers Stephen Greer and Tina Morris in England studied 160 women undergoing breast biopsy to determine whether or not they had cancer. They asked them a series of questions before these women knew the result of the biopsy. Sixty-nine of these women were found to have cancer, and of these, almost half were also found to be extreme suppressors of anger—the type who would say that they "had never or not more than twice during their adult lives openly shown anger." This pattern was not typical of the women whose biopsies were normal. This does not mean that you grow a tumor if you do not express anger. It simply indicates that for some reason those who turned out to have a malignancy were less likely to report getting angry. There is a growing body of research, spawned by psychologist Daniel Weinberger at Case Western Reserve, showing that some individuals may experience a good deal of distress, but they are so conscious of social requirements that they repress expression of these feelings of discomfort: He calls them "repressors," in contrast to "sensitizers," who feel no constraints about giving vent to even minor discomfort. Repressors may themselves be unaware of how much discomfort they experience, which could lead to delays in seeking appropriate medical diagnosis and treatment. This could account for a higher proportion of malignancies—the symptom had progressed farther before it was noticed and attended to.

FIGHTING SPIRIT

The same British cancer research group, joined by Keith Pettingale, turned their attention to personality factors that might help in coping with cancer once it had been diagnosed. They studied a group of sixty-nine women who had breast cancer and classified their responses to the illness in one of four categories:

1. *Fighting spirit.* These individuals accepted the diagnosis of cancer, but were determined to fight it and were realistically optimistic about the outcome.
2. *Denial.* These individuals pretended they did not have cancer or if they had it there was minimal threat to their health.
3. *Stoic acceptance.* These individuals simply accepted their lot and were fatalistic about the outcome, doing little or nothing to change it.
4. *Helplessness/hopelessness.* Overwhelmed by the diagnosis and its implications, these individuals basically gave up.

All these people with cancer were followed for several years. The investigators found that those who demonstrated fighting spirit or denial were *twice* as likely to survive for the ensuing five years than those who demonstrated stoic acceptance or helplessness. These findings have persisted ten to fifteen years later. In my opinion, the "fighting spirit" finding is the important one. These individuals recognized the threat, but were determined to cope with it as effectively as possible. Both the stoics and the helpless/hopeless individuals were aware of the problem but saw no avenues of control, so they were perpetually uncomfortable and unhappy. That those who employed denial fared well is puzzling to me. Clearly their conscious distress was lower than that in the other groups, except perhaps for those with fighting spirit. It is indeed possible that for some people the pretense works. Whether or not these means of responding to cancer influence its progression in some way, or are a sign of those whose bodies are more capable of fighting the illness, the results make sense. Stick up for yourself and you'll stick around.

Individuals with a fighting spirit are not head-in-the-sand optimists. Rather, they seem to have a quiet determination to do whatever they can to deal with their illness. They seek and evaluate alternative means of medical treatment, insist that their questions be answered, get diagnostic tests to clarify any problems, and have a "take-charge" attitude about conducting their lives as well as their medical treatment. They illustrate the difference between positive expectations and false hope. They are determined realists.

Our own findings are consistent with those of the British researchers. We took pains to interview the family members of the four women from our early studies who had survived the longest (three were still alive). We wanted to understand what they had been like. In general, they were quietly assertive, determined to live life the way they wanted to. They said "no" to treatment they did not want, and told friends and family how and when to help them. They would insist on diagnostic tests, and at times would refuse aspects of medical treatment they did not feel they needed. We found that they were rather restrained in expressing emotion, especially anger, serious but with a low-key sense of humor. They were extremely determined, independent, and were not prone to be easily frightened.

Jane's sister told us about Jane's control over her medical treatment. She had refused a mastectomy and had argued with her doctor. "She said, 'I just told him that that was my body and I was in charge of it and that I would make the decision about it, and what he said wasn't going to make any difference. If I didn't want that done, I wasn't going to have it done.' "

Jane took charge of her care and was quietly determined. She might at times be the last to volunteer information in the group, but she held to her opinions firmly.

The brother of another of these long-surviving women described his sister as being utterly resolute:

> My sister Evelyn was a very tough, determined person who had to have her way. That's her main characteristic. That's the most important thing about her, because she was a determined person, and it was her way or no way at all. And she had her husband pretty much buffaloed, you know, in that regard. And she was the boss— let's put it that way. She had the control. . . . She decided she wasn't going to let some little thing like breast cancer take her.

Thus there is evidence from several studies that charting your own course, a kind of quiet determination or fighting spirit, is a good style of coping with the illness, and seems to typify those who do well. This does not mean that yelling at everyone will make you survive longer or better. It does mean that, if anything, a dose of assertiveness is good medicine.

This does not mean that refusing medical treatment is a good overall strategy. Many effective treatments are unpleasant, and many patients have an understandable impulse to avoid them. Healthy assertiveness means finding out what you need to know about the benefits and risks of treatment. In some circumstances, your doctor and you may agree that the possible benefit is not worth the discomfort or risk. Fighting spirit means making choices, not just saying "no."

"TYPE C" PERSONALITY

The research on personality correlates of people with cancer has been reconceptualized as a coping style complementary to Type A, called "Type C." Psychologist Lydia Temoshok defines this style as involving appeasement, suppression of negative emotion, and a focus on the needs of others rather than on oneself. She reported that this self-effacing style is common among cancer patients and that it predicted faster progression of malignant melanoma, a cancer of the skin. In a study of fifty-eight such patients, she reported that the more emotionally expressive malignant melanoma patients had more slowly growing tumors and a stronger immune response to them. Thus, this finding would suggest that denying illness is not good for you, while giving vent to strong feelings might help. These results led Dr. Temoshok to conclude that there is a relationship between emotional suppression and inhibition of those aspects of the immune system that are involved in cancer surveillance. (I discuss possible mechanisms by which psychological and social factors may translate into effects on the body in Chapter 4.)

This whole area of research is fascinating but controversial.

Several large-scale studies have failed to demonstrate any relationship between personality variables and the course of cancer. Psychologist Barrie Cassileth from the University of Pittsburgh administered personality tests to two large samples of people with cancer and then followed the course of their illness. She found no relationship between any of the personality measures and the rate of disease progression or survival time. Psychologists Robert Jamison, Thomas Burish, and Kenneth Wallston at Vanderbilt University tested the mood, sense of well-being, self-esteem, proneness to experience hostility, and sense of being in control over health in a sample of forty-nine women with advanced breast cancer. There were no differences on these measures between the women who survived less than sixteen months and those who lived longer. In other words, proneness to anxiety, depression, hostility, or helplessness did not seem to predict how long these women survived with cancer. Similarly, in our own studies, we have not found any personality variables that predict the rate of disease progression. While the concept that certain personality attributes such as anger suppression may be more common in cancer patients is interesting, it lends itself far too easily to the problem of blaming the victim. If suppressing your anger makes tumors grow more quickly, then any growth of the tumor might be considered your fault. There is no proof that this is the case. Furthermore, even if there is a relationship between being sicker and suppressing feeling, it could well be that the illness causes the emotional suppression rather than the other way around. You may simply not feel well enough to be your usual irascible self. Far more research and less finger pointing is needed in this area.

In the meantime, the psychological and social meaning of these personality styles deserves attention. Regardless of a possible effect on the rate of disease progression, at the least this research suggests that a take-charge attitude in response to serious illness is a good idea. Many people with life-threatening illness may be less likely to put their own feelings and needs first, especially the strong feelings and new needs that arise after the diagnosis and treatment of the illness. Just when you may (and should) feel angry, frightened, and frustrated, your resources for handling such feelings may be sorely taxed.

If you have learned over the years how to recognize, express, and use such strong emotions, you may do it well when you become ill. If, on the other hand, you are one of those people who don't allow themselves the luxury of experiencing or expressing strong emotions, then the flood of feelings that comes with serious illness will make you even more uncomfortable and more likely to suppress them. This can lead, in turn, to a kind of deep personal confusion in which you are puzzled and frightened by your own uncharacteristic emotional reactions. You then struggle more desperately than ever to suppress and avoid them. Those emotions in turn, seek expression, and on the cycle goes.

The same problem may emerge if you have a built-in tendency to put the needs of others first. There is something almost reassuring about doing this when you have new and upsetting needs. There is a kind of soothing comfort in the repetition of old patterns. It is as though you could recreate a time before you had cancer, somehow make it go away. Addressing your needs means acknowledging that you have a serious illness, and this in and of itself is frightening. Initially, it may feel better to look after others.

Francine is a hardworking, sweet, but somewhat remote office manager for a group of physicians. Unmarried but devoted to her family, she habitually put aside her needs to attend to her responsibilities. This included putting off a visit to an oncologist for eight months after she noticed a lump in her breast, because "I couldn't take time off from work, and that was the only time when the doctors could see me." Alas, this duty-bound and denial-based delay may have allowed the cancer to spread.

After some months in a support group, during which she learned by watching others some "tricks of the trade," Francine proudly recounted an interaction with a patient in the practice where she worked: "He was yelling at me on the phone, complaining that we had not filed some health insurance papers we were supposed to have sent. I was explaining that we were doing the best we could, but he kept yelling. Finally, I said: 'Look, I have cancer and I'm not going to take this anymore.' It stopped him in his tracks. He apologized and that was the end of it."

Francine had a big, shy smile on her face as she told the story. She had finally succeeded in recognizing and accepting her own perfectly reasonable anger and putting her needs first, and all in a few well-chosen sentences. The group was proud of her.

As this story illustrates, not only is a life-threatening illness stressful, but other stressors have a way of coming along and demanding attention. Psychologist Amanda Ramirez studied the effects of severe stress on breast cancer patients in England. She compared breast cancer patients who had experienced a recurrence of the disease in some other part of their body with those who had not. She found that those with a recurrence were far more likely to have had a serious stress, such as a death in the family, loss of a job, or being forced to move. More minor stressors, however, were unrelated to disease progression. This study cannot prove causation, but it does suggest that additional major stressors are not helpful. The body's resources are finite, and coping with one major stressor may limit its ability to cope successfully with others.

Our group participants often joke among themselves about the personality characteristics that are supposed to make you vulnerable to cancer. At one meeting they were discussing their fears about dying, and the talk revolved around how uneasy they felt at the thought of other people having to do things for them. They defined themselves to a great extent by their ability to do things for other people: family, friends, colleagues. Lucy then asked: "Say, where are all those women who like to have someone hold the phone for them? I guess they don't get cancer."

EXPLAINING CANCER TO YOURSELF

Joan described her life of service to other people, and how she had always put others' needs first. To her, cancer seemed unfair: "I have led a good life helping other people. It isn't fair that my reward should be to die so young of cancer."

It is not uncommon to spend time trying to explain to yourself why you got a terrible illness—the "Why me?" syndrome—especially after you have had it for a while. Illness is often experienced as a punishment, since indeed there is suffering associated with it, and the treatments often seem "punishing." We like to believe in a world with some kind of justice and logic to it. Furthermore, it is hard to comprehend chance, the idea that bad things may happen for no good reason at all. This is the problem depicted in the biblical Book of Job. Job is a good man who suffers every conceivable loss for no good reason. Suffering is not fair. It simply *is*. After all, it is *your* body that is betraying you and changing for the worse. Hence, if a punishment is being meted out, there must be a crime. What did you do to deserve this?

When asked by researcher Carolyn Gotay why they believed they had gotten cancer, cancer patients most frequently cited "chance." Their other explanations were past behavior, the opportunity to find positive meaning in the illness, and God's will. Social psychologist Shelley Taylor found that less than a third of women with breast cancer in her study considered the question of what had caused their cancer important at the time of initial diagnosis. Taylor's patient group suspected stress, a specific carcinogen, heredity, diet, and an injury to the breast as causes. Her research showed that one kind of explanation for cancer seemed associated with poorer adjustment to the illness: blaming it on someone else. However, women who believed that they had some kind of control over the cause of disease did better emotionally. This finding is important, since it is consistent with the theory that a fighting spirit is helpful: Blaming someone else, which is a passive stance, gets you nowhere, while taking responsibility for your past, present, and future makes you feel and do better. These findings suggest that feeling in control is good for you, while placing blame elsewhere just makes you feel helpless.

However, the *type* of control you believe you have over your illness is crucial. Research by psychologist Maggie Watson and her colleagues at the Royal Marsden Hospital in London (1990) provides evidence that those cancer patients who feel in control over the *course* of the illness and its treatment feel better emotionally. However, those who feel responsible for *causing* their cancer through some presumed personality flaw or inability to handle stress are burdened with needless guilt and fare poorly. The famous "serenity prayer" written by theologian Reinhold Niebuhr would seem to be especially apt:

Lord grant me the courage to change what can be changed,
the serenity to accept what cannot be changed,
and the wisdom to know one from the other.

My colleagues and I asked the women with metastatic breast cancer in our group how they understood the causes and means of coping with their illness. Their answers fell into four categories, presented in order of the degree of personal control they represent.

1. *Personal/Psychological.* Many of the women believed that their mental attitude, emotional state, and coping behavior played the central role in controlling and explaining their cancer's onset and course. An example of this psychological type of explanation is: "My inability to handle stress better was responsible for my cancer's spreading." The women who espoused this viewpoint were prone to self-blame.

2. *Religious.* Some women believed that prayer and faith in God both control and explain cancer. An example of the religious explanation is: "Prayer helps my body fight cancer."

3. *Medical/Biotechnological.* Some women gave scientific explanations of what caused their cancer and how it could be controlled. An example of the medical/technological explanation is: "The rapid advance of medical technology is my best hope for overcoming my cancer."

4. *Fatalistic.* For some women, chance and the arbitrary nature of the world explained their cancer. A typical fatalistic statement is: "My cancer and its spread have no meaning except that we are all mortal and life is limited." The women with this viewpoint were prone to a grim realism.

We found that, initially, the women who explained their cancer using the first three categories all suffered considerable anxiety and depression. During the course of the subsequent year, however, those who subscribed to personal/psychological explanations tended to become less disturbed. By contrast, those who increasingly expressed a fatalistic attitude became more anxious and depressed. We also found that many patients yielded to fatalism as they became sicker, and at such times they (naturally) showed more emotional upset. As we followed these women over time, it became clear that those who thought that they had some control over the course of the illness did better emotionally. They did not do well when they felt helpless.

We also compared the beliefs of those women assigned to our support groups with those of the women in the control group, who just had routine cancer care. The women in the support group did best emotionally when they believed in the utility of psychological factors in managing their illness, while those in the control group felt better when they believed in the power of medical and technological influences. In other words, they were less anxious and depressed when they believed in what they got.

Yale psychologist Judith Rodin conducted an important series of studies in nursing homes. Older patients were given training in stress management and then given small tasks to perform, such as caring for plants. She found that those who received this experimental treatment approach were not only rated as happier and more sociable, but also lived longer than those who were not treated. Rodin also measured decreases in the amounts of cortisol, a stress hormone, produced by those patients who received education in stress management.

All of the studies cited above point in the same direction: You do better when you learn to take charge of the course of your illness realistically. You cannot control everything, you cannot undo what has been done (like getting the disease), but you will benefit by taking hold of your current situation in whatever way is possible.

MANAGING THE ANXIETY

People with serious illness often *do* feel helpless and may become consumed with anxiety about the possibility that the illness will return and spread.

Karen developed breast cancer in her twenties and told me that she feels she has lost her youth. She watches the carefree attitude her friends have, their untroubled lives, their spontaneity, and resents the fact that she faces every day worried about cancer: "I don't mind not having a boob. But I regret the worry. I wonder if I ate too many french fries. I will never again have that freedom to do and eat and be whatever I want." Karen is determined to live as full a life as she can, and travels widely. However, her determination to keep her body in shape is so strong that she awakens at 3 A.M. to get to the gym and have a two-hour workout before she reports for her job. Her determination and discipline are admirable, but the spontaneity is indeed gone from her life.

Each new ache and pain, every new lump, could be a sign that your illness has come back or is spreading. It helps to have developed a plan in advance for dealing with such problems should they arise. Usually the next step after the discovery is a series of inner battles:

1. Is it real? Do I feel anything or is it just my imagination?
2. Should I tell anyone? should I let my husband know or not? Telling him seems to make it more real, and makes it more likely that I will have to do something about it.
3. Should I tell my doctor? Do I call and make an appointment, or just wait for my next regular checkup? If I make the appointment, it seems as if I am making a big deal about it. Maybe it's nothing. But if I wait and it is something, I have all that anxiety for a longer period of time, and I may delay necessary treatment.

My general rule of thumb is, *if it is on your mind, do something about it.* You treat anxiety by doing something. Even if you are just humoring yourself, you are still reducing your anxiety and that in and of itself is worthwhile. If your doctor thinks you are worrying about nothing, he or she can tell you so. But doctors count on their patients to be good reporters of what they feel in their bodies.

Thus, plan in advance that if you feel a new pain or lump, you will not agonize over what to do. You will call and make an appoint-

ment to see your doctor. You can't stop the worry, but you can minimize the discomfort of indecision. Furthermore, earlier detection can
make a critical difference in outcome: If you find the cancer sooner,
less treatment will be more effective.

Research shows that seeing the illness as an occasion to make
positive changes in your life beyond the disease itself is a creative
adaptation to a major life threat. Furthermore, taking charge of as
many aspects of your life as possible, including the disease and its
treatment, will help you feel less anxious and depressed. Your illness
is an occasion to reevaluate life—a wake-up call, not a death knell.
When your life is threatened, take hold and make the most of it; don't
give up on it.

Jane takes genuine pride in her newly acquired skill of getting her
large health maintenance organization to respond to her—no small
task. She discovered that if she gets her X ray or bone scan order at
the beginning instead of at the end of her doctor's appointment, she
can put it in downstairs and save herself half an hour or more waiting time. She learned that she can obtain initial reports of the results
right after the scan. She finds doctors who will talk directly with her
and actively seeks information about new treatments. She used to
think of herself as a typical "good patient." Now she considers herself an "expert patient." She is realistic about the illness, but determined about how to manage it. She is cultivating that fighting
spirit, a determined realism, and others in the group are being infected by it.

4. Does Living Better Mean Living Longer?

SOCIAL SUPPORT AND HEALTH

Our answer to the threat of nonbeing is not just being, but being together. Some of the hardest moments in our supportive/expressive therapy groups occurred when we saw how close death was, and yet at those very moments we relied most upon our caring about one another. Our answer to the ultimate loss of human contact was a reaffirmation of that contact.

There is a mounting body of scientific data that suggests this answer was a wise one: Research shows a positive link between health and the social support in our lives—our friendships, marriage, family, and the like. Several large-scale epidemiological studies have found that the number of regular social relationships is associated with a lower risk of dying at a given age.

Lisa Berkman, now a Yale professor, and Leonard Syme, an epidemiologist at the University of California, Berkeley, for example, studied the relationship between four types of social connection: marital status, contact with extended family and friends, church membership, and other group affiliations. They found that each type of social connection, and all of them put together, predicted how likely a subject was to die within the next nine years. Indeed, all other things being equal, those individuals who were least socially connected were *twice* as likely to die as those with the strongest social ties.

Similar studies in Michigan, Georgia, Sweden, and Finland have yielded comparable results. For example, when epidemiologist James House of the University of Michigan obtained data from interviews with 2,754 adults after they visited physicians, he discovered that those with more social relationships and activities had lower mortality (likelihood of dying). The more socially active men were two to three times less likely to die than those who were most isolated, while the risk for socially isolated women was one and a half to two times as great. These studies make it clear that daily contact with people is good for your health.

The relationship between social isolation and mortality is as large and statistically strong as the relationship between smoking or high serum cholesterol and mortality. Based on the strength of these data, it may be as important to your health to improve your social relationships as it is to stop smoking or reduce dietary cholesterol. Whether or not changing the number of people you see every day would change your risk of dying in the same way as stopping smoking or reducing dietary cholesterol remains an open question. Nonetheless, it is strange indeed that a factor that is so strongly related to health outcome is so widely ignored.

Internist James Goodwin and colleagues, now at the University of Texas at Galveston, studied the relationship between marital status and survival among several thousand cancer patients. They found that married cancer patients did better medically than unmarried cancer patients. Similarly, Yale epidemiologist Lisa Berkman found that the quality of social support available to patients who have suffered a heart attack significantly predicts their odds of surviving. People who are socially isolated are three times less likely to recover from a heart attack than those who have an extensive and caring social support network.

I recall Thomas Hackett, a professor of psychiatry at Harvard, who taught me my first hypnosis course, telling the class about "one of those studies I just couldn't publish." It was a randomized trial conducted at the Massachusetts General Hospital to evaluate the effect of having a psychiatrist pay a visit to patients recovering from heart attacks. As expected, they found that the patients who received such consultation felt better—they were less anxious and depressed. Unexpected was the finding that the patients who had received the consultations were more likely to survive their heart attacks and leave the hospital alive. Dr. Hackett was so stunned by the finding that he could not bring himself to publish it; he "knew" no one would believe it. Since he had not predicted the result, he had good reason to wonder whether the difference in survival was a chance finding. Nonetheless, given subsequent evidence over the years of the relationship between social support and survival, his early finding is less surprising.

Of course, there are many things that can account for the differences in survival that are related to our social network. In general these studies have been careful to eliminate the obvious confounding variables, such as smoking and alcohol abuse and differences in socioeconomic status. Thus, both the quality as well as the quantity of social relatedness has been shown in large-scale studies to be associated with mortality and demonstrates that more and better social support from family and friends is associated with lower odds of dying at a given age.

Humans are social beings. It is no mystery, nor is it surprising, that our skill at maintaining social relationships should have survival value. Two obvious examples come to mind. The first is the necessity of forming alliances to protect groups from predators and to provide stable sources of food, clothing, and shelter. In primitive times those who were more adept at communicating with one another and forming relationships were more likely to survive. Second, the human infant is not a particularly robust specimen. Indeed, humans have the most prolonged period of helplessness and dependency in infancy of any higher organism. To survive to reproduce, humans are dependent upon the physical and social skills of their parents. The infant must engage in a certain amount of social behavior to attract parental attention and support in order to make its needs known and survive. Thus, in a basic sense, social support has always meant survival.

Let's examine a related but different question: What effect does social support have on health and survival in modern, industrialized cultures? As humans we are not especially splendid physical specimens. Bears are stronger, leopards faster, dogs smell more keenly, eagles can read newsprint half a mile away. Other than the opposing thumb, humans have little in the way of physical advantages over many other species in the animal kingdom. Indeed, some attributes set us below: We are the only species that kills so recklessly that we wipe out entire species. When asked what he thought of Western civilization, Gandhi is said to have replied: "I think it would be a very good idea."

What sets us apart in a positive sense is the large neocortex that sits on top of our bodies and allows us to think, remember, plan, talk, and interact in very complex ways with other humans. Mental agility seems more important than physical strength in coping with modern civilization. Does it not make sense that there might well be survival advantages associated with the large brains we have evolved? Could they not be useful in transforming our skill at social relations (and lapses in that skill) into mechanisms for coping with disease and the deterioration of our bodies?

CANCER SUPPORT GROUPS AND SURVIVAL

Given all of this research, I was highly interested in the question of what effect group support might have on the course of cancer. If you had asked me in 1980 what the effect of support groups might have been on the course of the *disease,* rather than on the patients, I would probably have said, "not much—maybe a month or two in survival time. But it will be too small a difference to mean anything statistically."

I was invited to speak at a conference in New York sponsored by the excellent psychiatry division at Memorial Sloan-Kettering Cancer

Center in September of 1984. This is a pioneering program, run by psychiatrist Dr. Jimmie Holland, that has helped to establish the field of psychooncology, the psychiatry and psychology of cancer. Research from Holland's group has demonstrated that depression and anxiety are common among cancer patients and has provided important guidelines for medical and psychotherapeutic treatment.

I spoke about our finding that hypnosis and group support were effective in reducing cancer pain (reviewed in Chapter 11). I had a few confrontations with neurologists who felt that I was really dealing with patients who had minor pain or that I was overlooking neurologic problems in my patients while focusing on the psychiatric ones.

The presenters and attendees were abuzz about the growing popularity of visualization and other "wish away your cancer" techniques, espoused most prominently by Dr. Carl Simonton. Increasing numbers of cancer patients were being taught to meditate on their white blood cells killing cancer cells. Many were being made to feel guilty for getting cancer in the first place, or for not curing it once it happened. Indeed, many professionals at the conference expressed concern that such approaches would constitute an obstacle to the development of psychosocial support for cancer patients, because we would be identified with the medical "fringe."

In his book *Getting Well Again,* published in 1978, Dr. Simonton and his colleagues made very strong claims about the positive effects of his visualization program:

In the past four years, we have treated 159 patients with a diagnosis of medically incurable malignancy. Sixty-three of the patients are alive, with an average survival time of 24.4 months since the diagnosis. Life expectancy for this group, based on national norms, is 12 months. A matched control population is being developed and preliminary results indicate survival comparable with national norms and less than half the survival time of our patients. With the patients in our study who have died, their average survival time was 20.3 months. In other words, the patients in our study who are alive have lived, on the average, two times longer than patients who received medical treatment alone. Even those patients in the study who have died still lived one and one-half times longer than the control group. (p. 11)

This paragraph, quoted in its entirety, is worrisome. Dr. Simonton's group talks about developing a "control population," yet by the end of the paragraph they are already basing results on the unfinished process. They never describe this control population, which is one basis for the claim that their visualization patients lived longer. The other comparison is to "national norms." It is quite unlikely that the 159 people with cancer who had the time, money, interest, support, and energy to come to Simonton for treatment are typical of all cancer patients. Just based upon who they are, rather than the visualization treatment they practiced, they would be likely to do better than most people with cancer.

Despite this shaky base of evidence, Dr. Simonton goes on to claim the following:

The results from our approach to cancer treatment make us confident that the conclusions we have drawn are correct—that an active and positive participation can influence the onset of the disease, the outcome of treatment, and the quality of life. (p. 12)

The question Dr. Simonton raised is a provocative and important one—does attitude or psychotherapy of some type influence the course of cancer? However, to make strong claims, you need strong evidence, and that provided in his book and subsequent publications is weak indeed. Although it is fifteen years old, I quote from the book because it is still widely cited and the authors have not published any more recent data.

I felt (and feel) an obligation to the field and to my patients to be, if anything, more cautious than ever in what we put forward as an effective intervention. I had gone to a meeting for the public led by Dr.

Simonton in San Francisco some years earlier. The Veterans Memorial auditorium was filled to the rafters with cancer patients in wheelchairs, on walkers, and on crutches. It had the atmosphere of a tent revival meeting, and the speeches did not disappoint. One man talked about how he had been at death's door with cancer, and his wife had said to him: "If you die on me now, I'm going to follow you up to the afterlife and kick your ass back here." "Now," he added, smiling, "I am the North Carolina state racquetball champion." With stories like that, I could see how much hopes were being raised—and knew how much they would be dashed.

Stephanie Matthews-Simonton is currently conducting a study of the effect of imagery on a small group of patients with a rare and serious form of cancer at the Cambridge Hospital in Massachusetts. The crucial issue is developing a body of systematic research that documents whether or not such imagery techniques have any effect on the course of cancer.

A similar "take-charge" approach is recommended by Dr. Bernie Siegel, a former surgeon who advocates *Love, Medicine and Miracles,* the title of his best-selling book. He instructs patients that they need to take charge of their lives, and that they can control the course of their cancer if and when they are willing to live rather than die. This is another kind of false optimism. While there is some evidence that cancer patients with a "fighting spirit" may live longer than those who are docile and helpless, there is again no proof that simply changing your attitude changes the disease. Indeed, Dr. Siegel collaborated in a published study (the senior author was Dr. Thomas Morganstern) that showed that patients who went through Dr. Siegel's Exceptional Cancer Patients Program did not live any longer than a comparison sample of cancer patients, once researchers took into account the time from initial diagnosis of cancer.

A more recent study, published in the *Journal of Clinical Oncology,* by Dr. Siegel and colleagues provides a longer-term follow-up and confirms the original finding: Patients enrolled in the Exceptional Cancer Patients program did not live longer than a comparison sample of patients with similar disease. Thus, as judged by his own follow-up studies, there is no evidence that Dr. Siegel's version of love and medicine yields miracles.

In *Love, Medicine and Miracles,* Dr. Siegel asks patients to answer four questions for themselves:

1. *Do you want to live to be a hundred?*

   Dr. Siegel argues sensibly here that many people don't conceive of their lives going much beyond sixty-five and ignore the need for sensible diet, exercise, and other health-promoting activities.

2. *What happened to you in the year or two before your illness?*

   This is a more dangerous area, implying that stress may cause cancer. Stresses occur, and handling them well makes sense, regardless of whether or not they have anything to do with the onset of a disease.

3. *What does the illness mean to you?*

   This is an important question, and Dr. Siegel argues appropriately for "frank acceptance" of death and other realities of our lives. In the next paragraph, however, he gives examples of patients who seem to live on because they expect to live, not die. How can one face death and yet not expect it?

4. *Why did you need the illness?*

   This question is deeply disturbing to me. It implies that the illness occurred to fill some emotional need in the patient, that a miserable biological reality has been turned into a virtue by the ill person's mind. Even worse, it suggests that the illness was caused by this need. Dr. Siegel gives the example of Gladys, who "had learned to manipulate her whole family" through her intestinal disease. He told her that he had "a new drug that would cure her cancer" and invited her to come to his office. She never did, despite repeated phone calls. He takes this as evidence that she did not want to get better. That might be the case. On the other hand, Gladys may not have liked his approach or may not have believed that he indeed had a drug that would cure her. This is a weak basis upon which to rest a claim that people are sick because they want or need to be.

Dr. Siegel tries to distinguish between guilt and "a realization of one's *participation* and responsibility in the disease process.... Of course few ever really want a life-threatening sickness, but it usually functions as a message to change or gives patients something they are not getting from their lives" (p. 110). Indeed, as I have tried to illustrate in this book, the threat to life posed by a serious illness can become an occasion to rethink life priorities and to make some very positive changes. That, however, has nothing to do with the false belief that you got the disease because you needed to give yourself that message. It is common for people to blame themselves for events over which they have no control—"If only I had not gone to the party, I wouldn't have been in the accident"—as though they could have known it would happen. We don't need theories that reinforce this irrational self-blame. What I would ask you to ponder is "What can I learn from this illness?" You don't *need* the illness, or question number 4.

In the afterword to his later book, *Peace, Love & Healing*, Dr. Siegel mentions my study in a sentence and then goes on to oversimplify the complex relationship between mind and body:

How can we explain this [Dr. Dean Ornish's research on reversing coronary artery disease, my study, and one by Dr. George Valliant showing that mentally healthy men are less likely to become physically ill]: To simplify it, feelings are chemical and mind and body are a unit. A ten-pound weight on a clothesline is no problem, but the same weight on a piece of string breaks the string. Bringing your pain to a group that shares it with you makes the load bearable, that is what all these studies are revealing. When we express ourselves and dump the garbage, our bodies respond. The body is receiving a live message. Denial of our needs is a die message. We must begin to confront our unhealed life. To understand that our childhood abuse is stored up in our bodies and is affecting us.

Dr. Siegel admits that he is simplifying things—but would that it were so easily simplified. Indeed the mind affects the body, and the body affects the mind, but the relationship is nothing like dumping garbage. This old "cathartic" method, the idea that simply giving vent to bad feelings eliminates the problem, was abandoned in psychotherapy a century ago. Simply dumping feelings does not guarantee the removal of any negative effects of emotion on the body any more than positive images automatically produce positive change in the body. Dr. Siegel deserves credit for asking us to think about the connection between mind and body, but some of the questions he is asking are wrong, and some of the answers he is providing are too simple. The mind and body are related, but they are not the same.

Again, this approach could seem harmless enough, but it has been used to scapegoat patients. A businesswoman from New York called me to inquire about supportive resources for families of cancer patients. She had a seven-year-old son with leukemia and had called a cancer support program for help. She was told by them: "Any child with cancer is an unwanted child." This worried mother was being told that her son had developed leukemia because he felt unwanted by her. His disease was thus a solution to her problem, a means for her to get rid of him. That is damaging nonsense. While we want to overlook nothing in our efforts to help people with cancer help themselves, there is no excuse for blaming them (or their parents) for their disease or misleading them into thinking they can simply wish it away.

Sarah, a lovely but frail older woman with cancer, sat in my office struggling for breath. Weak as she was, she was more concerned about her husband and grown daughters. She had lung metastases that were so widespread that she could not breathe lying down and had to sleep sitting up. Yet she adhered to the belief that the disease was in her mental control and that in dying she was "letting my family down." This seemed so tragic to me that I called her daughters into my office and asked them: "Does any of you believe for a moment that your mother would not do anything she could to stay alive and be with you?"

"No," they responded.

"Will any of you blame her when she dies?"

"No," was again the firm response.

In front of the daughters, I turned to Sarah and said: "Then let go and allow yourself to die when you are ready." She died quite peacefully several weeks later.

There are people, physicians among them, who would say that I killed that woman by making it more emotionally comfortable for her to die. I frankly believe that an approach that teaches people with cancer that they mentally control their fate is quite cruel, even if well meant, and I was determined not to make the same mistake.

I thought about Susan, a feisty, round woman with a cherubic face and a halo of gray-white hair. She had been to a Simonton-based visualization program and had become so convinced that she was "visualizing" effectively that she had decided to stop her chemotherapy. She understandably disliked the side effects of her chemotherapy, and was certain that the medication was doing her body harm and that visualization was doing her body good. I argued vigorously with her in the group: "Visualize all you want," I said. "Just continue with your medical treatment as well." She refused, and even stopped coming to our group. Susan died within a year.

Martha, as well, weighed on my mind. She was a brilliant woman who had published several books on computer programming. She had a restless, curious mind, and wanted to try anything, which she explained to the support group:

"Today is the day when I was supposed to return to Texas for my follow-up group. I'm not there. I did meet a lot of people I liked very much. I had been doing the Simonton meditation exercises for a while, and I wanted to have my imagery checked out by Simonton. I liked the Simontons very much, but I did not get along at all with the person who is responsible for most of the day-to-day operation of the program. I really disagreed about their philosophy that if you can use your mind to control the cancer, you must have brought it on by not handling things properly. That is the reason I broke with the group. I called after having left and was asked about my bone scans and other tests. They indicated a progression of the cancer. This 'counselor' said: 'Well, why did you want to have the cancer spread?' "

Another group member chimed in: "That's really laying quite a guilt trip on you, isn't it?"

Martha replied: "Yes, I sent them a letter outlining these complaints, but I have not heard from them."

There are other dangers to the prevalent simplistic mind/body approach that holds that stress leads to cancer.

Jane has a grown son who lives at home, and rather erratically at that. He is an accomplished carpenter, about which she takes great pride. However, he drinks, smokes, and does little or nothing to carry his own weight at home, leaving it to her to look after him. She was told in an alternative support group that stress from her son had "given" her cancer.

When I heard this story, I clarified for Jane that there is indeed real hurt in recognizing that her son was damaging his own body. Her helplessness to stop his self-inflicted harm must feel like her sense of helplessness over her own cancer. But to add to this real hurt the unnecessary and incorrect accusation that her son was giving her cancer was unconscionable. To tell her this is to create a barrier to their relationship, to invite her to unjustly blame him for a deep imaginary hurt—giving her cancer—instead of helping her to deal with a real but lesser hurt—his apparent indifference to his own and her well-being.

Thus, when the conversation at the New York meeting turned to the destructive effects of these mind/body approaches, I wondered what I could do about it.

STUDYING SURVIVAL

Dr. Irvin Yalom and I had spent years in the late 1970s at Stanford working with women who had metastatic breast cancer. As a psychotherapy trial, we had randomly assigned eighty-six of them either to attend weekly support groups or to receive routine cancer care. (This is what is known as a "randomized clinical trial.") We had administered standard measures of anxiety and depression to these women, all of whom had metastatic breast cancer, before they entered our study, and then at four-month intervals for the following year. We found a year later that there was a highly significant difference between the women who had been given the support group experience and those who had received only standard care. The latter group had shown increases in anxiety, confusion, fatigue, and overall mood disturbance. By contrast, the women in the support groups actually *improved* on these measures; they were less disturbed emotionally at the end of the year than at the beginning. They were also using denial less, were able to face their problems more directly, and were less frightened. Thus by the end of the year the breast cancer patients in support groups were emotionally better off, whereas those in the control group had suffered emotionally.

We had published the results in psychiatric journals: The fifty women who had received support of the type described in the next several chapters had proved to be less anxious and depressed, and in addition had considerably less pain than the thirty-six women in the "control" group. After the psychooncology conference, I realized that I could do a terrific experiment. We knew that in our study we had helped the women with breast cancer psychologically. Nobody could argue that we had no effect on them. I decided to find out whether or not their cancer had progressed in the same manner as it had among the control group. Usually, you plan experiments to prove a point. This would be the unusual case in which the *absence* of a difference between groups would in itself be worthwhile; this would be a "negative experiment." Normally you cannot find a journal to publish a negative result; I thought I would have no trouble with this one. I was highly skeptical of the claims of the "mind over matter" community, and since I was sure this analysis would show no difference in longevity between the two groups, I thought the analysis would be a worthwhile, scientifically grounded contribution to the debate.

I had met a businessman during one of the breaks at the New York psychooncology meeting who told me that he was developing a small cancer research fund (named the American Cancer Research Fund). He had been interested in my talk and wondered if I had a small research project that could use some funding. That is the kind of question any researcher likes to hear, and shortly after the meeting I sent him a letter describing our plan for finding out about the fate of the women in our original study. (It was now almost ten years since the original study. Sadly, most of the women in that study had already died.) The Fund agreed to provide support. We wrote to various state death registries and obtained death certificates for eighty-one of the eighty-six women who had been in the study. (At that time, three were still alive, and two had died of other causes—one from a stroke, the other, sadly, was a suicide.) I then sent the painstakingly acquired data to Laiani Kuspa, my computer programmer, for analysis. I asked her to plot out what are called "survival curves"—they show the proportion of each group who are alive at a given time after the study began.

I had to sit down when I got the first (of what would prove to be hundreds) of printouts. The two survival curves overlapped initially, but diverged markedly at twenty months. By four years after the point at which the women were enrolled in the initial study, it turned out that all of the patients in the control group had died, but fully one third of the patients who had received group therapy was still alive. The three women who were still alive had all received support group therapy. Laiani had also calculated the average survival time for the two groups: 18.9 months for the control sample, and 36.6 months for the treatment group. In other words, on average, patients who had been in the experimental treatment program had lived *twice as long* from the time they entered the study as did the control patients. This was a difference so significant that statistical analysis was almost unnecessary—all you had to do was look at the curves. And I had been expecting no difference at all!

We then began what turned out to be three years' worth of reanalysis. I thought that there must be some mundane way of explaining the difference. Perhaps the patients were, by chance, at a different phase of the disease. If so, naturally one group would die before the other. However, it turned out that they were both, on average, five years past the initial diagnosis. Perhaps one group was sicker than the other. Here, the analysis became more complex. On the one hand, the two groups were similar in many ways. They were virtually identical in age, fifty-five on average. Likewise, the period of time from the initial diagnosis of cancer to the occurrence of metastasis, an important measure of the aggressiveness of the disease, was very similar in both groups (three years on average). They had also had comparable amounts of surgery and chemotherapy.

However, there were two variables that did differ between the two samples, albeit not enough to produce statistical significance. One was the initial staging of the cancer. It turned out that fewer of those that got group support had been initially diagnosed with Stage IV cancer (the most widely spread disease). In other words, when they were first diagnosed, their cancer was in a less advanced stage. By the time they entered our study, of course, all patients had, in essence, Stage IV disease. Nonetheless, this was worrisome, because it could indicate that somehow the patients receiving intervention were initially less ill. The other variable was number of days of radiation treatment, which was less in the intervention group, potentially biasing the study in the opposite direction.

It turned out that neither of these differences could account for the difference in survival time. We consulted with Helena Kraemer, Ph.D., professor of biostatistics in psychiatry, and a coauthor of our study, who suggested several other ways of analyzing the data. We performed a type of analysis that controls for the differences in staging and radiation and statistically tests to see whether there was still a significant difference in survival time. In both cases, there was. We plotted out the treatment/control differences in survival time for all the patients who had Stage I, Stage II, Stage III, and Stage IV cancer initially. While the numbers were small, in each case the intervention patients outlived the control patients. Thus, these differences could not account for the difference in survival times.

We studied those patients who were more actively involved in the study as measured by their willingness to provide us with more than one set of questionnaires. Within this subgroup of fifty-four, treatment patients had lived longer than control patients. In a randomized trial such as this one, you have to count as a treatment patient everyone who is assigned to treatment, even if he or she never goes to a single treatment session. This is because in a random assignment study, the only thing that can differentiate the treatment from the control group is the computer's assignment of them to either group. If you allow their behavior in going or refusing to go to treatment to affect which data you analyze, you are now studying the effects of patient choice of treatment rather than random assignment.

Nonetheless, we did compare the survival time of patients who were assigned to the support groups but who never went in contrast to those who went to between one and ten sessions, and to those who went to more than ten sessions. The survival time of those who went to no sessions was 26 months, that of those who went to 1 to 10 sessions was 36.5 months, and that of those who went to more than 10 sessions was 41.5 months. In other words, there was a dose/effect relationship: The more support you got, the longer you lived, on average. You would expect to find this, since one reason you would not attend many groups is that you were not well enough to do so. But if those who were randomly assigned to the support groups but never actually attended any lived as long as those who went to ten sessions, it clearly could not be the therapy itself that produced the effect. However, such was not the case. Attendance and survival time were related.

One afternoon I had a chilling thought. We had been conducting hundreds of analyses, but all on the same data. Perhaps there was some systematic error in the way the data had been entered into the computer that could explain the consistent but startling results. With my heart rate up and sweat on my forehead, I dug out the data sheets on which we had recorded by hand when patients entered the study. I located the death certificates, and compared the dates of study entry and death with those in our computer files. I began to breathe easier as I found only a few minor errors. I calculated the mean survival times for patients in the treatment and control groups using a hand calculator and got the same differences as in the first analysis. I slept well that night.

What to do now? I decided to do something I have never done before. I knew the study would not be ignored. However, I also knew that if there were some technical error that we had not detected, the study would be both misleading and embarrassing. I therefore decided to send the paper to a number of people in the field who would be predisposed to dislike the finding. Henry Kissinger once said: "The reason academics fight so bitterly is that the stakes are so low." Having been through my share of academic wars, I understood what he was talking about. Nonetheless, I wrote to more than twenty people, enclosing a copy of the paper. I was surprised and moved by the nature of the responses. I received long, thoughtful letters and lengthy phone calls. There were numerous good suggestions for further data analyses, which we conducted. However, none of the scientists I had consulted could find a fatal flaw, some obvious reason other than the group treatment that could account for the survival difference. At that point, I decided to publish the paper, and the fine British medical journal *The*

Lancet accepted it. In addition, the editors published a very thoughtful editorial about the study in the same issue, noting that what distinguishes unorthodox from standard medical treatment is not so much the treatment itself, since that varies from culture to culture, but rather the nature of the proof offered that the treatment is efficacious (*The Lancet,* October 14, 1989, p. 901):

> . . . [I]t is not so much the treatment on offer that determines whether the medicine is orthodox or alternative but the quality of evidence adduced in its favour. . . .
>
> In this issue (p. 888) Dr. Spiegel and his colleagues in California report that psychosocial intervention can enhance the survival of patients with metastatic breast cancer. These results will undoubtedly reinforce the prejudice of all those who subscribe wholeheartedly to the mind over matter nexus—they do not even need to read the paper critically and their response will be "I told you so." However, we would encourage our readers to adopt the same healthy skepticism about these claims as they would about the claims of any other breakthrough in the therapy of metastatic cancer. The methods adopted by the Californian workers seem to be beyond criticism, so they have indeed subjected their claims to the hazards of refutation. . . .
>
> Finally, even those who are left with a residual degree of skepticism about the life-prolonging capacity of these holistic approaches would have to agree that the measures described by Spiegel et al. are at least life-enhancing. . . .

That paper has provoked considerable interest and discussion of the possibility that group psychotherapy be included as a biomedical treatment for cancer. I had expected a storm of criticism, which has not materialized, although some oncologists find it difficult to believe (as did I) that support groups could have such an effect. I have received invitations to lecture across North America, Europe, and Japan about the finding. Most audiences have been open and curious. Many are planning similar research programs of their own. Currently, for example, research trials similar to ours are being planned in the Netherlands, Denmark, Canada, and the United States, and several studies of the effect of psychosocial treatment are already under way in Canada, Great Britain, and the United States.

An interesting debate ensued in the letters section of *The Lancet.* Several physicians wrote suggesting possible mechanisms for the observed effect. Others wrote in (as the editorial had predicted) saying, in essence, "We all knew that psychosocial support can ameliorate the course of cancer—what is new about that?" In science, any novel research finding is inevitably criticized on one of two grounds: It is not true or it is not new.

A conference was organized at Stanford by the Symington Foundation (no relation to the Simontons) to review and explore research on this issue. Stanford oncologist and breast cancer authority Dr. Frank Stockdale pointed out that while the survival differences were substantial, they only affected half of the treatment group; the other half died as quickly as control patients. Oncologists often look for differences in *median* survival, and there were none in this study. He also noted that this is just one study in a sample of moderate size. He called, quite reasonably, for more studies designed from the outset to test the idea that support groups may affect survival.

We had not, of course, predicted that our support group participants would live longer. Therefore, examining their survival time would, in the parlance of the research world, be a *post hoc* investigation—that is, it looks for the difference after the study had been done. Such data analyses are often problematic because they enable researchers to "go fishing," searching for any relationship they can find, rather than adhering to the discipline of making a prediction at the beginning and testing whether or not the result supports or refutes the expected difference. It is indeed true that we did not look for or expect survival differences when we began recruiting patients in 1975. However, when we acquired new data by writing for death certificates in the mid-eighties, we were testing a new and specific question: Would participat-

ing in a support group affect survival time? Thus, we had a hypothesis
—that there would be no survival differences—when we obtained the
additional survival data. We acquired new information about an old
study and tested a new hypothesis.

CONVERGING EVIDENCE

Several other studies since ours have provided evidence that psychological intervention has measurable physical consequences. Jean Richardson, a psychologist at the University of Southern California, studied
the effect of supportive and educational home visits for patients with
lymphomas and leukemias (cancers of the blood and bone marrow).
Patients were assigned either to routine care—the control group—or
to one of three educational and home-visiting supportive interventions.
The patients in the control group had significantly shorter survival
time than those assigned to the intervention group. There were also
differences in patients' adherence to medical treatment, which involved
taking a medication called allopurinol. Dr. Richardson examined the
effect on survival of psychosocial support above and beyond the effect
of the drug. The treatment effect persisted, even when differences in
medication use were taken into account.

More recently, Dr. Fawzy Fawzy, a psychiatrist at the University
of California in Los Angeles, and his colleagues published intriguing
data about psychological and immunological results of a randomized
trial involving eighty patients with malignant melanoma. Half were
assigned to routine care and the other half to a highly structured series
of six weekly support groups. These weekly meetings were designed to
help patients better cope with the illness and its effects through group
discussion of drawings that depicted typical problems confronting such
cancer patients and their families. While much more structured, these
support groups addressed many of the themes discussed in our Sup-
portive/Expressive therapy for breast cancer patients, which I describe
in the next chapter. The Los Angeles researchers found that the group
that received support showed much less mood disturbance using the

same measure we had employed. The patients in the intervention sample also used more active coping strategies.

In a companion report published in the *Archives of General Psychiatry*, Dr. Fawzy's team observed significant differences in immune function between the two groups at a six-month follow-up. They measured a special class of cells, called natural killer cells. Natural killer cells are a type of white blood cell that is involved in killing invading cells, including some cancer cells. Fawzy's team found an increase in natural killer cell activity (cytotoxicity) in patients who had been offered the group therapy, as compared with control patients. In other words, the group support seems to have had an effect on patients' immune systems. In addition, Fawzy has recently found that six years after his study began, those patients who were assigned to the support groups had a substantially longer time to recurrence of disease, and fewer of them have died (three of forty in the intervention sample versus ten of forty in the control sample). This finding is consistent with ours among women with metastatic breast cancer.

Not all studies have shown a positive effect of psychotherapy on the course of cancer. Drs. George Gellert, Roberta Maxwell, and Bernard Siegel (the latter is the author of *Love, Medicine, and Miracles*) published a long-term follow-up study of thirty-four cancer patients who had been treated in the Exceptional Cancer Patients program in New Haven. The medical outcome for these individuals was compared with that of 102 others who were not in the program but who had similar types of cancer. The authors found no statistically significant difference in survival time: "The evidence of this study does not support a favorable impact of the ECaP program on survival with breast cancer" (p. 69). In other words, those who had participated in this program of "weekly cancer peer support and family therapy, individual counseling, and use of positive mental imagery" (p. 66) did not live longer than those who had routine care. It should be noted that, unlike the studies previously mentioned, this was not a randomized trial. Thus the result depends on the successful matching of control to treatment patients.

Nonetheless, taken together, these studies provide evidence that the type of intervention that seems to be most helpful is one which focuses on facing directly the threat posed by the illness and increasing social support, rather than positive mental imagery. Facing bad possibilities does not, according to these studies, convert them into bad probabilities.

MAKING SENSE OF THE FINDINGS

I had undertaken the study to see whether or not group support had any effect on the course of the disease. We had found a difference that was too large to be ignored and that seemed to show that patients assigned to our group treatment lived longer than those who got routine care.

How does this finding reflect on the work of Carl Simonton and Bernie Siegel? I thought back, then, to the nature of our groups, and compared it with their treatment programs. There was an important difference. Never at any time had we told our patients that what we were doing would have any effect on their survival time. Our focus had been on facing death, detoxifying fears of dying, living as fully as possible. We tried to teach these women not to control their cancer but to control their lives and their treatment. We used hypnosis to help them control pain and manage anxiety, not to visualize white cells killing cancer cells. If the support groups influenced their survival, they did not do so because of any intention or suggestion on our part or theirs that we would help them live longer. Instead, the focus was on how to live better. The outcome was not what we expected, but the means was not what Simonton or Siegel would have employed. We focused on controlling living, not the course of the disease. The result —that the women lived longer—reminded me of the Zen parable of the archer. If he focuses on the target, he misses it. If he focuses on his relationship to the bow and arrow, he gets a bull's-eye.

Nonetheless, the issue of power and responsibility cannot be avoided. If patients in a support group can affect the length of time they live, someone might come along, look at our results, and use them to blame other patients for dying too quickly. This is wrong, if not downright destructive. First of all, there is nothing in our research that suggests that cancer patients give themselves the disease. To whatever extent personality, stress, and isolation play a role in vulnerability to cancer, we were not studying the *cause* of cancer, we were examining its *course*. Second, the minute you admit that there is anything you can do to alter the course of cancer, the patient has some responsibility for getting it done. If chemotherapy affects survival time, then the patient's cooperation with the treatment program will affect survival time. This does not mean that we have the right to blame the patient when the disease progresses. Would we blame a patient for not taking the next round of chemotherapy or for not trying a new experimental form of immunotherapy? Should we ignore any avenue to deal with disease because some will misinterpret these opportunities as occasions to blame the victim? If people with cancer can help one another live better and perhaps longer, we are providing an opportunity, not an occasion for inducing guilt.

THE SCIENCE OF MIND/BODY CONNECTIONS

How could being married, living with others, and participating in a support group affect how long we live? What is the route by which the psyche influences the soma? We are coming to a much more complex and interactive understanding of mind and body, seeing it not as a bottom-up system in which the mind is merely an afterthought, nor as a simple top-down system in which good thoughts lead to good bodily deeds. Rather, each may influence the other in ways that are being deciphered now and have important implications for health and health care.

The output of the brain comes through four basic pathways: (1) nerves that stimulate muscles to act, thereby controlling physical behavior; (2) nerves that control involuntary actions, such as the rate and contraction of the heart, the size of arteries and bronchi (larger passages in the lungs), and the movements of the intestinal system, the so-called autonomic nervous system; (3) the secretion of hormones that travel through the circulation and affect organs such as the adrenal glands, breasts, ovaries or testes, and kidneys; and (4) the secretion of neurotransmitters such as norepinephrine and endorphins, which affect various body systems, including the immune system. We will explore a number of possible explanations for how psychosocial support, which affects the brain, is translated to the body, keeping these pathways in mind:

- Social support may affect behavior. It may get us to do the things we should do: eat well, exercise regularly, and get plenty of sleep.
- Perhaps cancer patients who benefit from group support interact more effectively with their physicians, eliciting more vigorous medical treatment.
- Support groups may act as a buffer against stress, cushioning our bodies from its effects on the autonomic nervous system and on the production and secretion of stress hormones such as cortisol and prolactin.
- Recent research suggests that the brain and the immune system are closely intertwined, each producing substances that influence the other. Perhaps feeling understood and supported affects the function of the immune system in some way that allows it to fight cancer more effectively.

Social Support and Behavior

Grandmothers are always right. They tell you to eat well, get plenty of sleep, and exercise. We often ignore them just because they are right (it is said that the reason grandparents and grandchildren get along so well is that they have a common enemy—parents). There is no doubt that these three factors are essential for good health.

Diet is a matter of considerable current debate in regard to cancer. There is evidence that a diet low in fat and high in fiber may help to reduce the risk of getting certain cancers, especially of the colon, and perhaps of breast as well, although some major studies have cast doubt that fat in the diet increases the likelihood of getting breast cancer. There is clear evidence that being overweight makes it less likely that a woman who has breast cancer will do well. Thus, lowering fat in the diet and in other ways keeping your weight under control may help slow the progression of breast cancer.

Such caution about diet seems sensible anyway. In the United States and many other cultures, we eat a diet that is far too rich in fats, often obtaining more than 40 percent of our calories from a food source that increases our risk for heart disease as well as cancer, the first and second leading killers, respectively, in the developed world. It is simple common sense to restrict caloric intake from foods high in fat.

On the other hand, some cancer patients have the opposite problem. They find themselves uninterested in food, and their weight falls dramatically. Other cancer patients eat well, and still their body weight falls—they cannot keep up with the metabolic demands of a body that is fighting cancer, and whose cancer cells are growing at a rapid rate. For these people, the problem is eating enough to keep up with the body's needs.

It is possible that being in support groups encourages people to eat better and more sensibly, thereby giving their bodies the fuel they need to more effectively fight cancer. On the other hand, studies of systematic dietary interventions in the treatment of breast and other cancers have not shown that such dietary changes have a big impact on the course of the disease.

Some people with cancer have subjected themselves to rather extreme and strange diets, from macrobiotics to specific fibers, fruits, apricot pits (laetrile), and other unproved remedies. Such measures, as an editorial in *The Lancet* (October 14, 1989, p. 901) described, lead to " . . . life impoverishment suffered by many terminally ill patients subjected to the vile diets, costly placebos, and exhausting introspections recommended by the more lunatic fringe among alternative practitioners."

Diet is important for people with cancer, but it is not the whole story. Similarly, sleep is a necessity of life. Studies show that if you deprive animals of sleep for several weeks, especially rapid eye movement (REM) sleep in which dreaming occurs, they stop regulating internal temperature, stop eating, and die. In higher mammals, sleep is a necessity of life.

People with cancer do have sleep problems. They are worried and have the typical difficulty getting to sleep that most anxious people experience. Some are depressed, and wake early in the morning, which is a common symptom of depression. Some are awakened from sleep because of pain. It is certainly possible that by providing a time and place to deal with anxiety, depression, and pain, thereby reducing it, support groups help people with cancer sleep better. While it has been said that "losing sleep is nothing to lose sleep over," such is not the case with cancer, and teaching people with cancer how to sleep better can only help. That improved sleep alone accounts for differences in survival time is unlikely, but it does not hurt.

Exercise is another good habit that might help the body cope with disease. There are important impediments to getting regular exercise in cancer: the aftermath of surgery, pain, weakened bones, the reduction in energy that results from the disease, chemotherapy, radiation, and depression. Nonetheless, efforts at sensible regular exercise, in consultation with your doctor, clearly make sense and may help you feel better. Again, however, it is unlikely that differences in exercise alone could account for the eighteen-month difference in survival time we observed in our study.

Social Support, Doctors, and Dosages

Another important possible source of differences in the way cancer patients responded to treatment is the amount of treatment itself. It is possible that by making our patients more assertive consumers of health care, they elicited more vigorous treatment from their oncologists. After all, chemotherapy and radiation are at times taxing treatments. Judgments about how much to give are based upon a number of considerations: the location and amount of the tumor, the patient's white blood cell count, his or her general ability to tolerate more treatment, his or her level of pain and other symptoms, and the patient's desire to treat the disease vigorously. It may be that confronted with two patients, one of whom is rather depressed and hopeless, and another who is full of determination to get on with life, a physician might choose to treat the second patient more vigorously, thereby affecting his or her survival time.

Another far less palatable explanation for our findings is that our patients were more assertive in *refusing* unwanted—and perhaps unhelpful— treatment. Since chemotherapy is something of a tightrope walk, balancing therapeutic against dangerous side effects, more treatment is not always better, and avoiding excessive treatment could, at times, help rather than hurt.

Unfortunately, we do not have complete evidence about how much chemotherapy and radiation the patients in our original study obtained after the intervention was completed (we do know what medical treatment they received before the study began). It is possible that participating in the group affected the kind of medical care patients received afterward. Indeed, I would not be disappointed to learn that our intervention was as effective as it was because of its impact on doctor-patient relationships. That would still be a powerful reason for people with life-threatening illness to utilize support groups as a routine part of their medical care. Nonetheless, chemotherapy and radiation for patients with metastatic breast cancer are aimed at reducing symptoms rather than at effecting a cure. The overall increase in survival time for women with metastatic breast cancer since the current modern combined chemotherapy regimens have been introduced is on the order of only three to four months, and cure rates have not been affected. Thus, it is unlikely that differences in medical treatment alone account for the difference in survival time that we observed in our groups. It could also be that some combination of this with other factors enumerated here may be responsible. Clearly the type and amount of medical treatment is critical, but it is probably not the whole story.

Social Support and Stress

During episodes of stress, the brain produces and secretes hormones such as cortisol and prolactin. These hormones cause proteins to be broken down into components and stimulate production of glucose, a type of sugar that provides fuel for increased activity, especially muscle contraction, and for the brain. The stress response neurotransmitters also function as hormones, traveling via the blood to affect distant organs. These substances, such as epinephrine (more commonly known as adrenaline) and norepinephrine, also stimulate the production of glucose, thus strengthening the action of cortisol. This system is designed to help us deal effectively with such acute stress as a physical threat. These chemicals ensure that you have plenty of sugar available in your blood to fuel the muscular activity required for a physical response, such as fighting or fleeing.

However, this system is also designed to "habituate"—that is, to become tolerant to repeated stimuli so that one can temper one's responses appropriately. In other words, over time the same stressor will not elicit the same response. Presumably this is so that we do not deplete our reserves of energy once a situation has become familiar enough to be mastered. In his research with air traffic controllers, psychiatrist Dr. Robert Rose found that those with the most stress actually had the *lowest* levels of cortisol in their blood. He reasoned that over time they found a way to distance themselves from the arousing aspects of their stressful jobs and thereby teach their endocrine systems not to react.

In some people, however, the opposite seems to happen. They enter a state of chronic arousal. Their bodies act as though they were constantly facing an acute crisis even though there is no external stress. Dr. Philip Gold, director of the Clinical Neuroendocrinology Laboratory at the National Institute of Mental Health, has observed that people who are depressed are also in a state of chronic, uncontrolled anxiety and arousal, secreting high levels of neurotransmitters associated with stress.

In depressed people this stress response system is overworked. Levels of stress neurotransmitters in the fluid surrounding the brain and in the blood are unusually high. In addition, psychiatrists Dr. Alan Schatzberg of Stanford and Dr. Charles Nemeroff of Emory University have found that depressed individuals have chronically high levels of cortisol and of precursor substances, such as corticotropin releasing factor (CRF), that lead to the production and secretion of cortisol. Not only does cortisol regulate the use of sugar in the body but it also suppresses the immune response. Thus when people enter a state of depression, they leave the stress response system on all the time. Their brain no longer regulates it to fit the situation, which tends to deplete their reserves of energy, leading to many of the symptoms of depression. Antidepressant medications, which effectively treat depression, reduce the levels of these substances.

This is of special interest because many people with cancer, especially those with pain, are significantly depressed. In one study of ours, 28 percent of a sample of cancer patients with substantial pain met criteria for major depression, the most serious kind, compared to the 4 percent of the normal population that is depressed at any one time. It makes sense that at least a substantial minority of people with cancer would be depressed and so have the associated effects on their nervous and endocrine systems. This offers another explanation of the physical effect of our groups. We found that women in our support groups became less anxious and depressed over time. It is possible that participating in the groups reduced their chronic oversecretion of stress hormones such as cortisol, prolactin, and epinephrine.

Indeed, animal studies conducted by Dr. Seymour Levine, a noted physiological psychologist at Stanford, have shown that social support may serve as a buffer against the physiological consequences of stress. In a series of experiments, a squirrel monkey was exposed to a mild shock paired with a light flash. The shock was discontinued, but the light flash continued to elicit a response from the monkey like that when the shock had been given. This response included a sharp increase in the amount of cortisol in the monkey's blood. The amount of cortisol in the blood often increases shortly after an acute stressor, such as a physical threat. Levine and his colleagues found, however, that the same light flash produced only half the increase in cortisol when the monkey had one of his friends with him. In another experiment, the monkey had five of his friends with him, and there was no increase at all in the animal's blood cortisol after the light was flashed. These results suggest that the presence of friends may buffer the body from the consequences of stress. Consider how you might feel walking through a dangerous neighborhood after dark if you were alone, with one friend, or with five friends. While you might not actually be much safer with a group of friends than you would be alone, you would feel far different, both emotionally and physically.

If people with cancer secrete excessive amounts of these stress hormones on a chronic basis, those hormones might affect the course of cancer in one of several ways. There could be a direct effect on the growth of tumor cells. For example, if breast cancer patients experiencing stress secrete excessive amounts of prolactin, it might cause the tumor to grow faster. Prolactin stimulates normal breast tissue to grow and produce milk (hence the name "prolactin"). It also causes breast tumor cells to grow more rapidly in tissue culture. By analogy, patients in support groups might secrete less prolactin because they manage stress better, therefore reducing the amount of a tumor-enhancing stimulus hormone. This is nothing more than theory at this point, but in our current research we are examining the effects of participating in support groups on the production of these stress hormones and their relationship to the progression of breast cancer.

Social Support and the Immune System

Another possibility that might account for the beneficial physical impact of social support is the effect of such stress hormones on the immune system. These substances, cortisol in particular, suppress immune function. Indeed, corticosteroids are used to treat diseases such as rheumatoid arthritis, in which the immune system is hyperactive and attacks the body—a so-called autoimmune disease. This leads to another possible pathway by which group support could influence the body's ability to fight the progression of cancer. The evidence for this comes from the newly emerging field of "psychoneuroimmunology," or PNI, the study of links between mind (psyche), brain (neuro), and the immune system.

There is growing evidence that the nervous and immune systems communicate with one another. In a series of pioneering studies, psychologist Robert Ader at the University of Rochester demonstrated that rats could be conditioned to show suppression of their white blood cells. Initially, they were given food with a distinctive flavor (the artificial sweetener saccharin) along with a drug that suppresses the function of the immune system (like many chemotherapy agents which selectively attack rapidly growing cells). He found that after several exposures to both, rats given just the saccharin showed reductions in their immune function. They had somehow "learned" to respond as though they had been given the immunosuppressive drug, even though they had not.

Indeed, the nervous system and the immune system are the two memory systems of the body. The brain remembers names and faces, facts and figures, while the immune system remembers the cell surface structure of substances that invade the body, the better to destroy them if they try again. An example of this is delayed hypersensitivity, the skin rash you get from poison ivy and other allergens. Your body becomes sensitized to a substance it is exposed to and will react more strongly with cells trying to destroy it the next time it is exposed. This is the basis of immunization against viral and bacterial illness: Your body remembers the structure of the antigen injected into it, produces antibodies to it, and will respond if exposed again, destroying the invader.

Immune organs such as the spleen are heavily laced with receptors for a variety of neurotransmitters, such as norepinephrine and endorphin, as are the cell membranes of white blood cells, lymphocytes.

Recent research from the laboratory of noted immunologist Dr. David Felton at the University of Rochester indicates that norepinephrine in the blood, for example, may influence the way natural killer cells, which are involved in fighting cancer, stick to the walls of blood vessels, making them more available to attack invading cells, viruses, or bacteria. Similarly, there are receptors on the surfaces of nerve cells in the central nervous system (CNS) for cytokines, substances produced by white blood cells that stimulate immune function, such as interferon and interleukin, thus allowing the immune system to influence the CNS.

Psychiatric illness, such as depression and bereavement, often brings a gradual decrease in immune function, especially in older patients. And short-term stress—e.g., taking an exam—is also associated with a lessening in aspects of immune functions, such as natural killer cell activity. These suppressive effects of stress on the immune system are not as strong in people who have good social support. For example, psychoimmunology researchers Drs. Ronald Glaser and Janice Kiecolt-Glaser found that those medical students who lived with supportive friends and/or families showed less reduction in the activity of their natural killer cells during examination periods than those who were essentially alone. They also found that social stress reduces the function of the immune system. For example, being the caregiver for a family member with Alzheimer's disease led to poorer immune function in the caregivers. These observations suggest a mechanism by which psychosocial support might positively influence the body's ability to fight off infection or cancer.

Parallel studies are being conducted among individuals who have been infected with the human immunodeficiency virus, commonly known as the AIDS virus. They have unique problems with their immune systems, since the virus specifically targets and destroys certain cells of the immune system. There is some preliminary evidence that being more assertive, tough-minded, and showing less negative mood may be related to improved immune function, fewer symptoms, and slower disease progression in HIV-infected individuals, according to research from Drs. George Solomon, a psychiatrist at UCLA, and Lydia Temoshok, a psychologist at the Armed Forces Institute of Pathology. In studies at the University of Miami, Dr. Michael Antoni and his colleagues have found that exercise training and support groups for stress reduction increase the number and responses of white blood cells to antigens in normal individuals, and to a lesser extent in those infected with HIV.

IN MAY OF 1992, I had the opportunity to speak to the National Cancer Advisory Board, a group of distinguished citizens, physicians, and scientists appointed by the president to advise him on cancer research and treatment. They had organized a meeting on Living with Cancer, and heard from experts on physical rehabilitation and psychosocial support. I was concerned that there would be some hostility to our "soft" approach. Indeed, Dr. Samuel Broder, director of the National Cancer Institute, expressed his quite understandable irritation with the widespread tendency to blame victims by telling cancer patients that they "caused" their cancer by having the wrong attitude or could cure it by wishing it away. Another member of the board raised his hand after I had reviewed our research and asked: "If you got that much of an effect with patients who had advanced breast cancer, don't you think you would get a bigger effect if you worked with women who had earlier-stage breast cancer?" That question was music to my ears. Members of the National Cancer Institute staff spoke to clarify their current interest in and plans for this kind of research. They are now supporting it. It would seem that perhaps the clear need for investigation into new means of helping people better cope with this disease is finally being recognized. We spend billions of dollars fighting cancer; why can't we spend even a fraction of that helping people cope with it? I find it alternatively puzzling and sad that techniques that are both effective and inexpensive are not made more widely available to people with serious illness and their families.

Modern medicine has suffered from an artificial distinction be

Peanuts characters: © 1950, 1952 United Features

tween mind and body. We have assumed that only physical interventions can influence physical problems. Yet in psychiatry we are learning that mental and social problems can be influenced by physical treatments, such as medication. In medicine, we are learning that physical problems such as high blood pressure and heart disease can be influenced by psychological interventions such as relaxation training. Indeed, the Food and Drug Administration issued a report recommending these nondrug approaches as the treatment of choice for milder forms of hypertension. Mind and body are connected and must work together, and this should be a powerful asset in treating medical illness.

In formally defining the mind/body dichotomy, the French philosopher René Descartes wrote the famous dictum "*Cogito ergo sum*" (I think, therefore I am). By this he meant that his physical being was secondary to his thought processes, and that the two are distinct. In fact, mind and body are never so separable, except perhaps during the French revolution, thanks to a physician named Guillotin. It is high time we recognized that mind and body work better together.

5. A Little Help from My Friends

While chatting with a friend at an elegant garden party in posh Atherton, California, Esther suddenly realized that she was holding a plastic cup. She looked around and confirmed what she had feared: Everyone else was drinking out of a glass. She alone had been served her drink in a plastic cup. She realized that her hosts were so frightened by her breast cancer that they were afraid they would catch it if they drank from the same glass. Esther had learned several years earlier that her breast cancer had spread to other parts of her body. Despite her vigorous treatment regimen, which involved chemotherapy and radiation, she had always done her best to maintain an active family and social life. Suddenly, at the party, Esther felt very much alone with her illness. It seemed as though everyone else belonged to the world of the worried well, and she to the world of the dying. This feeling was further intensified when she sat in a restaurant struggling to sip soup. She could not eat solid food because of radiation burns in her throat. She looked around the restaurant and thought, "All these people do not know how lucky they are to be able to eat."

Social isolation is the frequent lot of people with life-threatening illnesses. We are social beings. Think about how you feel when two people in a row fail to return your morning greeting. We depend upon networks of family, friends, neighbors, colleagues, and coworkers for help, love, companionship, and affirmation of our worth. We depend upon others for more tangible things such as food, shelter, and physical affection, as well as for emotional support, and even for our health.

Serious illness in general and a terminal illness in particular are frightening and isolating experiences for patients and their families and friends. One woman with breast cancer commented: "When I shut my shades as it gets dark, I feel cut off and isolated from the rest of the world." Her death anxiety intensified her sense of aloneness.

A VIP checked into a New York hospital and was given the red carpet treatment, with visits from every prominent official in the hospital and a variety of concerned doctors, nurses, and friends. He had been admitted for a diagnostic biopsy. The day after the biopsy he suddenly noticed that the only person who was still talking to him was the cleaning lady. This was because she was the only one who did not know that the biopsy had revealed that he had a serious malignancy.

At a time when people need support the most, they often get it the least. Furthermore, they quickly come to feel excluded from the happy everyday flow of life. Isolation radiates from two directions. Seriously ill people sometimes withdraw from the world of the healthy, and healthy people in turn often do not know how to react appropriately or are frightened by disease and avoid the sick.

Many people with serious illnesses note that initially they are besieged with food, flowers, and calls, sometimes to the point that it feels like a painful intrusion. One woman's husband had the clever idea of hooking the new technology of voice mail to their telephone line with the following tape: "Thanks for calling. Jane slept well last night, but is feeling poorly this morning. If you are interested in learning the results of her latest scan, Press 1. If you want to know when her next round of chemotherapy will be, Press 2," and so on.

On the other hand, frequently the calls and gifts begin to disappear as people desperately want to go back to things as they were before. Relationships at a time of such illness don't stay the same—they either get better or they get worse—and many people avoid their own fear of dying by avoiding those who are dying. This can be doubly painful: It does not help people deal with their own fears and only makes those fears worse by keeping them out of view. The more need there is to suppress them, the more horrifying they come to seem.

Jane said, "I think it's just this big front that we put on because we don't want to make everybody feel bad." She recounted resting in her bedroom at home while the furnace repairman tinkered in the basement. After they'd discussed the bill, he asked her, "Are you all right?" "And I said, 'Well, not really. I've been on chemotherapy and I'm not feeling very well.' And he said: 'Isn't that—don't they give you chemotherapy for cancer?' 'Yes,' I replied. And then he said, 'Well, I'll say a big prayer for you.' You know, I just broke down and cried. Here's a stranger who I've never seen before in my life, and it's easier to break down in front of people like that than it is with your own family or with our close friends, because everybody kind of expects you to be a stalwart and handle it."

Jane was surprised by her own deeply felt but hidden need to be cared about—the tears just erupted. Why had Jane been so profoundly touched? Why had Esther felt so desperately alone? The plastic cup had made Esther feel as if she were already dead. There is an old spiritual about dying entitled "You Got to Walk that Lonesome Valley by Yourself." The nature of death is very difficult to grasp, but one way we comprehend it is in terms of being separated from our loved ones. Thus, anything that isolates us from other people makes us feel already a little bit dead, especially when we are fighting an illness in our bodies that threatens our life.

Support groups are a powerful antidote to the toxin of social isolation that besets those who are seriously ill.

At first Esther was not fully aware of how deeply upsetting her sense of isolation was. However, when she sat in a room with nine other women who had breast cancer that had spread to other parts of their bodies, and talked about these incidents, she was greeted with sympathetic and knowing looks. Each of these women had been through her own version of isolation from the world of the living. Strangely enough, it drew them together. They responded to Esther by saying "I know what it feels like" and chimed in with their own stories. "My husband won't let me talk about my cancer." Another said, "Sometimes I cry and then he tells me I'm giving in to the cancer and letting it spread, so I even feel alone with him. He treats it now as if it's my problem. He was great when I had the mastectomy and the radiation treatments, but now he wants me to act as though it were all over."

The response to this woman's report was a mixture of recognition, understanding, and anger so strong that the group's therapists concluded that it was fortunate for the husband's sake that he was not in the room at the time.

It is common to react to the withdrawal of old friends and acquaintances with a flurry of self-doubt—"Perhaps it's because they really don't like me that much." "Perhaps I have not been such a good friend recently." "I have been so preoccupied with my illness that I have not paid enough attention to my friends." These thoughts are natural enough—we want to explain problems to ourselves in a way that makes them potentially fixable and controllable. The price of this is blaming ourselves for things over which we have little or no control. When other people in your support group exclaim, "The same thing happened to me; some of my friends just backed away," it dawns on you that your friends are reacting to your disease rather than to you. This makes the estrangement more their problem than yours, and you blame yourself less. You begin to look elsewhere for support or at least to choose your support more carefully.

It is natural for those with a common experience to reach out to one another, given the opportunity. Janice recalled a "wonderful nurse who had had a mastectomy herself in 1943 and who took a special interest in me and helped me get fitted for a prosthesis." This nurse helped her get through her mastectomy; she used her experience to help others in the same boat. The sense of commonality, of struggling with the same problems, is a powerful therapeutic tool. Marilyn described her experience in one of our support groups:

> "It's a chance to explain my feelings about having a terminal condition with people who really understand. A chance to help others in a similar situation. An opportunity to benefit from solutions I might not have thought of that have helped other women cope with this damn disease. A chance to learn and practice relaxation exercises that actually do help me relax and calm down. A chance to meet people I know well and care about a lot."

THE PRISON OF POSITIVE THINKING

Support groups are a safe haven for expressing the feelings that others may not want you to express. The pressure put on ill people to keep their spirits up and think only good thoughts isolates them. In a recent lecture, British psychologist Lesley Fallowfield described how desperately alienating a man with cancer of the colon found the forced cheerfulness and superficiality that surrounded him:

> "The fact that you've got the dreaded big C, that you've got to have an operation, wear a bag and you might die anyway, that's not the worst of it, you know. It's being treated like a changed person and

not being able to talk about it. Everyone sort of clammed up or they were so overly nice it drove me crazy. I just wanted to be me; to cry about it; be angry about it; say how scared I was, and sometimes even be brave about it, but no one wanted to listen. They all just wanted me to be a good patient. I had to listen to them talking about how lucky I'd been that they'd caught it early, what a good surgeon Dr. X was and don't forget all those endless conversations about the bloody weather or my nice flowers and cards when they changed the dressing. Did they really think that could make you feel better about it all? Then everyone who visited did the same sort of thing—this great big game of pretend. I just wanted someone to ask me how I felt, I didn't want to play let's pretend this nasty thing hasn't happened. It had and it was real for the rest of my life and no one could help. I've never felt so alone."

Even worse, many people with cancer are taught that they can control the disease by maintaining the right mental attitude. Don't give in to pessimism or your body will give in to the disease, this line of thinking holds. This means that when cancer patients become aware of the *normal* despair that occurs with a serious illness, they are made to feel as though they are responsible for allowing their disease to spread. The group members referred to this as the "prison of positive thinking." Even if you could eliminate negative thoughts, fears, and concerns, this would not stop cancer from spreading in your body. And you cannot do that anyway—the anxiety is your way of preparing to cope with a serious problem. The last thing you need is to feel bad about feeling bad.

Hope is important, but we have been too limited in the kind of hope we prescribe. Just as modern medicine has focused on cure at the expense of caring for pain and suffering, our idea that the only kind of hope is hope for a cure limits what we can offer. There are, in fact, many kinds of hope: hope for a good period of life ahead, hope for enriching relationships, hope for control of pain, hope for a strong sense of care and support from your doctors. Hope for cure is but one of many, and even that does not eliminate the risk of illness or death from some other source. Your doctor does not "remove hope" by telling you of a potentially fatal illness. He or she puts your life in a new perspective, alerting you to dangers and recommending courses of action. It is better to face the worst realistically and place it in perspective than to pretend it is not there.

There is an important difference between true and false hope. False hope is wishful thinking, investing your energy in a vain effort to deny that something bad is happening. It is one thing to do what you need to do to feel "I am doing everything I can to fight this illness and live my life as fully as possible" and another to insist "I will not let this illness get me." Doctors are in a similarly awkward position; it is painful to pretend to "go for a cure" when that is not a realistic possibility. Realistic hope means that you and your doctor believe in what you are doing, but that you are honest about the goals. False hope means pretending to seek a cure when that is impossible. It is important to believe in what you are doing, but what you are doing must be believable.

Embarking on an effort to control cancer through your mental state can isolate you from others as well. You may find yourself brooding on your own sense of failure, ashamed to let others know if things get worse, because you see it as your fault. You may feel that you are letting your family and friends down by not controlling the cancer, even if they do not believe that themselves. Or, you may find yourself in a group that expects that everyone will control cancer in this way. If your illness progresses, you are suddenly a "bad example." I have known of many cancer patients who were asked to leave "support" groups when their illness worsened, on the theory that they were demoralizing to the other patients. This is like being sent to the principal's office for failing to do homework that you cannot do. Anything that has the power to help, like a support group, also has the power to hurt. Feeling rejected by a group of people who should understand and sympathize with what you are going through can be very hurtful. The positive opportunities for mutual caring in support groups are so important that it is sad to divert a group's energy toward a false focus on willing away the disease.

THE TICKET OF ADMISSION

The fascinating thing about a support group is that it converts a liability into an asset. The very thing that isolates you from others—having a life-threatening illness—is your ticket of admission. You feel understood by others, and you can take pride in being able to understand them. A group of women from a northern California town who had all had mastectomies formed a very "exclusive" group that met weekly for lunch. They called themselves the "Bosom Pals" and told other friends that they met to "keep abreast" of things.

In July of 1991, I spoke at the annual National Cancer Conference organized by Y-Me, a very effective support group for women with breast cancer. Established just a few years ago, they have provided informational services and support groups, and have applied some political pressure to ensure that women with breast cancer benefit as much as possible from health care services and research programs.

> Maureen, a woman in her early thirties, told me, "When I got breast cancer, I was the kind of person who thought I could take care of everything by myself. I didn't like psychotherapy and I didn't like groups. I was very anxious about my cancer, but figured I'd just have to handle it on my own. Then my uncle, who is a doctor, sent me a copy of the article you published in *The Lancet*, telling that patients in breast cancer groups lived longer. That got me to my first Y-Me support group, and a few months later I was running that one and organizing others. The odd thing was that I felt so close to a group of women who were strangers, but it seemed to me that only they could really understand what I was going through."

Some groups have members with fairly similar illnesses and prognoses, for example, cancer patients who have been newly diagnosed, or those with more advanced disease that has spread throughout their bodies, often of a particular type, such as breast, colon, or lymphatic cancer. Others are made up of people with any kind of cancer or heart disease.

Many of these groups are designed to be more educational and structured. For example, they might invite physicians to come in and give talks on the latest in diagnosis and treatment. Others emphasize emotional support, helping members deal with the rigors of treatment and fears about worsening illness and death. They provide a means of conveying information and expressing the care and concern of health care professionals. They offer a place for the expression of strong and often hidden feelings. They allow for the sense of caring and belonging that people can provide for one another.

"A WOUNDED HEALER IS A WHOLE HEALER"

Won't a group of people with the same disease just frighten and demoralize one another? That is a common question asked about support groups, especially those involving people with serious medical illnesses. (In the next chapter I discuss how fears of dying and death are confronted.) But many are worried that merely seeing others with a similar illness will be too upsetting. Interestingly, that is usually not the case. Members of our support groups are often pleasantly surprised that their companions do not look at all like the walking wounded:

"It is surprising how healthy and chipper everyone looks—I expected the group to be more depressing," said one group member. Another woman chimed in: "I realize that there are many worse things to get than cancer. I have a friend with Parkinson's disease and another with severe arthritis. That puts my cancer in perspective. I intend to carry on living. I value every day a great deal more than I used to."

Psychologist Shelley Taylor at UCLA has observed that women in such support groups often find ways of making themselves feel better, not worse, a process she labels "downward comparisons." A woman with rather advanced disease will think, "I may be quite ill, but at least I have a loving and supportive husband," while a single woman in the same group will obtain comfort by saying to herself, "I may not have a husband, but at least my illness is in remission."

Another way of understanding what happens in support groups is to realize that you get a fuller picture of a problem when you see a person in front of you dealing with it. Let's say we're picturing someone with breast cancer. We usually form in our minds a rather two-dimensional image of a woman beset with weakness, fear, and pain. However, when you see a real person with that problem, you observe her strengths as well as her weaknesses, her coping capacities as well as her problems, and it helps to put the illness into perspective. Thus, just being and talking with others who have similar problems can deepen our understanding of them. We can learn to give and receive help from those who have plenty of relevant experience.

On the other hand, most of us have mixed feelings about asking for help. We derive so much of our self-esteem from helping others that it seems almost demeaning to ask for help. Not only that, it amounts to an admission that the cancer is real.

Jane complained sadly that her twenty-seven-year-old son, still living at home, as mentioned earlier, was no help at all. He left the house littered with dirty dishes, his room was a mess, and worst of all, he smoked. All of this deeply pained his mother. Yet when we asked her what she had asked of him, she said little. She found it too hard to ask things of him, fearing disappointment. We noticed how hard it was for her to ask for things in the group; she was not clear about what she wanted. Did she want sympathy, advice, or to be left alone? We came to realize that it was hard for us to know how to help her, which likely meant that it was hard for her son (even were he so inclined) to know what to do. You may not get what you want even if you ask. But if you don't ask, the odds are far worse.

Jane had in fact been a vigorous, athletic woman before she got cancer, enjoying skiing, taking long walks, going to concerts. She had great difficulty accepting the physical limitations imposed by the cancer —the pain in her neck, the lesions in her bones—which made physical activity uncomfortable and risky. She wanted to do for herself, yet increasingly could not. To directly ask for, indeed even insist on, the help she needed meant accepting the limitations the cancer put on her. In fact, Sheila pointed out to Jane that it made Sheila feel good to be able to be of help. Jane had been taking so much pain medication in recent weeks that she had been afraid to drive because of the side effects, so Sheila had been taking her to the group on Wednesdays. "It makes me feel like I am doing something to help you—I like it."

If friends and family feel helpless about your illness, you do them a service by organizing something for them to do to help you. Far from imposing on them, you are helping them feel competent in the face of your illness. They are still free to say "no," but they have a better chance to say "yes," and you have a better chance of getting the help you need.

Marianne talked about how she had mobilized support from friends. She found it easier, she said, to write letters asking for specific help than to call on the phone. She wrote suggesting that if friends wanted to help, they could make a little extra of a favorite meal and bring it over, but no more often than once a week. People seemed happy to do that. She showed similar skill in eliciting (and giving) support in the group through her warmth and openness. As she reflected on her experience in the group, she said: "There is no support as useful as from people who have had a similar experience. A wounded healer is a whole healer."

SUPPORTIVE/EXPRESSIVE
GROUP THERAPY

The program we have developed at Stanford is called Supportive/Expressive group therapy. Patients with cancer in our groups provide a good deal of caring and support for one another, hence the term *supportive*. In addition, the groups are a place where members' deepest fears, resentments, and joys are shared, hence the term *expressive*. We meet once a week for one and a half hours.

We generally assemble groups of people with similar diseases and similar prognoses—for example, women with metastatic breast cancer —although some prefer to convene groups of people with any type of cancer. While there are no hard-and-fast rules, we try to start out by acknowledging the common bond. One group might consist of people with primary cancer when tumors have been diagnosed and removed. For about half of those people, the tumor will never recur. However, the disease will come back for many, sometimes near the original tumor (a local recurrence), or elsewhere in the body (a metastasis).

Frequently, those with an initial diagnosis of cancer use the group to deal with the shock of it, to learn about the disease and its treatments. They want to make their illness a temporary stopping point in their life so they can go on to being "former cancer patients." People with metastatic cancer have to come to terms with having a chronic illness, dealing with the threat and reality of recurrence, and accommodating the physical and mental changes that the progression of the disease and its treatment produce. They more often deal with dying and death as well. Nonetheless, we have also run groups that combine patients with both types of illness, and it has worked:

> Pam, who has metastatic breast cancer, reached out and took Barbara's hand during one of the last meetings of their group. Barbara has primary breast cancer, but spent a good deal of time in the group discussing her husband's recent diagnosis of Alzheimer's disease (a

progressive loss of memory and other cognitive functions). Pam said: "Even though our cancer is different, we're in the same boat. The issue we're facing is being robbed of the time that remains to us. I have metastatic disease and an eight-year-old son, but I have a good deal of time to do what I want. You have been robbed of the time that you have by your husband's illness as well as your own."

The common ground is established early on in such groups. In more diverse groups, members must reach a bit further to find it, but in the right atmosphere it can be done. Unfortunately, groups can go to extremes in insisting on common ground to the exclusion of members whose experiences diverge too far from those of the majority.

Jane spoke with considerable bitterness about a time in a support group she had been in when her doctors discovered that her cancer had recurred in her hip. When she told the members of the group, instead of receiving concern and support, she was given the message by the leaders and the members that she was no longer welcome. The leaders felt her presence would be a "bad example" to the other members, and would frighten them. She left.

The group leaders who treated Jan this way showed extremely poor clinical judgment, not to mention outright unkindness. There is not a person with cancer alive who has not thought that (a) the cancer might come back, and (b) that it might kill him or her. This is not new information, and the presence of someone to whom it has happened, while frightening in one way, is not the source of this most basic anxiety. Furthermore, ejecting such a person from the group is not only terribly unfair, it conveys two unfortunate messages to the other members: first, that "a recurrence of cancer is too terrible for you to confront," and second, that "if it happens to you, we will want no part of you, either." This is hardly reassuring. Once you assemble a group, you must be committed to the people, not the disease.

Our Supportive/Expressive groups are led by a pair of professionals—some combination of a psychiatrist, like myself, a psychiatric resident or fellow, a psychologist, and a social worker. We try to have in each group someone with considerable skill in running groups and someone who is knowledgeable about cancer. We find that two therapists are helpful in other ways as well. In a good group meeting, there is simply too much going on for any one person to be aware of it all. One leader may focus on developing a particular theme—fear of dying, for example—while the other notices that one group member is especially withdrawn and helps to bring her out. One leader can elicit reactions to a statement by the other leader. And they can provide support for each other, sharing the common challenges they face in bringing out and discussing difficult issues. A pair of leaders also permits continuity when one is away.

We start the group by taking roll, inquiring about any absences. It is crucial to make sure that nobody is overlooked, that no one can slip away unnoticed. If there is an unexpected absence, we plan who will call to find out what has happened. We use our attendance book as a place to record planned future absences so the group doesn't worry when a member is away on a trip. In doing this, we acknowledge that we *do* worry: Like the parents of teenagers who are driving for the first time, we have reason to fear absences and what they might mean. We are also sending the message that every member of the group matters, that we care enough to make sure everyone attends.

We then touch base with any members who might have news—a new bone scan, an evaluation of pain, a report on how chemotherapy is going. I try to elicit the meaning of the medical treatment—the fears it stirs up or puts to rest, not simply the results. We try to avoid extensive discussions of the niceties of treatment, and comparisons of older and newer protocols, although some of this is inevitable.

We then find the theme of the day, and I try to draw as many members as possible into the discussion. The topic is not predetermined, but rather arises from the issues brought to the group that day by the group members. One member might have some news about a diagnostic test, another family problems.

Rachel reported that her headaches had been evaluated using an MRI scan, and they had found evidence of four new metastases. "I am worried about this, and I don't like the thought of radiation treatment," she admitted. Sheila talked about how successful her treatment had been, and wanted Rachel to know how well she had come through it. Jane had some new headaches, and was about to undergo a scan. Thus, all three were at different points of the same process, and this became the opening theme of the group.

The major themes that have emerged repeatedly in our clinical and research groups over the past seventeen years form the substance of many of the chapters in this book. They include "detoxifying dying," developing a life project, revising relationships with family and friends, clarifying communication with doctors, and so on.

Finally, we end with a five-minute self-hypnosis exercise, in which we show participants how to induce physical relaxation and control pain. Then we review the major theme of the day.

What goes on is far more than hand holding and good wishes. The groups are also a place where these women's deepest fears and concerns can be shared, and strong emotions emerge. The women come to care deeply and personally about one another, visiting each other in the hospital, writing and calling between group meetings. They share their victories, such as a lesion-free examination, and their defeats, such as learning of another recurrence of the illness. The group creates a time and a place to express some of their darkest fears. One woman described it this way:

That sense of waking up at three in the morning with an elephant sitting on your chest. I wonder if I will live to see my son graduate from high school or my daughter get married. I have to keep up a front everywhere else and that's so hard.

There is a good deal of crying in these groups as well as laughter. Interestingly, these two emotions are often not far apart. There is a kind of release that comes from being able to feel any feeling, no matter how painful. The groups allow participants to feel positive feelings that have been suppressed along with the negative ones.

THE VOICE OF EXPERIENCE

In one group of breast cancer patients, Susan looked at Mary, who had lived through a recurrence of her illness, and said: "I thought at first that getting cancer would be the end of my life. I lived through that and found that it wasn't. Then I thought that having the cancer come back would be the end of my life. But I look at you and see that it isn't. That comforts me."

The task of coping with life-threatening illness is putting the threat into perspective, neither denying it nor blowing it out of proportion. We deal with threats every day. Those who have been through this one can offer enormous comfort to those who have not. Just seeing someone who has lived through the same situation and seems to be beyond the sense of panic is profoundly reassuring. "Veteran" patients have a kind of authority in asserting that you can get through this because they have done it themselves, something even the most experienced and sympathetic physician lacks.

More than that, though, support from other people who share your illness is an example of having your cake and eating it too. The more you give, the more you get. The ability to offer such help makes the helper feel better as well. Indeed, this newfound ability to assist others gives genuine meaning to the tragedy of grave illness. Consider what it means to bear the burden of struggling with an illness that could shorten your life. What good could there be in it? Yet when you come to the point when your experience in dealing with it is of use to someone else, when you can say something that brings real comfort to someone who is where you were, you have found a positive dimension to your illness. It does not make the illness any better than it was, but it broadens its meaning. Because others suffer with it too, they can help you, and you can return the favor. Your own struggles with the illness can be turned into a tool to help others with similar problems.

Here is how Ellen described her support group experience:

"This program has provided a safe place for me to feel about me and cancer. The support of my fellow members and the staff have helped me think beyond everyday concerns and the general denial I live with. I'm in touch with reality with all its discomfort—but it feels good."

BUILDING BONDS

Group support is a powerful means of helping people with serious illnesses to mobilize their resources and face the illness with courage. Ironically, being in a support group with others who are in the same position frees you to feel more like ordinary people: "Since you have cancer and I have cancer, we understand one another better. But more than that, our differences are not due to cancer." Our groups are a natural and powerful response to the social isolation these cancer patients experience. Feeling cared about is deeply reassuring to everyone, and especially to those who sense that they are slipping away from life.

Donna, who struggled with depression as well as cancer, mentioned in one group meeting that she continued to smoke, despite her doctor's admonitions not to. Jane turned to her, and with emotion that surprised even herself, said, "Donna, I would do anything to get you not to do that to your body. I'd come over and stay with you. Please don't give up on yourself like that." On the surface, Donna had been asking for acceptance of her habit. Underneath, she was really asking whether or not anybody cared about her statement of despair.

Indeed, Donna was touched by Jane's concern. She talked about how much better it made her feel to be in this group, where the worst things were faced, than in another group she had been in. There, everybody seemed to be putting on a façade of doing well. It just made her feel guilty for feeling bad. "Here," she said, "everybody feels bad and you can talk about it. I no longer feel guilty when I have these feelings. I just know I'm having a bad day."

This interaction was important for Jane as well. She was advocating for Donna what, in different form, she needed for herself— the will to keep going. She was doing battle against that part of herself that wanted to give up, to give in to despair. She said that her strength came from having moved constantly as a child: "I was always prepared to deal with the new. I forced myself to go swimming right after chemotherapy. I can't let myself give up."

Sheila had been ambivalent about joining a group. Her religious faith was very important to her, and she was convinced that she had been "miraculously cured" on three occasions, including one in which she had a seizure due to spread of the cancer to her brain. Despite these episodes of serious illness, she insisted that her faith would save her. Nonetheless, she gradually allowed the group to coexist with her faith:

"The group has been an opportunity to share my fears and deal with a possible recurrence of the cancer. Hopefully, I have been able to give hope to the members who are currently in treatment. I am presently disease-free and I thank the Lord for my healing. It has been difficult for me to readdress my past experiences with this disease. But I have been assured by the group it has been appreciated ... Drawing from one another's experiences has encouraged me to the extent that I am not so alone. Being able to share with one another gives me a sense of belonging."

The effort to "put up a front" is draining, isolating, and counterproductive. Support groups can be a powerful way of letting down those fronts a bit at a time among people who understand and feel the same conflicting pressures—to act as though everything is all right when it is not. Gradually, when such groups run well, the fronts dissolve because everyone there is trapped behind the same façade and wants to be free of it. Participants also find that the group provides a stable and deep sense of connection at a time when friends, fearful of cancer, may fade out of the picture.

> Sometimes group members found themselves avoiding certain friends, even when the friends were not avoiding them, claiming they were "tired of being labeled a cancer patient." Sandra commented: "One of the values of this group is that when friends drift away, particularly people who are not very close, the group provides a kind of support."

There are many ways to manage the seemingly permanent label of "patient," and support groups can provide a setting for sharing ideas and trying them out. Understandably, most people want periods of normalcy. On the other hand, the best way to dispose of the role of "patient" is to address it head on: "Okay, I have cancer. Now let's get on to whatever else we need to deal with." Stanford psychologist Al Hastorf studied how people in wheelchairs could best manage the complex social problems their disability provoked. Some of the problems would not occur to an able-bodied person: "You're always looking up at everyone else." Striking up conversations is often awkward. Dr. Hastorf found that the best approach is for the person with the disability to get the word "wheelchair" into his or her opening sentence. It was a way for the person in the wheelchair to say, in effect, "I know you are thinking about it and are relieved that you are not in one. I am in one, so let's get on to something else." If you feel comfortable enough to say the word *cancer,* you free those you are talking with to use the dreaded word as well. You are really saying to them: "I can handle this. We don't have to pretend it isn't true." Rather than denying it, say, "Yes, it is true, but there is a lot more to me than my illness."

Despite the need for support and closeness, most people have mixed feelings about letting down their front, and some are initially uncomfortable in groups. Some of our members have wanted us to function more like a social group. Others were uncomfortable watching another member cry. "I want to do my crying at home," said Claire. More often then not, this kind of reaction represents some initial anxiety that is overcome as new members feel more a part of such groups. Nonetheless, there are some people who simply do not want to open up and who are uncomfortable in such groups.

Fortunately, such reticence is the exception rather than the rule, and our group members receive considerable comfort from discovering that many of their deepest fears and sources of sadness are not unique.

Susan made a point of telling us how supportive her husband was. "Despite this," she said, "now that I am no longer performing my jobs as a housewife and mother I feel useless." She also felt terribly sensitive to any hints from him that he "wasn't getting what he had married."

Marianne had devoted her life to helping others—first as a nurse, and then as a psychotherapist. As the illness progressed, she turned inward, exploring her own feelings, fears, and goals. "If I can no longer be a psychotherapist for anyone else, at least I can be a therapist to myself," she mused, sadly. Still, she was torn between these two sides of herself. She found it very hard not to be able to be self-sufficient. Friends would say: "I like to do things with you—let me go to radiation treatment with you." "Go away," Marianne would respond. "I want to do it on my own." She realized that out of frustration with her own limitations, she was producing the opposite of what she wanted; she was driving friends away. She enjoyed her friends' concern, but was angry with herself and her body for needing and wanting it.

Receiving help from friends is both a relief and an admission, a help and a confirmation that the illness is real, that your life is changing.

Laura listened to Marianne with her usual quiet intensity (she looks like a Modigliani painting, with a long neck, her head bent slightly to the side, absently staring but deep in thought). Then she said: "Marianne, I can just see you as a teacher." The following week, Marianne started the meeting by saying to Laura: "You helped me so much last week. With what you said you lifted some weight within me about having crossed the line from 'one of us to one of them.' " She then reached out and took Laura's hand.

Marianne was coming to terms with having become a patient instead of a therapist, the helpee instead of the helper. Laura had helped her by acknowledging the part of Marianne that was indeed so good at helping others, showing her that she could do both, that the therapist in her had not died when she became a patient.

Strength and caring flow in these groups at the strangest times. Just when members are admitting weakness, despair, and sadness, they draw others to themselves and receive affirmation.

The deep sense of caring that develops in these groups is striking. It happens quickly, and it lasts.

Doreen had developed inflammatory breast cancer, which is, unfortunately, a rather aggressive form of the disease. It is treated by chemotherapy first and then surgery or radiotherapy. Thus Doreen was in one of our groups for several months before she faced her mastectomy. She was bitter about her illness, feeling she had been robbed not only of life, but of even a respite from the relentless progression of the disease (not without reason—she has since died). We found it difficult to console her. Despite a good deal of attention, she seemed to feel as though she had received little from us. It was thus all the more striking when she spontaneously commented on Nancy's visit to her in the hospital on the morning of the surgery. "Your visit meant more to me than anyone else's, because you knew what I was going through." This, even though they had only known one another for a few months.

JOINING SUPPORT GROUPS

De Tocqueville called America "a nation of joiners" and fortunately the medically ill are becoming no exception. People with cancer, heart disease, arthritis, and neurological illnesses, among others, are increasingly meeting regularly with those who have similar problems. They meet to counter their own personal sense of isolation, learn techniques for dealing with the illness and the side effects of treatment, get tips on how to get the most out of the health care and insurance systems, and cheer one another up. These support groups are never a substitute for medical treatment. Rather, they are a companion to it, providing knowledge about the illness and its treatments in a supportive setting. I believe—and there is a growing body of scientific evidence to support this—that this kind of support is not merely a "feel-good add-on." Although it is not a cure, psychological support is so valuable that I hope the medical community will come to see it as every bit as essential a part of the treatment of life-threatening illness as the latest chemotherapy, radiation therapy, or surgical technique. As it is now, we spend more time learning to drive a car than learning to live with life-threatening illness.

Such support groups are often run by social workers, nurses, physicians, or psychologists who work in medical clinics or doctors' offices, and meetings can take place in hospitals, private homes, or public meeting areas. Ask any of these professionals to recommend a local group for you to join. If there is no such group in your area, consider getting together with other patients and finding a professional leader through your doctor or a local hospital or oncology treatment program. A more informal gathering can provide an important arena of support, but I think it's important to join a group led by one or more professionals as well. These experts can draw on a pool of experience you may not have access to.

Finding or Forming a Support Group

Support groups come in many shapes and sizes. Here is what to look for:

1. *Similar problems.* Find a group of individuals who are facing problems as similar as possible to yours: recovery from a heart attack, breast cancer, bereavement, etc. If there is a choice within type—for example, separate groups for newly diagnosed breast cancer and for more advanced disease, try to match your situation to that as well. Look for people who are going through similar difficulties and who are about at the same stage of coping with it as you are. However, some diversity is good, it helps to have some group members who have already "been through it" to give others the benefit of their experience.

2. *Excellent leadership.* In general, I recommend groups led by well-trained and licensed professionals. These include doctors, nurses, social workers, and psychologists. Look for those who have experience in group psychotherapy and/or with the particular problem to be addressed—e.g., breast cancer, heart disease, etc. I have great regard for self-help groups, and there are some fine ones for people suffering with medical illnesses, but because of the complexity of the medical issues and the depth of emotional response to them, I prefer professionally led groups when possible.

3. *Comfortable setting.* Many good health care programs are offering support groups as part of their services. This includes oncology and radiation oncology clinics, inpatient services, group practices, and volunteer organizations. Find a solid program, and you are likely to have found a good support group if they offer it.

If they don't have one where you are receiving medical care, ask them to start one.

4. ***Reasonable payment.*** Many support groups function without charge to participants. Costs are often absorbed by the programs that sponsor them. On the other hand, it is neither unreasonable nor expensive to pay a modest fee to participate, since there are costs for the therapists' time and the facilities used.

5. ***Supportive atmosphere.*** You don't need to commit forever to a group until you see and feel what it is like. You should feel respected, understood, and comforted. There may well be times that are upsetting, but you should feel rewarded for this discomfort with a new perspective on the problem, a sense of support, and growing confidence in your ability to handle difficult situations. You should come to care about the others in the group, and feel cared about by them.

How do you know if a support group isn't right for you? If the group feels judgmental, insisting on "one way" of handling tough situations, challenge it if you can. If you cannot, or they don't respond, leave. If the group is scapegoating one or more members, blaming all their problems on one or a few members of the group, point out what the group is doing, and leave if they don't stop. If they "kick out" members whose illness progresses as a "bad example" to others, it is the group that is setting the bad example. Find another one. If they make false promises—the right attitude or visualization will cure you of cancer—look for a better place to spend your time. Finally, if they are charging a great deal of money or insist that you "buy in" to some long-term package, use the money for something else.

We all like to have a sense of belonging. Groucho Marx commented that he would never join a club that would accept him as a member. The interesting paradox of all self-help and mutual support organizations is that they combine the exclusivity and sense of belonging that comes with membership with the stigma and sense of exclusion that is the lot of those with serious illnesses.

Ed Roberts, currently the head of the World Institute of Disability in Berkeley, California, was transformed in forty-eight hours from star high school baseball player to permanent quadriplegic on a respirator by the polio virus. He has come to lead a remarkably independent and full life despite this. After several years of deep despair, with his mother's help, he applied to the Department of Rehabilitation of the State of California for entrance into its training program. He was rejected, with the comment that he was "unrehabilitatable." He went to school anyway, gained considerable experience, and twenty years later he became the commissioner of that same department! He is an energetic, outgoing man, who seems to project himself beyond his wheelchair, attendant, and breathing apparatus. He took steps to see that the disabled had control over those who helped them—making them, rather than the state, the primary employers. And he rails against the exclusion the disabled feel. (He hates the term *handicapped*—it comes from being "cap in hand.") Looking up at a roomful of bright young Stanford medical students, he said: "I think of you as the temporarily able bodied." By mobilizing the disabled to share and work together, he was able to redefine the world of the able bodied, and change it. "The doctors told my mother that I would be a vegetable," Ed commented. This was quite a mistake—the poliomyelitis virus attacks motor neurons, not the part of the brain that thinks. "But it turns out they were right—I am. I'm an artichoke: prickly on the outside, with a big heart in the middle."

Ed's transformation from a socially isolated, depressed, despairing young man who had lost "everything" into an effective, vital man who boasts about the quality of his life despite his serious disability, came in part through his contact with other people with disabilities. Through them he learned that he did not deserve what had happened to him, that he was not less of a person for it, that he could find other ways to build his life. This resulted not from denying or hiding from his disability, but rather from making it the starting point of new relationships and a new perspective on life. People with life-threatening illness do the same thing every day, and many more could, if they stopped suffering in silence.

Sandy described how her experience in a support group influenced her view of herself, her cancer, and her life:

Being part of this support group has been a reality check for me. Cancer has come to be not the death sentence I first believed it, but part of my life—and the women in my group have helped me learn this. The joys, the tears, the love, the support—they're all there, and we share. What a thing to live for!

6. Detoxifying Dying

I was nineteen when my grandfather lay in a hospital dying of heart disease. We were friendly with one another, but had not been especially close, largely because I had chosen not to follow in his orthodox religious footsteps. I knew that disappointed him.

During our last conversation he asked me about my plans in life and I talked about school and my future. He turned and looked at me and said, "You know, David, we each have to thank God in our own way."

I have always been grateful for that benediction, in which my grandfather expressed his respect for my way of life and at the same time tied it to his. How sad it would have been had I not had the opportunity to have that final discussion with him. Yet very often our denial of the imminence of death deprives us of such opportunities.

A patient of mine with cancer whose husband had died five years earlier remains bitterly unhappy over such a missed opportunity. Her husband called to her from his hospital bed and said, "Look, I know I don't have long to live. There are some things I want to discuss with you." "No, no," she replied, "things will be fine—you just get some rest." He went to his grave with what he wanted to talk over with her, and that plagues his widow to this day.

Think back to a time when you lost someone you cared deeply about. Consider how precious were the last moments you spent with that person, and the sense of things left unfinished after he or she had died. You could no longer correct a mistaken impression. You could no longer express your appreciation for what he or she had done for you. You could no longer share with him or her the exciting new events in your life or commiserate about a problem.

Most people, looking back, find the last moments of life spent with someone they care about an especially precious time, one they treasure later in life. Such moments can steady and guide us later on. Just as the law recognizes that there is something special about a death-bed statement—that people are liable to speak the truth when they are facing the infinite—there is a kind of directness and importance to the time one spends with the dying person that gives it a weight, a staying power with the living.

Ellen was quite ill with advanced breast cancer. She had been an adventurous and physically vigorous woman all of her life, relishing hiking and the outdoors. Just prior to a long-planned trip to Death Valley when the cacti were in bloom, she hesitated to go. During a long conversation, her grown daughter asked her whether she had any regrets about not having done things. Ellen's daughter is thinking of joining the Peace Corps in a year or two and was identifying with her mother, trying to balance in her own life risks taken versus opportunities missed. Their conversation got Ellen thinking about her priorities, and she ended up taking her journey to Death Valley and enjoying it. The image of blossoms in that arid land is an apt one for Ellen; the vast, sandy landscape highlights their beauty. Ellen and her daughter had an important discussion, one that will guide her daughter, because they both acknowledged that Ellen's life was limited. She died eight months later.

Death is so absolute and overwhelming that the last moments can be precious, even if there is barely a relationship between people.

Two years after an accident in which a section of a plane blew out at twenty-two thousand feet and nine passengers were sucked out of the plane to their deaths, a flight attendant cried as she recalled having had the last conversation with a young man who was about to die. She had made a noise that had woken him from a nap. As he opened his eyes sleepily, she said, "I am sorry." That was all. But she tearfully reflected that it was his last human contact before being swept out of the plane less than a minute later.

Such moments are transforming. We feel deeply for the person who died and we also profoundly experience our own vulnerability. There, but for the grace of God, go I.

DEATH ANXIETY

What could be more terrifying than the prospect of dying? It is a topic that most people don't like to talk about, much less think about. Indeed, we lead our lives pretending that it will never come to us. We use words and phrases that belie nonexistence: "He passed away." We tell children that the favorite pet "went to sleep." This not only provides the false comfort of denying the absoluteness of death, but could cause a young child to be fearful of sleeping. The reality of dying is far more stark than the language of disguise we use for it:

Mary, on the verge of tears, talked about how she would awaken alone at night and stare at the ceiling in dread. Others in the group described similar experiences and talked about their belief that they would sink into their fear and never emerge from it again or ever be able to think of anything except cancer.

Who could blame anyone for wanting to avoid confronting the end of life? It is the ultimate limitation, the supreme fact that confronts us with our inability to order things in the world the way we would like them to be. Death is not pleasant, and confronting it elicits strong feelings—terror, sadness, rage—with which few people are comfortable. We often rationalize our reticence to deal with these feelings with the fantasy (and it *is* a fantasy) that expressing such feelings is "bad for you." Indeed, I sometimes think that doctors are trained to treat crying as if it were bleeding, to be stopped at all costs as soon as possible. I tell the medical students at Stanford: "If you see a patient crying, don't just do something. Stand there."

A man with alcohol-related liver disease was dying at Boston City Hospital. We had resuscitated him once when his heart stopped due to an imbalance of electrolytes in his blood. Less than twenty-four hours later, his heart stopped again, and this time we failed in our desperate efforts to bring him back to life. His desolate fourteen year-old daughter stood at the foot of his bed and wailed: "This can't be. This can't be. He's not dead."

I, just a medical student at the time, thought her reaction seemed quite appropriate. The head nurse did not: "She's upsetting the other patients."

"Let's take her into another room," I suggested helpfully.

"No, she needs a shot of Valium," said the nurse.

"If this upsets you, *you* take the Valium," I said, less helpfully. I thought this poor girl was doing the grieving she needed to do, and that if she did not do it now, she would be doing it later in a psychiatrist's office. The nurse convinced the intern to give her a shot of Valium.

This difficulty in dealing with the strong emotion that is naturally associated with serious illness is all the more tragic because, when handled well, the support can be so powerful.

Jim, a forty-two-year-old man, was dying of leukemia. He had become suddenly ill several months earlier, and the disease was advancing so rapidly that a variety of intensive treatments had failed to arrest its progression. He lay in his hospital bed, conscious of his situation, while his wife sat beside him. A nurse who had been off duty for several days entered the room, took his hand, and said, quietly: "Jim, I love you. We all love you." There were tears in everyone's eyes, and he died quite peacefully later that day.

In these few words the nurse acknowledged what we all knew, that he was dying, and found a way to help everyone face it together rather than separately.

We physicians have been all too good at shutting off strong emotional reactions. We have a range of medications to calm anxiety and depression. Please do not conclude that they should not be used at times. But their appropriate use is to treat *pathological* anxiety and depression, not normal fear and sadness.

Sandy described how she had suppressed her reaction to her father's death: "I just put aside the strong feelings, thinking I would deal with them later. The trouble is, I never did. I paid a price for that, and my brother and sister, who were much younger than I, never got a genuine picture of our father as a result.

"But I think I see why I do it with my cancer," she added. "It is my way of trying to control the effect the illness has on me. If I don't get upset, it is as though the disease can't get to me. But it does, anyway."

We doctors often think we do patients and their families a favor by "protecting" them from the reality of death. But ultimately we cannot, and what we really do instead is hobble them, making it harder for them to understand and cope:

> Laura was hospitalized because of a pathological fracture in her leg due to a metastasis of her breast cancer. She watched a man dying in the room across the hall. She noted with interest how his family was reacting and found herself quite curious about the details of dying, how the body was prepared, who took charge of it, where it went. When she awoke the next morning, the room was empty. She asked two nurses, who were foreign but had spoken good English the day before, what had happened. Suddenly, they spoke no English. They were apparently more anxious about the death, or its effect upon her, than she was.

Death anxiety is a fundamental part of human existence. Existential philosophers, such as Kierkegaard and Sartre, have emphasized that we come to know ourselves as best we can only when we confront the possibility of nonbeing. The term *existential* itself comes from the belief that there is no "essence" of human experience that is truer than "existence." We can understand what it means to live when we contemplate what it means to die, not to exist.

The nineteenth-century Danish philosopher Søren Kierkegaard begins one of his most famous works, *Fear and Trembling,* with several retellings of the Abraham and Isaac story from the Old Testament. He describes it in terms of Abraham's disappointment that God for many years seemed disinclined to fulfill his promise that Abraham would become father of a great race of people. Finally Abraham had a son, and God then asked him to make a sacrifice of that son. Abraham is thus asked to sacrifice not only his son, but his cherished and promised role. When the crucial moment comes and he finds that he is willing to make the sacrifice, he sees a ram nearby and sacrifices it instead. Kierkegaard calls Abraham a "knight of faith," in part because he obeys the word of God, but in part because he confronts the meaning of his own existence in the possibility of his and his son's nonexistence.

He had elevated his role as the father of a great race above the fundamentals of his being, and was losing himself. He saw his son, Isaac, as nothing more than a means to an end. It was only when he was willing to give him up (i.e., give up his ambition in Isaac) that he could truly have him. When he was willing to die without having fulfilled his cherished role, he was finally able to live.

Kierkegaard contrasts Abraham with Agamemnon, who, according to Greek mythology, sacrificed his daughter Iphigenia in order to appease the gods and obtain favorable winds for a military victory against the Trojans. Calling him the "knight of infinite resignation," Kierkegaard noted that he subordinated the truth of being to his role as a leader. He lost himself in fulfilling a role, only one aspect of himself. We play at roles and suddenly find that we have become them. I am reminded of watching the wonderful French mime Marcel Marceau. In one performance, he plays with putting on the classic comic and tragic masks of theater, switching his expression with stunning ease. After a few minutes of this, however, the comic mask gets "stuck." He cannot pull it off. The smile, now glued to his face, becomes painful. His whole body struggles to pull it off, but cannot. In this way he depicts how we become trapped in our roles. What seems like a game ceases being one.

Stanford professor Irvin Yalom, a noted authority on existentialism and psychotherapy, has observed that there are two fundamental ways in which we avoid confronting our own mortality. The first is what he calls our "immortality projects." We throw ourselves into various worthy activities with the idea that as long as we are doing them, and doing them well, we are somehow insulated from death. We could not possibly be allowed to die while doing such important things. Some throw themselves into work, others into raising children, all with the unwritten and unexamined idea that such continued noble activities are a defense against death. Doctors are famous for losing themselves in the myth of the immortality project. They studiously worry about everyone else's health and ignore their own. How could I possibly be taken away when I am doing so much good in the world, when

I am saving so many lives? That is why doctors make lousy patients, and even worse pilots. They imagine themselves to be invulnerable to illness and death.

The second way we sidestep the issue of our own mortality is to conjure up "the rescuer," some powerful person who provides insulation against the danger of dying. This is a role that doctors love to play and patients love to have them play. If I simply put my faith in you, you will magically save me from the inevitable. As doctors, we do not like to admit our limitations, and as patients we do not like to see them. I am not referring here to lack of skill or knowledge. I am referring to the ultimate limitation that sooner or later everybody dies, and yet we want to play the role of rescuer: the knight on the white horse who makes everything better, who has the solution that eluded everyone else. Every once in a while, a doctor does indeed manage to postpone the inevitable, but often he or she does not.

Because patients often view their doctors as rescuers, they fear provoking or contradicting them in the belief that their doctor's willingness to rescue them will be withdrawn. We often have a sense of safety when we are with someone who cares about us; it is as though we believe that nothing could happen to us when we are with them. We seek out leaders, even some who lead us into danger (remember Jim Jones?), in the belief that they provide some special protection from the inevitable. If death is close, the rescuer will keep it at bay. This is indeed a realistic assessment of what parents do for children, who are extremely vulnerable and who need their protection. But as adults we continue to long for the safe haven our parents provided.

In *The Sickness Unto Death*, Kierkegaard describes the price paid for avoiding a confrontation with death: despair. A person in despair lives life as though it differed little from death, with no vibrancy, no important choices, no risks. Such a person avoids the importance of the "moment." To make a choice that counts means recognizing that you have only so many choices in life. The vitality that comes from acknowledging the fragility of your own being, the preciousness of time, is an antidote to despair. We either live as though we could not die and never really live, or we live fully in the face of nonbeing.

Professor Yalom and I believed that if these existential ideas were correct, they should work in action. People who were quite literally facing their own deaths could actually live more fully, and imbue their lives with vitality by reordering their priorities. But first they had to learn to tolerate the considerable and deep anxiety that comes from staring into the bottomless pit of nonbeing.

Your personal recognition of death hits an entirely different level when you notice a lump or your doctor orders some tests and asks you to come back to his or her office for the results. From the certainty that you could live endlessly and happily, suddenly it seems that your life is over, that you have been, with a few words, removed from the world of the living. Suddenly it becomes difficult to pay attention to anything else. "The prospect of the gallows concentrates a man's mind wonderfully," said Boswell. We go from knowing too little to knowing too much.

THREE WAYS WE KNOW DEATH

How do we comprehend death, this incomprehensible fact of life? There are three ways. The first and least difficult is the *impersonal,* in which we understand it as an idea. We know that death happens, that people disappear. We read about death daily in the newspapers and watch it repeatedly on television. The way death is portrayed in the media at once makes it seem unreal and, indeed, unimportant. By and large, the people who die on television shows are bad guys. We have not gotten to know or care about them; their suffering, if portrayed at all, is brief and presumably well deserved. Death is an impersonal event and arouses little, if any, emotion. These matter-of-fact accounts tend to desensitize us to violence and death, making it seem commonplace. It is estimated that the average child in the United States spends more time watching television than being in school. By the time children have reached adulthood, each has witnessed tens of thousands of deaths on television. Does this teach us an existential lesson? On the contrary, it numbs us to death, or in tragic ways pushes us to act out fantasies of invulnerability—for example, by obtaining weapons. Teenagers—children—obtain guns with the fantasy that the ability to kill others with ease will make them invulnerable to death. In fact, owning a weapon makes it more likely that you yourself will die as a result of violence, and you are more likely to be killed by that weapon. Murder is the leading cause of death of young black males in the United States. Thus in these and numerous other dangerous ways, like smoking, we pretend to avoid our vulnerability to death rather than face and accept it.

Teenagers seem to have lost what little comprehension of death they had in childhood, which is what makes them so dangerous to themselves and others. They live an illusion of invulnerability, firmly convinced that they are immortal, that nothing can harm them, making them terrible drivers and excellent soldiers. The process of maturing into adulthood involves facing the reality of dying, and hence the need of defenses to help us manage that terror.

The second way of coming to know death is the *interpersonal*. Someone whom we know and care about dies and the meaning is brought home in a much more powerful way. Few people have grown up without the experience of losing someone they cared about—a grandparent, an aunt or uncle, a friend.

Our lives are profoundly changed by the loss of a loved one —it feels as though a piece of ourselves has died. At first it is hard to believe that person is gone. You expect him or her to walk in the room. When the phone rings, you are sure he or she is calling. Many even imagine they hear the voice of the deceased. You start to discover, at times like these, that what you *want* often has nothing to do with what *happens*. You feel as if someone you love has pulled away from you and your knowledge of what happened is deepened by strong feelings about it: loss, abandonment, anger, fear. Your own life is changed by the death of a loved one. If it is a parent who has died, you have also lost a protector, someone who, in a sense, "stood between" you and death, and you feel that much more vulnerable. If you lose a child, your ability as a protector, a guardian against death, is challenged. We often reassure ourselves about our strength by exerting it to protect others, and a failure makes us feel more vulnerable as well.

The third means of confronting death is the *personal*, the recognition that *your* life will be over, that *you* are not invulnerable and immortal. This is, of course, the hardest and most profound way to understand dying. And given how difficult it is, we find many ways to avoid it.

One way we become aware of the personal meaning of death is through envy of the living. Sarah talked in the group about her envy of her daughters:

> I am afraid of dying but have been unable to discuss my fears with my daughters. I envy them. One went away for a weekend at Lake Tahoe, and I was jealous of her. I know I shouldn't feel that way, but I wish I could go and enjoy it too.

These words led to an admission by Amanda of a kind of perverse pleasure in realizing that even people who were very much set apart from her came to the same end:

> I was reading *Citizen Hearst* and it gave me comfort to realize that even with all the important people Hearst knew, he is now dead. No matter what someone had done in his life, this is the common denominator. For example, I looked at all the people in a football stadium recently, and realized that fifty years from now they will all be dead.

Thus Amanda had discovered that the very thing that separates her from others—her death—ultimately unites humanity with her. Everyone's existence is fragile. She took comfort from combining the personal with the impersonal and interpersonal understandings of death.

DEALING WITH DYING

I sat talking with my friend Bryan a few days before he died. We were discussing what would become of his boys, aged eleven and nine. Quite suddenly he turned and yelled at me, "I'm so pissed off at you, Spiegel. You are going to get to see it and I won't. I hate you for that." It was hard to hear, but he was right, and I told him that I did not blame him, that I would feel the same way he did. Just as I was feeling cheated of his friendship, thinking about the football games I would go to without him, he was coming face-to-face with what it meant that I was far more likely to see his sons graduate from high school than he was.

What could possibly help somebody facing the end of his or her own life? Oddly enough, staring death right in the eye, rather than running from it, can help. Death can become not the problem, but rather a series of smaller problems, some of which have solutions. This is a process we have called *detoxifying dying*.

Marianne came to take her Muslim faith more seriously and made a journey to Mecca with her teacher. One day he said to her, almost casually, "It seems like a good day to buy our shrouds." She went with him, stunned at first. It is a Muslim custom to prepare for your death by purchasing and preparing the cloth that will be wrapped around your body. She said: "There was a little girl inside me, crying, 'I don't want to do this. Why should I have to buy and wash the shroud I will be buried in? I don't want to.' " But she did it, feeling her teacher's guiding hand and closeness, and she felt a sense of accomplishment. She was developing a new side of herself, a sensitivity to her own feelings and a directness in expressing them that made her a most valuable member of the group. She made it safe for others to reveal their feelings by being so open about hers.

I have asked hundreds of people what they most fear about death. Strangely enough, it is not being dead; rather, it is the process of dying. Fears of losing control of your body, suffering increasing pain, losing the ability to do things you love to do, being unable to make decisions about your medical care, being separated from loved ones: Those are the ways that fears of dying become real. Death is something that pushes the edge of our comprehension and we have personal, philosophical, or religious ways of understanding what it means, but the process of dying is something that takes far less imagination. Despite this, each of those problems can be addressed. You can do something to control pain, to make decisions about future medical treatment, to draw closer to loved ones, and thus make the process of dying seem less overwhelming.

Years before I went to medical school, I had the opportunity to visit an experimental cancer treatment program at Brookhaven National Laboratory on Long Island. They were studying the use of the large nuclear reactor there for radiating the blood of cancer patients. As we entered the ward, a gaunt woman sat up in bed, greeted us, and clearly wanted to talk. With barely a question to elicit it, she told us her story. She had been diagnosed with breast cancer, her breast had been removed, and she had been told that she was fine. Her doctor had later discovered a recurrence of the cancer in her spine after she had complained of back pain. He lied and told her it was not cancer, but muscle spasms. But he told her husband that she was dying of cancer. She noticed that her husband was becoming rather estranged from her, but she decided that it was because she was losing weight (this due to the cancer). She had concluded that she was less physically attractive to him, and that was why he was withdrawing from her.

In the guise of shielding her from death anxiety, her doctor had isolated her from the person who meant most to her in life. What a cruel thing to do to her! How sad that she had to think her husband had withdrawn from her because of her looks, rather than because of his sadness at her illness, and his (wrongly perceived) need to keep this to himself. This managed to turn his love for her into something destructive, separating instead of uniting them.

> For the experimental program it was required that patients be made aware of their diagnosis and prognosis. Thus, she was finally informed: "You have an illness that will shorten your life, but no matter what happens, there is something we can do to help you." The woman told us: "I felt so much better coming here and knowing what was happening to me."

Notice how that woman responded to the truth: It was less painful to her than the imagined loss of affection from her husband. Also, the message she was given was the right one, since it had two parts: (1) You have a serious illness that is likely to shorten your life; but (2) no matter what happens, your doctors will be there to help you. Certainly, anyone would want the doctor to say he or she has a cure, but most do not expect that. However, people with serious illness have a right to hear that their doctors will be there for them. This kind of support is threatened when doctors think their mission is only to cure rather than to comfort. More on that in Chapter 10.

HOW GROUPS CAN HELP

As a means of examining fears about dying in one of our groups, we went around the room one day asking each member of a group for women with mixed primary and metastatic breast cancer about their worst fears. Several spoke of increasing pain, having seen mothers or other family members die in great discomfort. Others spoke about the manner of dying, one saying that a lifelong friend of hers, who had died in an experimental treatment unit for cancer, had been consumed with anger, bitterness, and pain. "I do not want to go that way," she said. Others feared depending on people. One, who lives alone, found it frightening to think of depending on others for help even in getting to her doctors for treatment. Another talked about a brilliant man she knew who had turned his cancer into an intellectual puzzle, challenging his doctors at every turn. She hoped to be like him. Several women began to cry when talking about their fear of being separated from their families.

Many are so used to doing for others that the thought of asking others to do for them is not only depressing, it is frightening. Women who have nurtured their children, husband, and even their parents all their lives suddenly face the very real possibility of needing to be nurtured and cared for themselves. At first this seems too hard—asking is more than they can bear. Indeed, they do not even allow themselves to think of what others might do for them. Thus, the process of dying brings with it fears of helplessness, of entering into a position in which you depend on others and therefore become vulnerable to their willingness to help and their judgments of you.

One recounted how her family told her that she will make herself sicker if she even for a moment faces her fear of dying and being separated from them: "I guess I'm just not coping as well as the rest of you. I'm just not as strong and independent—my family is everything to me." The other group members wasted no time reassuring her that she was coping fine, and that they felt closer to her when she shared her fear. They pointed out that her family was protecting itself from their feelings. They were not helping her by insisting that she shut off her tears.

One situation, many problems. Yet each, difficult as it was, could be dealt with at least partially in the group. The group could address fears of isolation, pain, and helplessness. By facing these fears, the fears did not seem so overwhelming, and the feeling could be distinguished from the content of the problem.

Maria was the image of what every cancer patient fears. Always a tall and slender woman, she had become gaunt. Week by week she became thinner as the cancer spread through her body. Finally she developed metastases in her brain, which made it increasingly difficult for her to control her muscles. She developed weakness on the right side of her body and became confined to a wheelchair. She nevertheless kept coming to the group.

Maria talked a good deal, but mostly about the sense of having failed her mother, whose expectations of her had always been excessive. When she had been elected senior class president, her mother insisted that she be on the student council and Phi Beta Kappa as well—nothing was good enough. The group wondered if perhaps she was not setting excessively high standards for herself in regard to coping with her severe symptoms and expecting disapproval from us.

She had quite a different memory of her father. He had been taken to the hospital on a stretcher after having suffered a serious heart attack when Maria was eight years old. She recalled that he smiled and waved to her as he was being taken away: "It is unlikely that he really felt like smiling at the time," she said. "But it meant a lot to me that he did that for me."

There had been arguments in the group about Maria, criticism of her increasingly untenable denial: "I'm going to beat this cancer —I won't let it get me." However, the discomfort of some other members with her presence came to a head during the weeks after Nancy, who had attended only a few meetings, died of a similar type of brain tumor. There was relatively little discussion of Nancy, but a flood of criticism of Maria (who was not at this meeting) for being "defensive" and "closed." I wondered aloud whether it was not Maria's physical frailty rather than her psychological limitations that troubled the group. In retrospect, we had not spent sufficient time and energy grieving Nancy's loss and were displacing our anxiety onto Maria.

The next week, it did indeed seem that both Maria and the cancer had gone too far. She was barely able to walk into the meeting room and it became apparent that she was unable to hold her head erect. I became anxious, as did the group members, just looking at her. What effect would this have on them, seeing their worst fears so graphically before them?

But I had a more immediate problem: how to help Maria with her head. Years of psychiatric training that taught me to talk to patients about things rather than do things to them had to be abandoned because I couldn't bear to sit by and watch her head wobble uncontrollably. So I sat next to Maria and held her head erect throughout the meeting. She talked about her fear, mixed with an iron determination to keep coming to the group. She said: "I'm not having any more fear and feel very comfortable. I am surrounded by friends. I know that I may just have days ahead of me, but I don't want to spoil them."

Telling us that she was tired, she left the meeting a few minutes early, which gave the other participants an opportunity to unburden themselves about their reaction to her. At first disagreements emerged in the group. This bickering was followed by some anger directed at Maria for coming in that condition. "It upsets me to see her that way," one woman said.

Said another member, "She should have known better than to come."

Then another said: "There must be more than one right way to die. Perhaps some people will die screaming like a wet hen rather than in peace."

Judy suddenly changed the course of the discussion by saying, "It must have taken a lot of courage for her to come. I hope that when I am that sick, I will be as able as she is to make decisions about what I do. I think we are being so critical of Maria because she frightens us. We see her dying and we are really frightened that that is what will become of us."

Suddenly the group's image of Maria, and what she meant to them, had been transformed. The women shifted their focus from the disease's ravages on her body to her continued mastery over it. They saw her now not simply as a woman who was dying of metastatic breast cancer, but as someone who was struggling to live her life as fully as she could, as long as she could.

And instead of being an image of despair, Maria became one of hope for these women. Not the irrational hope that the disease would not kill them, but rather the hope that they could live their lives much as they would have chosen to right until the very end. This came from admiring how Maria coped with the threat of her own death, not from denying that she was dying.

The group then decided to hold the next week's meeting at Maria's home, knowing that it would be easier for them to go to her than for her to come to the medical center again. We had a touching and sad meeting around the hospital bed in her home, and a few days later she died, but not before dictating a note to the group saying how much she had learned from the meeting and appreciated everyone coming to her home to see her.

The group found a way to imbue what they most feared with a different meaning, one that strengthened rather than weakened them, even though it was sobering. We went through periods when it was quite difficult to discuss the deaths that had occurred or were impending. Toward the end of Maria's life, one member bolted out of the room, and we had to bring her back in and urge her to tell us what was upsetting her. It was knowing that Maria was dying, she admitted —she found it almost too terrible to talk about, although she finally did. It became a matter of facing but not yielding to limitations. In discussing Maria's dying and death later, group members commented on how alert and comfortable she had been until the very end. Thus they managed to focus not just on the fact of her death, but also on the quality of it. They were encouraged by her determination and control in the face of painfully obvious physical decline. They managed to extract, even from a very difficult situation, positive aspects of coping.

Maria's presence led the group to address head-on a number of important issues related to the fear of dying: They began to see death as a series of problems, many of which they could take control of.

Who Decides What
Medical Treatment I Receive?

Many fear that as their physical and mental stamina decline, they will lose the ability to decide about chemotherapy, radiation, and other treatments. We encourage members of our group to discuss clearly with their physicians what treatments they want, and when.

Planning with your families and attorneys includes filling out a "living will." This is a document in which you can state your desires regarding the kind of medical care you will receive if and when you become more ill. You can make it clear, for example, that you do not want so-called "heroic measures" employed when you are near death. Creating a living will is a concrete step you can take to set your mind at ease regarding the procedures that will be used and also to relieve your family of painful choices at a time of critical illness. ("Since I love her, shouldn't I tell the doctors to do anything they can to save her?")

Will I Be Left Helpless to
Deal with Increasing Pain?

Not all people with cancer suffer severe pain. Indeed, about a third of people with advanced disease do not suffer significant pain. Pain is not inevitable in many other serious illnesses as well. Nonetheless, all are understandably concerned about the possibility. In Chapter 11, I describe some simple self-hypnosis techniques that have helped many people with cancer control pain. In addition, doctors have become increasingly expert at using medications and physical devices such as nerve stimulators and infusion pumps to control pain. Talk with your doctor about his or her plans for helping you with pain. Knowing about your many options will allay your fears of helplessness.

Will Friends and Family Withdraw from Me?

Loneliness feels like a preview of dying. Death is, after all, the most profound separation from loved ones and friends. We don't need it any sooner than necessary. Yet many people are so frightened of death that they withdraw from dying people.

I believe that the best approach to keeping loved ones from withdrawing is to give them the license to confront the issue as directly as you are. If you insert the dreaded words *cancer* and *death* into the conversation, for example, you are telling your friend or family member that you are strong enough to talk about it. Such direct conversations can become treasured moments for both of you. The result is that you feel close, and far less alone, as the members of our group did. In the face of their worst fears, what they gave one another was comfort and closeness. It did not solve every problem, but it powerfully countered the sense of isolation that makes death seem to come sooner than it does.

How Do I Handle Unfinished Business?

When death anxiety is strong, people need to feel their relatedness to others.

Sheila was angry with herself after Donna, another woman in the group, died rather suddenly. "If I had been a better group member, maybe I could have helped her in some way. I didn't let her know how much I cared about her." If there is one regret that our groups have experienced over the years after a member has died, it is the sins of omission—not making members aware before they died how much they meant to us.

There is such an absoluteness to death. Harsh words cannot be taken back. Promises unfulfilled can never be completed. One cannot even say good-bye. Facing the absoluteness of death can be a tremendous stimulus to life. If it is important, do it now. This goes beyond writing a will and arranging for burial (although such tasks should be attended to). Say what you mean to say. Settle old grievances. Accomplish what needs doing, sooner rather than later.

Jim reflected painfully on his wife Jane's final year: "We put up a front for each other. I didn't want her to see how worried I was, and she didn't want me to know how scared she was. But one night, she woke up and told me how terrified she was. I tried to tell her not to worry. Now, I wish I had just held her more and that we had talked about how frightened she was."

Jane had been in considerable pain near the end. She could be more than a little huffy when she was uncomfortable and had sent Jim packing from the hospital room: "I don't want any visitors tonight—you just go on home." Sadly, she died that night, leaving Jim hurt and wishing that he had dealt more directly with her fear and pain.

While the phrase "Live every day as if it were your last" has become a cliché, it takes on real meaning when each day might indeed be your last. Make sure you have said what you want to say to loved ones and friends, that your possessions will be distributed as you intend, that you prepare others as you would like to be prepared yourself for the loss of someone you care deeply about.

Am I Strong Enough to Face My Death?

When the going gets heavy in groups, I frequently find myself at a loss. Death is so overwhelming that it is rather humbling. There seems to be so little one can do about it. Strangely enough, we always resort to the same comfort: our sense of caring about one another. In some sense, we huddle together. Our bond of caring forms a kind of talisman against the power of death. Although, ultimately, each of us has to face our death alone, it is a tremendous relief to do some of the work with someone else. A good hug or some shared tears may not save a life, but it will make you feel more alive.

It is one thing to express support and caring for the living, but maintaining that sense of caring and connection in the face of death is another matter. Madeline illustrated a series of cards on which she inscribed the following poem after the death of Ilene, a vital and delightful woman who died shortly after a long-planned final trip to Greece:

Dear Ilene,
Whenever the wind is from the sea
salty and strong
you are here.

Remembering your zest for hilltops
and the sturdy surf of your laughter
gentles my grief at your going
and tempers the thought of my own.

The last two lines of this poem capture an important point. Grieving losses in the group strengthened, not weakened, members. They were able to cherish the strengths of the departed member, identifying with her joys and abilities, not just her defeat in the face of the inevitable. Madeline had deeply admired Ilene's strength, her open-eyed acceptance of the inevitability of her death. However, there had been times when Ilene felt trapped by her strength, admitting to the group that she had been reluctant to come to meetings when she felt overwhelmed and depressed. Madeline pointed out to Ilene that it would be better if she could show them both sides of herself, since they would learn that, even in their frailty, they could also have strength like Ilene's. We tend to think of strength and weakness in simple arithmetic terms: Strength − Weakness = Coping.

In fact, all of us are strong and weak, and admitting to ourselves this duality does not weaken us. Admitting one's frailty to others helps them by allowing them to see that you do not have to be perfect to be strong. If a person you admire admits weakness, you can tolerate your own weakness much better.

Madeline's process of grieving was ultimately reassuring rather than threatening, because it was a reminder that she, too, would be missed and grieved when she died. The most frightening thing is to think that you might slip away unnoticed. The process of grieving helps you understand those aspects of life that remain with others after you are gone.

GIVING UP THE ESCAPE CLAUSE

Shortly after Ilene's death, the group members, including Maria, got into a discussion of finally coming to terms with "giving up the 'escape clause.'" Most had nurtured a secret fantasy that they would be the one to beat the odds. However, as the disease progressed, producing new symptoms, they became increasingly aware of its relentlessness, and came face-to-face with a recognition that what they *wished for* had nothing to do with what *happened*.

The irony of giving up this escape clause is that to do so is in an odd way invigorating. It makes you feel how precious and fragile your life is because you recognize that it can indeed slip away. This is what is so debilitating about approaches that hide from people the medical facts of their illness or make them pretend that they can wish the cancer away. They are handed an escape clause—denial or wishful thinking—and it puts them to sleep instead of waking them up. These approaches are examples of what anthropologist Gregory Bateson used to call a "dormifying hypothesis," one that "puts to sleep the critical faculty." When we come face-to-face with the idea that all of us will one day run out of escape clauses, we take what we have more seriously. This is what living beyond limits is all about.

This recognition is, on the one hand, deeply frightening, and on the other, necessary for coming to terms with life-threatening illness. It is part of a process of selecting goals that are attainable. The thought of death is overwhelming and at times terrifying (there is a reason why we use the phrase "scared to death"), but it is usually not first on the minds of people with life-threatening illnesses. They worry more about more proximate dangers. Bad as these are, there is something almost reassuring about being able to articulate them. As each takes shape, it suggests possible courses of action. You can learn about the expected course of the disease, and how you can prepare and compensate for loss of physical abilities. You can develop an ability to ask for help, something that comes easily to very few except the very young. You can plan with your doctor how to participate in your present and future medical care. You can even mitigate the inevitable separation from loved ones by intensifying your closeness to them now, while you can. Each of these problems (and many others not enumerated) is less overwhelming when faced directly.

Our group felt less passive as they thought of things they could do about each of these issues. Instead of denying or ignoring death, they looked it right in the eye and decided what to do about it. As Eleanor put it:

> What I found is that being in the group is a bit like that fear you have standing at the top of a tall building or at the edge of the Grand Canyon. At first you are afraid even to look down (I don't like heights), but gradually you learn to do it and you can see that falling down would be a disaster. Nonetheless, you feel better about yourself because you're able to look. That is how I feel about death— I am able to look at it now. I can't say I feel serene, but I can look at it.

CONFRONTING YOUR DEATH: DEMORALIZING OR INVIGORATING?

People with cancer in our Supportive/Expressive group therapy program spend a good deal of time confronting their own fears of dying and death. We have at times had more than an indirect confrontation with fears of death.

> Toward the end of one meeting, Lucy said that she was not feeling well. As we asked her to tell us what was wrong, she turned her head to the side and lost consciousness. We took her out of her chair and laid her on the floor. As I took her pulse and blood pressure, which were normal, she became conscious again. We brought her to the emergency room, and it became clear that she had fainted; because of recent chemotherapy, she had not felt like eating and drinking,

and had taken in very little during the preceding day. She recovered well, but the group had quite a scare. Leslie said: "We just saw what we most fear." Each group member interpreted what had happened in terms of her own recent stress. Rachel's sister had just suffered a stroke, so she thought that Lucy was having a stroke. Several group members thought Lucy was dying; others thought she had fainted. What the group found most unsettling was the unpredictability of the event—they wanted at least to have had some warning that something was going to happen. Focusing on one aspect of the event, and on how predictability could help them to be emotionally prepared, was a way of dealing with their death anxiety.

That such an event should occur was hardly surprising. After all, when you get people with a similar serious illness together, some will get sicker and even die. What effect will this have on other group members with the same disease? When we began this project in the 1970s, many clinicians were understandably concerned that we would make patients worse rather than better, that we would demoralize them through exposure to similar patients who did poorly. We were quite concerned about that and went so far as to compare those group sessions in which there was bad news about members to those in which the group was doing well.

We asked several Stanford medical students to observe a number of group sessions and classify the discussions in two ways. First, we asked them to rate the mood of the group each minute of the ninety-minute meetings. They used a list of emotions, including anger, happiness, despair, and frustration to determine whether the overall mood was positive, neutral, or negative. We also had the students rate the content of the discussion at each minute. The topics included death and dying, medical treatments, what was occurring in the group, what was happening to group members, the family situation, and small talk. We had several students provide ratings of the same meetings so we could assure reasonable agreement among different raters about these dimensions. We then examined the medical news about group members, and divided it into three types: good news (a clear bone scan, no sign of recurrence), neutral news (the disease has not progressed), and bad news (the scan shows new metastases, an increase in pain, a member died). We looked to see whether the medical condition of the group members affected the emotional tone or content of group discussions. In collaboration with Michael Glafkides, then a Stanford undergraduate student, and now a plastic surgeon specializing in breast reconstruction, we analyzed these data and found something interesting. The emotional tone of each meeting was relatively balanced, with about an equal amount of positive, neutral, and negative moments, and it was not heavily influenced by the medical news provided by group members. However, the content of group discussions was powerfully influenced by news of members' medical condition. When there was bad news, the groups spent a good deal more time discussing death and dying, what was happening to group members, and their medical treatment.

> Laura, whose illness had been progressing, talked tearfully about how her sister had become pregnant again. While she was happy for her (her sister had recently had a stillborn child), she admitted that the news reminded her of her lost ability to have children. Sheila had been quiet, but when questioned stated that she was still "clean," meaning no recurrence of the cancer recently. Then she burst into tears and said: "At the time when all of my friends were growing babies, I was growing tumors. I waited until my thirties to have a child and wound up with a tumor. I love my adopted children, but I wanted children of my own."

Bad news elicited serious discussion. When there was good news, there was a lot more small talk. Thus, the medical condition of members, by this measure, did not demoralize the support groups, but it did focus the content of their discussions, as we had hoped it would. It also gave a sense of peace to other group members facing death. The following was read at the memorial service for Jackie by Reggie Kriss, a coleader of one of our early groups:

I would like to tell you about Jackie, as I came to know her. A person seeking help to quiet her fear of the unknown, from the ravages of cancer, she came to a group of women who were all dealing with the thought of dying, of their life coming too soon to a conclusion. It is daring and usually taboo to discuss with others what it is like to die. Sad thoughts are often left in limbo, unexpressed, hidden in the night in silent tears. In this group it was different. The experts were the women with cancer. They were encouraged to probe the depths of their feelings and unexpressed thoughts, to mourn themselves and share in the good and bad events and happenings of each other's lives. The bonding came from mutual concern and caring for each other and Jackie was in the midst of it. As she learned to help herself confront even the most frightening and fearful thoughts, she became aware, as did the other group members, that letting go of oneself has riches in it that were often learned too late. Letting the trivia in one's life go and the "shoulds"—I should do this or I should do that, or he should do this or that. The process in the group became for Jackie and the others a new way of confronting life. A vitality and energy came from the group that made no issue too painful to disclose, and the deeper the group went into their feelings the stronger they became in helping themselves and their families deal with the inevitable fact that we must all die, and for many of us, sooner than we wish.

I do not need to tell you of the warmth, deep devotion and interest, concern and compassion that Jackie has for all of us in the group. For that was her nature and we all basked in the beauty of it. But I would like to tell you how we all learned from each other. One of the issues that came up in the group was having the courage to die. Jackie was particularly concerned that she would not be satisfied with the way she would conduct herself, that she would just weep and feel sorry for herself. I remember the afternoon Jackie came to the group, some months ago, and slowly and quietly told us she had finally come to the knowledge that she was going to die and probably would not live out the year. We were all stunned to hear one of our members make this kind of statement. We were deeply saddened but admired her courage to tell us and share this most intimate feeling. Jackie showed us that she trusted us, to support her in knowing this, and somehow from that day on she seemed to have an unlimited courage to offer her family and all of us.

Jackie said that Ilene gave her a gift and after that Jackie had no tears. Ilene, a fighter of no mere means, in the last week of her life became peaceful and unafraid and told us just before she died: 'I'm not going to push the river. I'm not afraid to die, I feel at peace.' Jackie, in turn, gave courage and love to all of us who knew her. Her tender and loving family gave and received her beautiful spirit, just as she wanted it to be. Jackie will be in our memory, always.

Jackie gave a gift to the group by making it clear to us how much we had helped her. She often referred (as Reggie mentioned) to the comfort she drew from the "amazing grace" with which Ilene had confronted her own death.

There is much in the popular psychology literature that suggests that true maturity about facing life-threatening illness means a conviction that it can never hurt you, or that dying is not to be feared. There is nothing unusual or incorrect about fearing death. The crucial issue is to face death in such a way that you can do something realistic about it: enriching life before death, taking control of your medical treatment, setting up a living will, reordering your priorities in life. If there is one thing worse than death, it is living as if you are already dead, something Kierkegaard called the "sickness unto death."

One of the things I learned in my training is that what should be the easiest thing in life, expressing love and caring, is indeed one of the hardest. It involves taking risks, learning tenderness, and being vulnerable to hurt because the person you express care for may not care back. No one does this easily, and men do it even less easily. When I learned that my friend Bryan was dying rapidly, I returned from a sabbatical trip to spend some time with him. We both knew why I had returned and hugged each other so hard we nearly fell over. We said in words something that had been implicit in our friendship, which is that we each felt the other was like the brother we wished we had had. Now that Bryan is gone, I am very glad that we had that discussion, because I now know that he felt the way I did, and that he knew that I felt that way about him as well. We had to say it to each other, because we knew that soon the opportunity to do so would be gone forever.

THERE IS A SENSE of power that comes from an unblinking confrontation with death. The words *sacred* and *sacrifice* have a common root. Many religious symbols involve the transcendence of death: the sacrament in Catholicism, for example. Battlefields are consecrated by the blood of the deceased. But there is a power in facing death in everyday life as well. Sandy called her daughter Katie's dean after the dean refused to allow her to take a summer school course in order to graduate from college early. Sandy said: "I want my daughter to graduate early because I have cancer. The doctors gave me two years to live. I've lived a year and a half, and I want to be alive when she graduates. The dean said what a wonderful person I was and that she would do anything to make it possible." Katie called her mother back and asked with amazement in her voice, "What did you say to the dean? I can't believe it." Sandy proudly attended Katie's graduation.

There is a kind of freedom that comes with a recognition that your time is limited. Long-term consequences seem less weighty (indeed, less likely). I have always admired the freedom of older people to speak freely, in contrast to those of my generation in the middle years who are still building careers and maintaining relationships. Older people often just say what they think. They seem to worry far less about the consequences of their words. This is frequently ascribed to "aging," but I suspect it has more to do with the proximity of death. Not only is time (and candor) precious, but whether or not someone else approves or disapproves seems irrelevant. There is a kind of authenticity that comes from a confrontation with the fragility of life that can be positively refreshing.

Rachel had been more quiet than usual for several group sessions, and finally, after repeated questions from leaders and group members, she admitted that she was not feeling well and was afraid that she was dying. She was about to undergo radiation for the first time and had a new and general sense of being unwell. "I just feel bad— like I'm dying," she said. And then, with a little of the old twinkle in her eye, she added: "Even when I have a good day, I figure this must be the time when you rally—two days before you die."

We ended that meeting in laughter.

7. Taking Time

Far from being restricted to "being a cancer patient," Dr. Spiegel's group has allowed me the chance to focus on life issues in general, which include cancer. There can be no substitute for sharing with other cancer patients. But what defeats the pain and scare is the existential moments true for all of us. Plus we learn a lot about laughter and fun in the jaws of death!

—LORNA BARATI

I am fond of backpacking, and have noticed that food and water carried in strictly limited quantities on your back take on a special quality. A package of freeze-dried stew can become the most precious and tasty dinner when you are camped near the top of a mountain and have nothing else to eat. Similarly, time acquires its true value when we recognize that it is not infinite. Elisabeth Kübler-Ross, who did pioneering work helping patients with dying and death, wrote that many engage in a process of "bargaining," an imaginary negotiation for a little more time to accomplish some important tasks. I mentioned earlier that most of us engage in "immortality projects," good works that seem so important that we imagine that they guarantee our survival. This notion of bargaining is an explicit extension of the idea that "I won't die until I finish." Unfortunately, life is not so fair. Nonetheless, turning the idea on its head can be a spur to creative living: If I don't have much time left, how can I use it most meaningfully?

TRANSFORMING TIME

Some people wonder whether they can experience joy in their lives once serious illness and the threat of death has intruded:

> Patricia, whom I mentioned in the introduction to this book, realized that her illness was worsening. She had to resist measuring its progress by not looking in the mirror each morning as she dressed. She had liver involvement, and found her belly growing. One morning she was trying on a jacket that wouldn't fit and just started screaming and crying in frustration, a luxury she had not previously allowed herself.
>
> "I've always been troubled by not having my body perfect," Patricia told us. "When I was nine I fell down and cut my knee. I still have a scar there and I felt my body was perfect before and now it isn't. The same thing when I was told I had to wear glasses. I guess maybe it's a problem I have—wanting things to be perfect."

The valleys and peaks of emotion Patricia experienced are not unrelated. Her abject frustration at the effect of the illness on her body challenged in the sharpest way her wish for a "perfect" body. Her anguished tears in front of the mirror amounted to an acknowledgment of what the cancer had done to her. At the same time, she knew that although her body was no longer perfect, it was all she had. Once she had dispensed with perfection, she was freer to enjoy what time she had. The irony is that the "imperfection" of mortality, the threat of death, can enrich as well as diminish our appreciation of the joys in life.

> Susan resonated with Patricia's story, saying she too had a perfectionist streak, but had recently stopped working so hard and had just learned to "live day for day." "When I was younger," she added, "I was more inclined to insist on having things perfect. Now I'm more inclined to settle for what I can get: Everything I plant in my garden dies sooner or later."

There is a poignancy to the beauty experienced when a threat lurks around the corner. It is a bit like being in the eye of a hurricane—it is more deeply peaceful because of the chaos surrounding it, but you cannot quite forget what is coming:

> Sally mentioned that she has some trouble living fully now because of her awareness of her future. Even if she takes the time to smell a beautiful flower, she cannot somehow experience its beauty, but is instead overwhelmed with sadness because she is so preoccupied with the thought that she may not be here tomorrow to smell that rose. Another group member pointed out to her: "You are not living in the present; you are living in the future."

So much of our training in life is based on controlling wishes, delaying gratification, denying satisfaction of urges—living in the future. Much of this is necessary to maintain the semblance of civilized life that we try to lead. Nonetheless, we often get so used to inhibiting our impulses that it becomes automatic, and we deny ourselves too much pleasure out of habit rather than rational self-interest.

> Eleanor, who likened death to the Grand Canyon in the previous chapter, was a proper and rather controlled woman. She told the group a pointed story about having been taught in a convent school

that when someone passes the chocolate bonbons around at Christmas time, a polite little girl would refuse the first time and then accept the second time they were passed around. "That's been the story of my life," she said. "The trouble is they never came around a second time, and I would sit there staring at them, wishing for one."

The proximity of her death challenged Eleanor's characteristic willingness to defer pleasure. She had come to realize that she did not have infinite amounts of time to await the return of the bonbons. Furthermore, she realized that there was nothing shameful about wanting something, and if she was going to get it, she had better reach for it. Politeness came to seem far less important than satisfaction. The oddly invigorating thing about recognizing your mortality in a concrete and personal way is that it can push you to savor each moment that remains. Furthermore, you have an "excuse" to change (if you need one). The illness has taught you a lesson, and you have no time to waste.

In the previous chapter I referred to "immortality projects," our efforts to feel invincible by making ourselves seem indispensable. The hidden goal of such a project is to lengthen life—I am such an important doctor, lawyer, mother, policeman, builder that I cannot die. Devotion to work is not an end in itself, but rather a means to an end. The kind of life project I describe in this chapter is an end in itself. It begins with the acknowledgment of how brief and fragile life is, and there is no pretense that doing the project will forestall death. Rather, a life project is a means of making the most of whatever time is left, or living better rather than longer. An immortality project attempts to defer death; a life project defers to it.

Frequently those seeking to avoid a confrontation with death redouble their efforts to carry on as though their illness meant nothing. They throw themselves into their work or family responsibilities as though they had all the time and energy in the world.

Sally, who had metastatic breast cancer, three young children, and a new house, said that she had no qualms about her own death: "It's my children, that's the point that gets me. I think of them needing a mother. I want my husband to remarry, but I worry about how much she can love them—she couldn't care for them the same way I do." Sally had painful metastases in her hip and walked with a cane. Despite this, she spent her spare time stripping floors and nursing broods of baby bunnies, waking several times a night to feed them. She desperately needed to feel necessary to the running of her household and able to do anything her family needed. It was as though she could will herself to do anything, despite the fact that she was draining her physical resources.

The life projects that follow are examples of careful choices made by women and men who are reassessing their lives and setting priorities based upon a realization that illness may well shorten their lives.

CHOOSING A LIFE PROJECT

Group members decided that if they had less time to live, they had better make good use of the time they had left. They found new purposes in life or resurrected old projects. Martha was a delightful, peppery, frugal woman. Slender, with a pinched face and "granny" eyeglasses, she seemed abrupt and often complained, but in an affectionate way. She was a "fussbudget," but was endlessly giving. She grew herbs, which she brought to the group as gifts in recycled jars (years before it was fashionable). Her gifts took the form of carefully chosen words as well. She had been a frustrated poet all of her life. She realized while she was in the group that if she did not write more poetry soon and publish it, she would be a poet in fantasy only. She determined to publish her work. Before she died, she published two small books of poetry. This work was not accomplished without stirring up its own set of regrets:

"If only I had written earlier in life, I would have been able to make my mark. I'm a damned good poet and will leave far less than I might have. I spent a year growing tomatoes. That was beneath me because I wasn't using my talent then."

We tried to point out to Martha that what she did before had made her into the person—and poet—she was now. Nonetheless, one of the great obstacles to change is the necessity to grieve the past. A decision to do something new and different is a rejection of what you were doing before. One of the reasons people delay stopping smoking (other than habit and the general inertia of human nature) is that the better the reasons for quitting, the worse you feel about not having done it before. If you are really destroying your lungs, elevating your risk of a heart attack, reducing your energy, burning holes in your clothing, and alienating your nonsmoking friends and family, you *should* have stopped years ago. To become a nonsmoker now means passing judgment on yourself as a smoker. To change means being able to cut the past loose, feel sad about your mistakes, and head off in a new direction.

If you do something good now, it invariably raises the question of why you did not do it before. Oddly, a life-threatening illness gives you an opportunity to bypass this standard roadblock to change, because it gives you a new reason: lack of time.

I visited Martha in the hospital a few days before she died. I told her that we were sorry she could not be with us in the group, that we missed her but understood why she could not be with us. She proudly handed me her second book of poems. I thanked her for it. With a gleam in her eye, Martha said, "You know, Doctor, I'm going to have to charge you two dollars for this book."

I laughed and said, "I'll gladly pay it," and did. A few minutes later I said good-bye. Retreating from the finality of my departure, she called out, "See ya," as I left the room. Martha made excellent use of her last years. She accomplished a goal that had previously eluded her and made herself an integral part of the life of our group as well.

Members of the group were frequent topics of Martha's poems:

Never Ask Us Why

Those of us who know, won't tell
So we build you a barrier
To cut out any probing of our scars,
Self-inflicted or not.

If you will love us a little
And let us weep when we must
We may find out who we are.

The last three lines are especially telling. Martha captured the importance of the group as a place where any feeling could be expressed and highlighted how crucial it was to feel cared for.

It is reassuring to know you can build something new even as life becomes shorter. This comes from recognizing the precious nature of the time you have left. Moreover, it is a concrete way of saying to yourself and those around you, "My life is not over yet!" Rather than winding down, you are gearing up, determining to accomplish something despite (or in an odd way because of) the illness that afflicts your body.

The life projects varied greatly.

Sandy reflected on her life as a wife, mother, and editor. It had been rewarding, but not easy. She had taken on her editorial career late in life, and found balancing her education and family trying at best. As she thought about this, she remembered that she had planned to leave money in her will to help other young women negotiate a career change into journalism. She thought, "Why should I leave all the pleasure of helping people until after I am dead?" With that, she called up her college and arranged to make the donation. She then visited the college, helped select and met with the recipients, and derived much pleasure from it.

Other group members made it a point to let their communities know what it was like to live with cancer. Their hope was to use their experience to improve the lot of others coping with this illness.

Jane agitated relentlessly about the needs of women with advanced breast cancer. She commented bitterly that what public attention there was went to screening, prevention, and women with primary disease: "They just write us off if it comes back." She recalled her experience of being dismissed from a group of breast cancer patients when her disease recurred.

Despite progressing illness, she devoted her energy to informing her community about her struggle with cancer. When her church devoted an evening to various life histories, she asked to present hers. What follows is an excerpt of her story as she presented it. This was also read a few months later at her memorial service:

> *It was now February 14, 1985, and we were packed to meet our family . . . for a little vacation, and as suddenly as Hurricane Andrew hit Florida, Hurricane Cancer hit me with no warning. Later, after the first four years of surgery, chemotherapy, radiation and hormone therapy, I found out that I had only passed the eye of the storm. The winds and waves now picked up; stronger radiation, deadlier chemotherapy that went on and on and by December 1990, I would no longer participate in most of my normal activities: Christmas shopping, decorating, cooking, cleaning, gardening, bike riding, skiing, hiking, teaching aerobics, walking, water skiing, sitting, typing, traveling, helping others, taking care of my tiny new granddaughter, and I could no longer comb my hair . . . it was gone! It was then that I started to find out who I really was,*

what I was made of and how I would make the best use of the resources that were inside me and surrounding me to handle the hurricane raging inside my body!

When something like Hurricane Andrew hits, it makes you feel like pulling the covers over your head, and you hope that when you look out again it will all be gone. I think it is like that with lots of tremendous challenges in our lives, like: earthquakes, hurricanes, tornadoes, floods, serious accidents, child abuse, losses of life, limbs and eyesight, and life-threatening diseases like cancer. If it happens to someone near and dear to us, we seem better able to take care of the situation. But if it happens to you yourself, you must learn how to make good, selfish decisions for yourself! And it is a difficult task to become a survivor instead of a victim!

While you are under that blanket (called denial), it's OK to feel sorry for yourself or to feel guilty that you didn't do this or that differently. To experience guilt about your condition doesn't mean that you are bad, in fact it can help responsibility to kick in. What paralyzes us is: not taking responsibility, even though it seems overwhelming. Having a disease out of control in my body and not being able to do what I'd always done, what I'd taken care of my body to do, was overwhelming for me. After the denial came much anger and then the search for my resources.

Here are six of my most important resources:

#1. Attitude: Be open and honest, don't exaggerate or try to hide what you are going through. More help will come to you if you are honest. A friend sent me this little poem that has helped my attitude many times:

> *Be pretty if you are,*
> *Be witty if you can,*
> *But be cheerful if it kills you!*

I try to live with that attitude.

#2. Determination: *My brothers taught me that one when they kept saying: "If you can't keep up, stay home." So when my family said that they guessed I couldn't go Christmas shopping, I shopped off the TV for presents and clothes for myself (I'd gained 30 pounds on hormone therapy and not one thing in my closet fit me). When numerous chemotherapies stopped working and the doctors wanted to try yet another kind, I found a non-toxic treatment in England and when I didn't have enough energy to get there, I convinced the doctor to give me a transfusion.*

#3. Set Goals: *Set very small goals and always have a PLAN B. I think that moving as many times as I did growing up and in early marriage helped me to realize that if something is not working, change and do something else . . . always have the next plan ready even if you have to create it in an instant. Besides doing my shopping off the TV, I let others do it when I'm not up to it. If I can't walk but I need to get out, I use a wheelchair. I drastically changed my attitude about taking pain medication, chemotherapy and radiation . . . they have become my friends and I work with them instead of being afraid. And I have learned to let go of the unnecessary things in my life like cleaning, cooking, worrying about things.*

#4. Take Care of Yourself: *Get your sleep, exercise no matter what (I changed from every exercise that I was doing to swimming because that was all that I could do). I'd never had a massage, a manicure or a pedicure, but I have now. Screen visitors with an answering machine, a note on the door or a family member. And find some humor . . . somewhere, anywhere, everywhere . . . find some humor!*

#5. Professional Help. *Get some help: Good doctors, psychologists and chiropractors. Change if you have to. And learn to use the system at your health care facility. Be assertive* *but not necessarily aggressive. Join a support group, I belong to a professional group at Stanford and have helped make a movie for national TV and we are now the subject of a book about breast cancer. I also have a group of ladies that became my support group when there was not one to be found . . . I adopted them. And I have my swimming support group.*

#6. Spiritual Support: *I put this near the end because I firmly believe that God expects us to do all that we can to help ourselves and others and that He will be there for us no matter what. These things I have been making use of all my life but I certainly have examined them and tried to use them more effectively and more often for the last 7 and a half years . . . priesthood blessings by family members, home teachers, many members of the Stake [a Mormon jurisdiction], missionaries and friends . . . music, and Temple sessions. I have leaned on my family, friends, my visiting teacher and my neighbors heavily for physical and spiritual support. At some point in my disease, I had to realize that I may have to live the best I can with my disease and that I may not beat it. We are all going to die some time and so I simply have to count the blessings that I have no matter how small or how great they are.*

There is not one path that we all can follow even if our situations start out the same. Each of us was put here on earth to find our way, with our free agency, and each of us must do it for ourselves. I sincerely believe that is why we are here!

Thus did Jane devote a substantial amount of her waning energy to helping others cope better with the same overwhelming forces that were eroding her life. She reached out at a time when many pull in and used her experience to provide guidance for others.

For some group members, the concrete task of leaving things to their children became the focus of a difficult piece of life's work.

Ellen put off writing a letter to be read to her children after her death that would help disperse her few belongings among them. She delayed doing this because it brought her into contact with her death, with the actual knowledge that her children will be reading that letter after she is no longer alive. When she finally brought herself to write the letter, she felt she had taken a "gigantic step." That she could *be* alive after so directly facing a time when she would not be alive was, in a strange way, invigorating.

For others, the group time was used to review family values and loyalties and make some important final decisions.

Marcy was caught in a dilemma about whether to be buried with her family or that of her husband. The problem, normally difficult, was complicated by the fact that his family believed in cremation and hers considered it a sin. She wanted to be with her husband, but recognized that he might later remarry, which left her feeling that she should be buried with her family.

Marcy then began to cry. She had a strong sense of wanting to impart values to her children. They identified with their father's values, which were in principle very liberal, but which had caused her and the family great financial hardship. He did not value money, earned little, and gave away what he had to "good causes." She felt that her husband had the luxury of living by his "principles," but that he inflicted the cost of them on her and the children. The group comforted her about the times when life seems overwhelming and also pointed out that children are usually good at detecting inconsistencies. Just because they admired his principles, they were not likely to be blind to the reality beneath them. She said she felt reassured.

People with serious illness adapt by doing everything they can to fight the disease, and by rethinking their priorities in life. When you undertake the hard mental work of relinquishing those parts of your life that are behind you, you also free yourself to take on new directions (Have you noticed how you cannot bring yourself to buy new clothes until you give away the old ones?). You can remain mired in regret about the things you can no longer do: "If I cannot ski again, I can't do anything—life is not worth living." You can pretend you can still do them and push yourself and your body beyond reasonable limits, in which case you will do damage. You can try to pretend that it all doesn't matter, but usually that rings hollow. What works better is grieving the loss, admitting the sadness that accompanies aspects of your previous life that are gone, and looking ahead to what you can do now. It will not be the same—it will be different, and it might even be better.

> Frank, who was a successful corporate financial manager, is rethinking his commitment to work (sixty to seventy hours per week) and making money. His family and time seem more valuable now. "I was a human shock absorber at work. I now see that I cannot infinitely absorb stress."

One means of living more fully in the present is traveling. I sometimes feel like a travel agent because of the number of trips that might not otherwise be taken that are conceived in our groups. Donna described her planned trip to Hawaii as "sweet but sad. I know it will be my last trip there, and I have been very happy there in the past. But I want to do it." Sadly, Donna never got to make that final trip.

Many group members have nursed a fantasy of that special trip to Europe or Hawaii or Mecca, and with vigorous encouragement from other group members, they carry them out. Sandy and her husband "did" New York as they had always wanted to. They stayed up late, rested when they needed to, hit the shows, museums, and restaurants, and had a wonderful time.

Not all of these trips turn out so well when they happen. Laura's friend, who also had breast cancer, became quite sick the day they arrived in Hawaii, and they spent most of the week trying to get medical help and feel well enough to return. "The vacation from Hell," is the way she described it. Other trips have been wonderful—the final grand tour to see something that gives a sense of completeness. Just engaging in such a project makes people feel that their life is not over, that they can do what they want. One woman talked at length with her husband about their priorities: Should they buy a house or travel? "I may not be around to enjoy the house—I want to live with that money." They did.

THE ORPHEUS EXERCISE

One way we encouraged discussion of limited time was by conducting an exercise designed to help members imagine giving up aspects of themselves, and examine what remained. It was developed and named the "Orpheus exercise" by existential psychologist James Bugenthal. Orpheus was the tragic figure in Greek mythology who was left so bereft by the death of his bride, Eurydice, that he descended into Hades and sang for her release. He so moved the darker powers that they released her, on the condition that he not look back to see her until he and Eurydice again ascended to Earth. He weakened, glanced backward, and lost her forever. He has become a symbol of resistance to accepting loss, which requires leaving the past behind and looking ahead.

The Orpheus exercise involves experiencing the loss of an aspect of your life in a very personal way. Picture several important defining aspects of your life, and then imagine that you could no longer fulfill one of those roles. Then imagine another role being stripped away, then another, and so on. Who would you be if you were not what you are now? Do you have value as a person outside of your career, your family role? Often, initially, the answer seems to be "no." The common response is, I am nothing if I am not accomplishing something;

hence the stockbrokers who leapt out of windows in the wake of the 1929 stock market crash. They felt they were worth nothing if they had failed at their jobs. Yet many of our group members discovered a new sense of personal importance—that they deserved to exist even if they could not carry on the work they had done before they became ill —by imagining who they were without being able to fulfill the many roles and expectations that had been the stuff of their lives.

Ellen, who had taken that final trip to see the flowers bloom in Death Valley (Chapter 6), loved hiking. She felt most alive out in the wilderness with a backpack. As she imagined life without being able to hike, she was shocked to realize that she would be the same person when the day came in the near future that she could no longer climb mountains. She ended her Christmas letter that year with the following: "The greatest joy in my life is the companionship of good friends. In second place I put the enjoyment of the out-of-doors. Third comes the reading of interesting books. Conscious of my blessing, I look forward to the New Year hoping, in the large, that it brings PEACE to our unsettled world, and, in the small, that it brings me together more often with you."

Ellen had found a way to savor life beyond the loss of her ability to hike, shifting her focus more to family and friends.

Karen had devoted herself to church committees, feeling "terribly preoccupied" with this important work. It dawned on her that, fulfilling as it was, it seemed less important. She found that she could imagine giving it up and shifted her attention to regaining contact with a number of old friends who were very dear to her.

The Orpheus exercise helped group members to realize that we are always absorbed in some things at the expense of others. When we give time and energy to one person or group, we withhold it from someone else, often without realizing it. The mental discipline of imagining letting go of such roles allows you to consider reallocating your limited resources.

For some, the roles given up seemed minor, but the meaning of the loss was deep. Jane, whose "six resources" were recounted earlier in the chapter, found herself thinking about living day by day as her illness progressed. She was an avid concertgoer, but could not bring herself to renew her season tickets to the symphony. She found it a bittersweet thought—sad that she could not count on attending so many concerts, yet a reminder of how much pleasure the music brought her.

Group members began the Orpheus exercise by making a list of attributes, aspects of themselves that were important to them—for example, teacher, mother, wife, hiker, skier, cook, journalist. They were then asked to rank them, from least to most important to their own sense of personal identity. We then took a few moments, with eyes closed, and imagined giving each one up, starting with the least important one. The question we asked was, "Who am I if I am no longer this?"

There were tears and considerable discomfort, as the women grappled with an exercise that was more than an act of imagination, since the illness was forcing them to give up long-cherished aspects of themselves.

"I found it so hard to give up skiing—it is something my family has loved doing together for years. But I just can't do it anymore," said Jane. "So many of the things that gave my husband and me pleasure together—going to symphonies, taking walks, skiing—are lost. I worry about my marriage—what is it without those activities?"

Marianne reached out and took Jane's hand, saying: "I feel so much closer to you now that you are sharing some of your pain and your fears about cancer." Jane had at first tried to present herself in the group as super-strong and very well supported. I had worried that she would make others jealous (she did), and would alienate them (she did not). Closeness grew in the group as the fronts—the pretend strengths—were discarded.

As we moved closer to the core, feelings ran even stronger.

"I feel that in some way I have given up my womanhood. Between the surgery and the tamoxifen [an estrogen-blocking medication], I feel what it is like to be and yet not be a woman," said Laura.

"I feel sorry for my husband," said Nancy. "I am not a sexual being now, and I used to love that." She added, "I used to focus so much on accomplishing things. Now I just exist—I have gone from doing to being."

Sandy reflected on her cherished work as an editor. She had struggled to achieve the position she had, worked extremely hard, and loved it ("I was Lou Grant," she said proudly). Yet she had recently been forced to balance her waning reserves of energy against the demands of the evening shift on a major newspaper.

"For the first time I could imagine giving this job up, being and yet not being an editor. At the same time, it made me realize how much I love doing it," she said. A few weeks later she added that she had found the exercise deeply touching. Sandy had decided to tell her boss about her cancer, and her boss had taken it very well. Sandy also realized that she had other resources. She and her husband loved to talk with each other after the long hours of work. She realized that she would still have that, even if she could not work.

Thus, the paradox is that the pain of picturing having to give up cherished aspects of your identity can help you redefine your values and point the way toward new and rewarding activities and goals.

Barrie had talked about her love of teaching, and how painful it would be to give it up. Four months after doing this exercise, she was offered the type of job she had wanted all her life. Sadly, she was by this time too ill to take it. She credited the Orpheus exercise with preparing her to manage her disappointment.

Laura discussed giving up her image of finding and developing a deep relationship with a man in her life: "Now I am fighting for my life, and that has to take precedence."

Sandy saw the idea of building a new relationship from a different point of view: "I have always had this fantasy that I would outlive my husband and children and live in a cottage by the ocean with a fire going, reading books, and maybe going to an occasional play. I love solitude. And furthermore, I wouldn't know how to open myself up to a stranger—I wouldn't have the patience to explain myself to someone."

Sandy did not want the novelty Laura sought; Laura did not have the energy to establish the stability Sandy had but could imagine living without. Thus they gave one another perspective on their wishes and losses—making them seem real but less absolute. Each cherished what the other already had: Laura had solitude; Sandy, companionship.

Many of these women had defined themselves in terms of their usefulness to others: helping parents, making a home for their husbands, raising children, doing a good job at work. Jane talked about how uncomfortable it was for her to take rather than to give. She insisted on driving herself to the hospital because she hated to ask people to do things for her. Sheila tried to reassure her that it gave her pleasure to help. For example, as was mentioned earlier, it made her feel good to pick up Jane at her home and bring her to meetings when Jane felt too sedated by pain medication to drive on her own. It was hard for Jane to hear this, because she was so uncomfortable at her loss of the role of helper.

Some members found it hard to be flexible about their roles, not only in their lives outside, but in the group as well.

Sheila, who had been so supportive to Jane in affirming how good it made her feel to be of help, found it much more difficult to let herself be helped. Her religious faith was very important to her, and she felt that she had been "saved" several times from recurrences of the cancer. She had defined her role in the group as providing a model of hope for others. Sandy confronted her indirectly: "I know I haven't been through nearly what you have, but I would like to feel that I can be a model for you too." Sheila admitted that she did worry that she would have another recurrence of cancer and wondered how she would face and deal with it: "I will certainly need the group then." She seemed to be asking us whether we would want her if she was not a model of strength and health. Sandy and others were asking her to see herself as more than that role, to allow herself to be a follower as well as a leader, vulnerable as well as strong.

That session was not all tears. Rachel, in her inimitable way, responded to the Orpheus exercise by saying: "I've been around so long I've outlived all my roles." As usual, her humanity and humor shone through. She was more to us than any of those roles she had lived. What is truly human is the capacity to relate, to choose. We tend to lose ourselves in our roles, to become a thing, a collection of attributes. The process of giving up old roles and taking on new ones puts us back in touch with that deeper truth about ourselves. Even in giving up what we are used to doing, we (and others around us) can come to a new appreciation of what we have accomplished. We can teach rather than do. We can select new tasks and savor the ability to do so.

The Orpheus exercise is not merely a preparation for giving up things you may no longer be able to do. It is an effort to get at a core sense of your self, at the person underneath the roles we play. We tend to lose ourselves in our various roles, even in our language: "I *am* a mother" (or friend, lawyer, painter, gardener, etc.). In reality, each of us chooses to be many of these things for some period of time, but we come to identify who we are with what we do. As you sit quietly in a group with your eyes closed and imagine giving up being each of these things, you not only experience the pain of losing that part of yourself, you also realize that a deeper part of yourself remains. You are the one who chooses to be or not be any of those roles. You adopt them, you can reject them. You exist even if you are not doing any of them. You can *be* even if you are not *being* something. This realization is both upsetting and exhilarating. You as a person are more than any of the things you thought you had to be. Sandy found that she loved journalism deeply, but for the first time could accept being without being an editor. Laura deeply enjoyed feeling feminine, yet found that she could enjoy life despite feeling "neutered" by her disease and its treatment. While taking on life projects can make the later portions of life more meaningful, giving up projects can also add meaning. We lose ourselves in the everydayness of life. It is also important to take time to stay in touch with the part of you that *is* rather than *does*.

8. Fortifying Families

No *man is an island, entire of itself.* . . .
Therefore, never send to know for whom the bell tolls,
It tolls for thee.

—JOHN DONNE

Pam is a vital, incisive, articulate woman with a loving husband, a rambunctious seven-year-old, and a responsible job in university administration. She looked every bit the part with neatly tailored suits, carefully applied makeup, stylish short brown hair, and wide brown eyes. I mentioned earlier her appreciation of a surgeon who acknowledged her frustration with a delayed diagnosis of breast cancer. Unfortunately, her doctor had chosen to observe rather than remove the lump for several years. Her initial relief turned to fear, then frustration and anger, when she learned that the illness was spreading through her body. She came to see me for help in reevaluating the course her life was going to take. She had her career, which meant a great deal to her, she had her son to think of—and she had cancer.

As we talked, it became clear that her career was important to her, but her son and her health meant more. She came to feel that she could not do justice to all of them as she fought the illness. So the first thing Pam did was recognize that her energy and time were not infinite. She decided that if something had to go, it was going to be her career. She announced an early retirement.

But when her colleagues and friends at work planned a retirement party for her, she became quite anxious about it, worrying that she might "break down."

"Suppose you did," I asked. "What would be so terrible about that? Does it bother you to see someone else who is deeply moved by what you've done?

Pam agreed to give that some thought. Still, it was with some apprehension that she planned her speech. The party was quite moving and her friends had collected some twenty thousand dollars as a scholarship fund for her son. As she got up to say good-bye to her friends and that part of her life, she did begin to cry, but kept right on going. Everyone there was deeply touched by what she had to say, and she left her job with a sense of triumph.

Any serious illness afflicts families, not just individuals. Family members are often overwhelmed with conflicting feelings. They are sad and frightened about the potential loss of a family member; they ask many of the same questions the sick person asks of him- or herself: "Why us?" instead of "Why me?" Family members have their anger to cope with as well. They are resentful that the jobs the sick person performed have to be done by someone else.

Consider the situation: As the spouse of someone with a serious illness, you are not sleeping well because of your loved one's problem. You come home after working a full day, ask how he or she is feeling, and then have to cook dinner. You worry about your partner's health, how you'll pay the bills, and how the children will be cared for. Life-threatening illness is like a pebble in a pond—it sends ripples everywhere. Not only does it cause trouble directly, it interferes with the family functions we want and need to perform. This chapter deals with ways in which patients and their families can help one another. The key is to face a common threat together and make the most of precious shared time.

The concept of "family" is in itself not a simple one, and I use the term broadly. In many cultures, "family" often includes an extensive network of aunts, uncles, cousins, and more distant relatives who provide support, sustenance, and nurturance for one another. In hospitals in many such cultures, the nursing care is provided by family. I often wonder whether the social services upon which we pride ourselves in developed countries are not rather poor replacements for the caring routinely provided by extended families in "less developed" cultures. In our culture the nuclear family (husband, wife, and children) seems to be what is meant by family, needlessly downplaying the importance of adult siblings and multiple generations. Our economic wealth, along with social and geographical mobility, has dissected the family, and contact among family members tends to be more often electronic than physical.

In addition, many in our culture have not formed traditional nuclear families, simply because they are not ready to or have nontraditional sexual orientations. They, too, often form networks of loving and supportive people, although with less social and legal reinforcement than traditional families have. When faced with serious illness, such as cancer and AIDS, their needs for such support are no less, and at times greater. What I say about family in this book applies to anyone, regardless of the type of family, kinship, or friendship network that surrounds them.

In working with cancer patients and their families over many years, we have found that the challenges they face are of three basic types: what you need to know, when you allow yourself to feel, and how you can help. We sought to understand how families mastered each of these domains and how they managed to feel less helpless and overwhelmed. I learned that the best outcomes, like Pam's, came when people learned as much as they could about their situation, waded into the strong feelings they had about it, and then decided how to help others in their family deal with it.

THE MOST HELPFUL FAMILIES: RESEARCH FINDINGS

In our research on those factors that helped patients and their families, we administered a carefully constructed measure called the Family Environment Scale, developed by Drs. Rudolph and Bernice Moos at Stanford. Patients answered a series of ninety true/false questions, which gave us information about the nature of relationships in the family, family activities, and how the family was organized.

This scale was developed to help family members describe the nature of their family life. It can be filled out by just one family member or several. While it helps to have more than one perspective, in relatively well-functioning families there is pretty good agreement among the members about what the family is like. Do they feel a sense of commitment and loyalty? Can they get help with their problems? Do they fight all the time? Do they enjoy recreational activities together? Is religion a big part of family life? Is the family highly organized or do people come and go independently? What intensity and type of feelings flow among family members?

We were especially interested in the degrees of cohesion, expressiveness, and conflict the families demonstrated. By *cohesion,* we mean a family atmosphere of shared supportiveness, a sense that people in the family are on one another's side, there to help, that they care about one another. *Expressiveness* refers to open, shared problem solving. By *conflict* we refer to arguments, fighting, and disagreement. In order to find out how cohesive the family was, for example, we would ask them to respond to statements such as "Family members really help and support one another" and "We put a lot of energy into what we do at home." To determine their degree of expressiveness, the family would respond to statements such as "Family members often keep their feelings to themselves" and "We tell each other about our personal problems." To detect the degree of conflict, they would respond to statements such as "We fight a lot in our family" and "Family members hardly ever lose their tempers."

As a measure of how the patients in our study were feeling, we employed a widely used scale called the Profile of Mood States. It contains sixty-five adjectives, such as "angry," "friendly," "tense," "sad," and so on, and you are asked to indicate on a zero-to-five scale how well you feel each adjective describes your mood. We were particularly interested in using the measure of a family's emotional environment to predict how well cancer patients would be doing emotionally at a later time. This would help us to answer the question "What can families do that best helps ailing loved ones cope with the illness?"

We found that certain types of family interaction at home predicted how well the sick members of the family felt over time. The more family members supported one another, talked openly about problems, and reduced conflict, the happier the sick members were. In particular, expressiveness, a measure of shared and open problem solving, seemed to be a reliable predictor of how both sick and well family members would cope with a variety of illnesses, ranging from Hodgkin's disease, a cancer of the lymph system, to breast cancer, to schizophrenia. The lesson is that it pays to solve problems together rather than struggle with them separately. Our tendency is to hide what worries us from ourselves and from those close to us. This creates isolation, impairs problem solving, and seems to make sick people sadder and more anxious. While it may be true that "misery loves company," it seems that company dispels misery.

Sandy's daughter fought back the tears as she admitted to herself and the family group what she would lose when her mother died of breast cancer: "I've had lots of troubles in my life, lots of failures. Mom is the only person who always believes in me. I don't know what I will do without her."

"Have you told your mom this?" was the question from several group members. "No," the daughter replied. "I just feel so selfish— here I am worrying about myself, when she is dying."

Ruth, Laura's mother, gently confronted her:

"You know, I felt the same way. As a mother, I tried not to let Laura know how bad I felt. Then one day I burst into tears and told her, 'I am not only losing a daughter, I'm losing my best friend.' Then I felt guilty. I didn't want to give her more to handle, but she turned to me with a shining look of gratitude on her face, saying, 'That's the most wonderful thing you have ever said to me.' 'Didn't you *know*?' I asked. 'Yes, but it makes all the difference for you to *tell* me.' So let your mother know how important she is to you. That's not being selfish."

Ruth could play the part of the mother to Sandy's daughter, reflecting how much it would mean to Sandy to hear her daughter say plainly what her mother meant to her. Similarly, Pam could help her family so effectively because she had dealt with the despair that washed over her when she realized that the cancer had spread to other parts of her body and would be a chronic and serious problem for her. But instead of giving up when she realized that her life would be shortened, Pam had changed it. She refocused her more limited time and energy on her husband and son, and on helping other cancer patients. She took on a new task: helping her son tolerate her illness. This not only helped him, it made her feel stronger.

WHAT, WHEN, AND HOW

For friends and family of cancer patients, the steps to being more effective in helping cancer patients are: (1) Know what is happening to your loved one and to you, (2) acknowledge and vent your own mixture of uncomfortable feelings; and (3) demonstrate your willingness to be of concrete help and support. Find ways to intensify what is precious in the relationships you have and work on correcting what is destructive.

KNOWING

Knowledge implies mastery, yet it also acknowledges reality. As a loving family member or friend, you want to know as much as possible about your loved one's illness, yet you fear what you will learn. It is certainly not something you knew or cared much about before your family member or friend was told he or she was ill. You are thrust into a whole new and frightening world of terms, treatments, side effects, threats. The sick person's body is changed by surgery, radiation, chemotherapy, and you see that directly. He or she is changed as well, and becomes preoccupied with the changes. These may be much more disturbing to the sick person than they are to you, although you also may find yourself grieving the loss of your lover's physical perfection. If your wife has breast cancer, can you talk about it with her? Will you hurt her? She will be upset and embarrassed about her hair falling out during chemotherapy. She may be weak and tired. If your husband has prostate cancer, treatment may have made him impotent. Can you bring the issue out into the open? Your partner will be concerned about his or her health and future. What *is* the future? What does the disease mean? Is it curable? Is it treatable? Is one type of treatment superior to another?

These questions and many more beset people with life-threatening illness and their families. A few short weeks or months ago, you would have had only the slightest interest in them—now they are matters of life and death. Yet you often approach the information as though it were a loaf of bread just taken out of the oven—too hot to touch. To go to the library and read about cancer is an admission that your partner *has* cancer. It somehow makes it real. Think of learning about the illness as a means of being better equipped to help your partner and other members of your family. Treatments and outlooks change rapidly, so it is important to get up-to-date information and check it carefully. A book that is only a few years old may well contain outdated information. Some good sources of information are recommended at the end of this book. Also, consult your doctor.

A biological researcher was diagnosed with Hodgkin's disease some twenty years ago. He did what he would do about any other problem: He went to the library and read about his illness. Unfortunately, the books he consulted were quite out of date. At the time they were written, Hodgkin's disease was almost uniformly fatal. By the time he had contracted it, 80–85 percent of patients were curable, due to new treatment protocols with radiation and chemotherapy. He thought his life was over before his doctors set him straight on his prognosis.

Learning about the illness is a good idea. Stress is better managed when it is anticipated. When you know whether or not new rounds of chemotherapy and radiation are in store, when you know what can be done if the disease spreads or causes pain, those events will be less overwhelming and traumatic for everybody. Anticipation takes some of the force out of trauma.

Go with your partner to the doctor, and bring a list of questions. Tell the doctor at the beginning of the session that you have some questions so he or she will be able to allocate time to deal with them. Being interested in your partner's illness tells your partner that you are interested in *him* or *her*.

One of my patients said: "I came to realize that it was useless to hate my cancer. I mean, I did hate it and what it was doing to my body, but I realized that the cancer was a part of me, and that if I was going to learn to love myself I had to learn to love my cancer."

Perhaps *love* is too strong a word, but interest and attention are not. It is not just your spouse's problem, it is your problem. Reading, talking with friends who have been through it, and seeking information from such sources as the American Cancer Society and the National Cancer Institute can only help.

Jack, an erudite, goateed man in his late sixties, lay in his hospital bed. His skin and eyes were yellowed from an attack of jaundice, the apparent result of a reaction to medication. He bemoaned his fatigue and his frustration with the slow course of recovery. He steadfastly insisted that his only problem was recovering from his current medical problems. However, he and his wife were far from recovering from something much more serious than the temporary loss of his health: Their grown son, a prominent and successful attorney, had died eight months earlier from complications of leukemia. Jack felt the loss keenly, reviewing tearfully with me what a successful student his son had been, how well his law career had gone, and what a tragedy the loss was. "I wish I could have done more for him," Jack added. When I inquired about what he meant, he said: "My son knew he was dying for seven years, but he didn't tell us until a few months before he died. I could have sent him to New York for another opinion. I might have been able to help him more. I know he didn't want to worry me, but I wish I could have done something." The pain of his loss was tangible; his beloved son had been cut down in his prime, and Jack grieved. Yet his grief had been compounded by his son's attempts to protect him. In retrospect, Jack wished that he had known sooner, had been able to satisfy himself that he had done everything possible to save his son. Given the seriousness of his son's illness, it would not likely have made any physical difference, but it would have made an important emotional difference. He would have had the satisfaction of knowing he had tried everything possible to save his son. This kind of silent "protection" of loved ones has long-term costs.

"He wanted to save us from the agony of knowing he was dying," Jack added. "He was so independent—even the people in his office who knew about his illness thought he would beat it. Maybe he even thought that himself." Jack's other son added: "He wanted everything to be 'just normal.' It was. He had an excuse for the swelling on his neck, for everything. I wish I could have done something for him."

A recent study by psychologist Sandra Levy and her colleagues at the University of Pittsburgh yielded a surprising finding. Levy compared the psychological adjustment of women with breast cancer who had undergone the removal of a breast (mastectomy) with the emotional state of those who chose the more conservative breast-sparing procedure of lumpectomy (removal of the cancerous and nearby surrounding tissue) plus radiation. She found that the women who had the less mutilating procedure were slightly *more* depressed afterward. This finding, while surprising, had also been observed by British psychologist Lesley Fallowfield in a follow-up of women who had been treated for primary breast cancer.

How can one account for this? Levy found that the women who had received only lumpectomy and radiation seemed to receive *less* emotional support from their husbands than those who underwent mastectomy. Thus, it may be that those whose scars are more visible receive more support from their husbands. "Out of sight, out of mind" may even happen with cancer, allowing a husband to forget or avoid dealing with an illness that threatens his wife's life.

There may be another explanation for this finding. Dr. Fallowfield observed that women who choose lumpectomy over mastectomy may suffer more anxiety about a possible recurrence: They worry that their decision to have more conservative treatment may have reduced their chances of surviving the disease. This concern is understandable, but talk in depth with your doctor before making a decision. For many women with breast cancer, lumpectomy and radiation yield long-term results that are at least as good as those after mastectomy. In any event, this research shows that a less damaging physical procedure is no guarantee of less emotional damage.

Marilee almost did not tell her husband before she went to the hospital to have her lump examined: "I don't like to worry people." We explored in the group whether this was her way of saying she was not worth the worry. She could not accept this explanation, but admitted that she feels much better now when she can bring herself to discuss her current medical situation with her husband and daughters.

SPEAKING THE UNSPEAKABLE

There seems to be a double taboo about discussing cancer: that about death and that about the disease. As writer Susan Sontag (who herself had cancer) described passionately in her book *Illness as Metaphor,* cancer seems to be the great taboo disease of our age, as tuberculosis (TB) was in the nineteenth century. While AIDS has emerged since her book was written, we have nonetheless constructed a special mythology around cancer, with many believing it to result somehow from suppressed anger. She notes that TB was supposed to be an illness of suppressed passion. That mythology dissolved when the tubercle bacillus was discovered, along with an effective cure. Sontag expects the same to happen when cancer is demystified. So far, that has not occurred. In *Brighton Beach Memoirs,* playwright Neil Simon depicts a family discussing an aunt's cancer in hushed tones. Even among themselves they did not want the word spoken loudly, as though they would be contaminated by it.

In many cultures, discussion of death and illness is discouraged. In Latin cultures, for example, you are warned against "tempting the evil eye" by discussing death, as though you would call unwelcome attention to yourself by mentioning the name (and could thereby protect yourself from such attention by avoiding the word). Such taboos may offer false protection and inhibit meaningful interaction within families and with others who could potentially provide support.

In the Middle Ages, it was generally believed that all of life was spent in preparation for its final moments. The "last will and testament" that has now become a dry legal term was an event of considerable importance. Friends and family members gathered around the dying person to take in the wisdom that life had imparted, intensified by proximity to its end. In the modern era we have tended to suppress our fears by denying death and avoiding the dying. This renders them marginal, separating them from the living and depriving their families of the support they have to give. It is debilitating to act as though we do not know the obvious, to pretend that we will live forever. Thus, it is crucial for everyone to know—together—what is going on and what the likely course of the disease will be. You must bring the unmentionable out into the open so everyone can deal with it.

EXPRESSING FEELINGS

Our research with the Family Environment Scale pointed out that in addition to expressiveness—open and shared problem solving—cohesion and conflict were crucial to the adjustment of cancer patients. Both involve the expression of feeling, one positive, one negative. Learning how to develop more of a sense of cohesion—the open expression of caring and support—is as important as learning how to have fewer arguments. If you love someone, a time of illness is no time to hide it. Let that person know it and then tell him or her again and again. Show your loved one that you care, and acknowledge the caring you receive. If you want more, make sure you reinforce what you have received. "Thanks for doing the dishes—I enjoyed the rest so much," tells family members how much you appreciate the respite from dirty dishes and acknowledges their efforts and caring support. Such small steps build family cohesion—the sense that you're all in it together. Similarly, find ways to minimize the inevitable battles that occur:

> Pam was in the middle of an intense argument with her husband when she suddenly looked at him and said, "I have cancer. I win." He was stunned and then they both laughed.
>
> He later told the family group: "I wouldn't wish cancer on

anyone, and I would give anything for Pam not to have it. At the same time, I have to say that these years since she got cancer have been the best years of our marriage." They had reached a new level of understanding and openness. They had learned to argue only about what was important, and to value more openly the loving moments in their relationship.

I had a piano teacher with whom I enjoyed talking more than making music. Mr. Multer probably felt the same way, since the music I produced was less than spectacular. He used to say that "the spaces between the notes are more important than the notes." I learned as a psychiatrist to listen for what I was not hearing, as well as to take in what I was hearing. If someone is in a situation in which the natural consequence is to be worried, angry, or sad, I wonder if I don't hear about it. Where are those feelings?

Many families facing the illness of one of their members try to act as though nothing is wrong, because they are worried about admitting to a taboo subject, fearful of appearing weak or out of control, or laboring to maintain a sense of pride and a desire to seem self-sufficient. They try desperately to maintain a semblance of normalcy when the illness is in fact disrupting their lives. While you may well want and need to maintain some sense of the old routine at home, life-threatening illness must and will cause stresses and strains that will come out one way or another. You *are* all going to have mixed feelings about the situation; that is fully human and normal. Facing the inevitable feelings of fear, anger, frustration, loneliness, and fatigue directly makes it less likely that they will contaminate relationships within the family and with those who can help you.

Lisa is a warm, straightforward, fifty-two-year-old mother of a twenty-two-year-old son, Sean. He had gotten his girlfriend pregnant and then married her, moving in with his parents because of financial difficulties. Thus he, his wife, and their two children lived with Lisa and her husband. There were many tensions in the home, including that between Lisa and her daughter-in-law, who feels threatened and controlled by her. Lisa often found herself mediating between Sean and his father, who is an amiable and hardworking man, but who is exceedingly authoritarian with his son.

Sean rarely talked about his mother's illness, but one day Lisa announced that she was going out to take a walk to the market. Sean tore her coat out of her hands, then threw an ashtray at a picture on the wall, breaking the glass. He yelled: "You can't go out! You will die! You will collapse on the road!" He then burst into tears and apologized and said: "I cannot stand the thought of your dying."

Lisa recalled a time when Sean had walked miles to see her in the hospital because his car had broken down. She remembers him looking drawn, and thought that he was far too dependent on her: "I can stand for something to happen to myself, but I can't stand the hurt it causes in other people." Nonetheless, she found herself reproaching Sean: "What are you doing to help me?" This may have been her way of indirectly struggling against his dependency on her. Lisa cried as she related this story, and it was clear that the complex and threatened interdependence she felt with her son was very much affected by her illness. Their failure to discuss it directly led to eruptions of overwhelming feeling that seemed to make matters worse, not better.

Families of people with serious illness are often on an emotional roller coaster. At times there is panic: Things seem to be disintegrating before your eyes, and there is no respite in sight. My friend Bryan, an articulate lawyer, described his feelings when he learned that his brain tumor was growing again: "It feels like I am in an earthquake." At other times, life can become strangely normal, and for hours, days, or weeks everyone functions almost as though nothing had happened. This alternation between intrusion and denial has been described by University of California psychiatrist Mardi Horowitz as a "stress response syndrome." People exposed to serious trauma often fluctuate between feeling overwhelmed and avoiding the subject altogether.

How do you deal with such an uncomfortable mixture of apparently incompatible feelings? It is perfectly natural that when so much has been taken away and more is threatened, family members should be both compassionate and angry, understanding and resentful that their lives have been disrupted. While family members, including small children, can come to see pitching in and helping out as a means of contributing to the well-being of an ailing loved one as well as to the functioning of the family, there will inevitably be times when they are resentful, when they look at friends and other families who are not so burdened and feel that they have been singled out unfairly. One feeling does not cancel out another. It is fine to have both: to be resentful at the imposition and proud that you are meeting a challenge at the same time. This mixture of feelings needs expression and understanding.

DEATH ANXIETY

But there is another, even more deeply rooted problem that family members struggle with: death anxiety. Seeing a loved one threatened challenges all of our senses of invulnerability, the comforting belief that if we live life properly somehow we will be treated fairly. We usually live as though there were an unwritten pact, a script, that says we can quietly go on about our lives and death will come suddenly, painlessly, and swiftly at some comfortable point in old age and take us in our sleep. To see your wife, husband, mother, father, sister, brother, or friend taken suddenly and unfairly reminds you in a painfully immediate way of your own vulnerability. Thus the way we deal with the ill person reveals much about the way we handle our own death anxiety.

One defense against this deep and understandable anxiety—seen in witnesses to tragedies from homelessness to rape—is blaming the victim. "She did something wrong." "She didn't conduct regular breast self-examinations." "He ate the wrong diet." "She had the wrong thoughts." "He didn't wish himself well hard enough." If we can somehow blame the sick person, it lets us off the hook. We would do it right and thereby avoid the same undeserved fate. However, since this defense is irrational, sooner or later it will occur to you that the blame is undeserved. You may have even contributed to something you blame her for: When she first mentioned the lump you may have said, "It's nothing—forget about it," to quiet your own anxiety. Blaming a loved one for his or her "attitude" about the disease only distances you from that person and ultimately makes you feel guilty. One day it dawns on you: "What right do I have to judge someone going through an illness like this?" You have a right to be uncomfortable—angry, sad, frightened—but so does he or she. Share your feelings instead of blaming each other for them.

Another defense is avoidance. "Just don't remind me that danger lurks out there." The calls from friends, frequent at first, become rarer. You become reluctant to bring up the illness, as though mentioning it makes it more real. Life returns to a kind of tense pseudonormality. But the problem is always there, often covered over, rarely discussed.

What can you do to help with these problems? If you haven't done it already start by making the unspeakable speakable. If you feel up to discussing the illness and what it means, you can set the tone for the discussion, as mentioned previously, by bringing up words like *cancer, illness,* and *death,* thereby letting friends and family know they are not taboo. Very often, others fear that they will set off a torrent of tears or other strong emotion by bringing up the words, as though somehow these fears were not daily occupants of the minds of many people who are seriously ill. Be prepared to cry together, to express strong feelings in a respectful way.

You may fear that you will be opening the floodgates, that once you start crying you will never stop. The fear is common, but it never happens. Of more concern is the expression of more dangerous feelings, such as anger. Some things are better left unsaid, and anger can get out of hand. Know yourself and put your frustration where it belongs—with the illness and not the person who has it or who is trying to help you with it.

There are some families in which anger, frustration, and even physical violence are the primary emotions. In these families, the targets of such anger feel overwhelmed, frightened, and, sadly, guilty. They often blame themselves for "bringing on" attacks from others, even though there is often little they can do to control them. In such cases, better support must come from outside the family. Ask yourself whether it feels safe to bring up a difficult issue. When you raise a problem in your family, do you feel helped with it or hurt? Do you feel closer to others or more alone with your problem after you have discussed it? Being ill limits your resources of energy and time. Find help where you can get it, and avoid anyone in your family who adds to the burden of your problems rather than helps you with them. If a family member just becomes enraged, then avoid that person and seek help elsewhere.

With serious illness, family members have every reason to fear the loss of their loved ones. Sadly, we often realize how much we depend upon someone who loves us when we are threatened with losing him or her. Bill put it quite clearly: "I am losing my buddy, and I don't know who will be there to love me anymore." A man can both grieve for himself and care deeply about his wife—he is admitting to himself how much she means to him.

If you are honest with yourself, even if you love your wife so much that given the choice you would gladly trade places with her and take the illness upon yourself, you must nonetheless admit that there is a part of you that says, "There but for the grace of God go I," with a sense of relief that the wolf is at someone else's door. This may not be a feeling to be proud of—it certainly is not one to act on—but it is human and natural. No one likes to be hurt and no one likes to feel vulnerable. And so relief that the lightning struck somewhere else is acceptable even if not noble. Being honest with yourself about this can help you better understand and relate to the feelings of the sick person: He or she not uncommonly envies the well, and is not especially proud of those feelings either:

Maria's aunt came for a visit, and Maria was moved to tell the group, "My aunt is seventy-eight and in perfect health and I am forty-one and I am dying and I am angry as hell about that. Why couldn't things be reversed?"

Many people are convinced that having such feelings makes them unworthy. Will, Rachel's grown son, admitted that he feels "guilty about enjoying a nice day when my mother is dying of cancer." The other family group members said: "You need to enjoy life too."

Many families worry about overprotecting a sick loved one. The danger is that suppressing that protective part of yourself can make the relationship rigid and stilted. The challenge is to say that the fear is real and to acknowledge that you can be even closer to a sick loved one by sharing the common fear of death. The tonic in relationships is not false hope, but rather caring and closeness. Time and again in our groups, we found that when members faced the worst—the imminent death of one of the group—or when we grieved someone who had died, all that we had to offer one another was our caring and concern. In some ways this seems so frail and irrelevant a response to the absolute finality of death. Yet it came to be a powerful antidote because it was a reassertion of what life is all about: the sense of caring and being with others that gives life much of its meaning.

DIFFERENT STYLES OF COMMUNICATING FEELINGS

Another major obstacle to reducing the distance imposed by a life-threatening illness is the differences between the sexes in the way feelings are usually handled. As with any generalization there will be exceptions, but as a rule men prefer to suppress feelings, and women like to express them. Men use words as a distraction, women as an attraction. Men relate to one another by doing things together, women by being together. Men tend to express affection by doing things, showing that they love, women by talking about their love.

These differences, to the extent that they apply to your relationship, would not be much of a problem as long as both sides knew them and could effectively translate: "He's telling me he loves me because he got my car fixed." "She's telling me how much she loves me—she must want to be with me." Instead, we often speak at cross purposes, with no translator to help us appreciate one another's language. In this case the ill will escalates, with both sides feeling unappreciated and misunderstood. This situation has been likened to the problem of sleeping in a double bed with an electric blanket that has two separate controls, only the wires are crossed. She is cold, so she turns up the heat. This makes him too warm, so he turns down the heat. She gets even colder, so she turns her heat control up more, and so on. Each thinks he or she is doing the best thing possible to fix the problem, yet the situation gets even worse:

> A woman with primary breast cancer complained about her "classical engineer-type" husband. He had evidenced little sympathy for her distress about having had a mastectomy and losing her hair due to chemotherapy. "You've just lost a boob and your hair. It doesn't mean you're not feminine." "What I wanted to hear from him is: 'I'm sorry you feel that way.' I wanted sympathy. Instead, he was telling me I was being 'illogical.' "

From her husband's point of view, he was being loyal and reassuring: "The loss of your breast and your hair is not important. I still consider you feminine." Yet his wife felt put down, patronized, and isolated. Had he been able to speak her language and add, "It's not important to *me*," it would have helped far more.

COMMUNICATING ABOUT DAMAGE TO BODY IMAGE

Many life-threatening illnesses and their treatments may at times lead to physical damage or disfigurement. For example, surgery to remove cancer often damages nearby tissues. Thankfully, cancer surgeons are becoming far more adept at removing cancer with less harm done to the body, and the increasing effectiveness of chemotherapy and radiation makes widespread removal of tissue less necessary. We have come a long way from the original radical mastectomy for breast cancer, which left a woman without a breast, chest-wall muscles, and lymph nodes draining the arm and resulted in marked disfigurement. Now women often have a choice between a breast-sparing procedure that involves removing the tumor and following up with radiation, versus a modified radical mastectomy, which involves removal of the breast and some lymph nodes, and the possibility of cosmetic surgery as well. I am convinced that as patients learn that cancer treatments are less disfiguring and damaging, they will seek treatment sooner. Indeed, one of the most important reasons for seeking early detection of breast and other types of cancer is not only the far better odds of curing the illness, but the need for less damaging surgery. If you find the cancer early, you can save your breast as well as your life.

Nonetheless, serious illness often still causes damage or dramatic changes in the body. In the case of breast cancer, it involves a part of the body that women associate with their femininity, a part of their beauty, and a means of nourishing infants. The loss is real, but not total, and it does become part of the dynamic between partners. Again, the challenge is finding the middle ground—acknowledging that a woman who has lost a breast has a right to feel damaged and sad about her body, and at the same time recognizing that her attractiveness and sense of herself as a woman has many components, of which the breast is only one.

The other major ramification of the physical damage caused by illness is how others respond to it. We put so much emphasis on our physical appearance that even minor damage may completely change the way we relate to others. Dramatic weight gains or losses, the loss of our erect posture or graceful stride, the need to use a cane or wheelchair—all can have profound effects on social life. Many people whose illnesses have disfigured them and who are unmarried hesitate to begin new relationships. They fear rejection and don't know how or when to mention their physical difference. They know that some people will be frightened, avoid them, or even be overtly unkind. Many experienced patients come around to the point of view that such people are not worth knowing, but the emotional cost of separating true friends from unthoughtful or uncaring ones can still be high.

Facing up to the damage caused by illness can thus be an occasion to reorder your personal values about appearance and take charge of your selection of friends. Not uncommonly, women who have lost a breast to cancer feel worse about the loss than do their husbands:

> "He's a leg man," said Sally. "But I don't feel the same. I don't like to get undressed anymore. And I avoid mirrors."

Part of what is so hard about such losses is that they are inescapable—they are everyday reminders of what has happened. A loving husband or friend can go a long way toward helping you feel attractive, yet they are not the ones who have had a part of their body removed or altered. Ultimately, it is your acceptance of your changed body that will be the most healing. If you cannot make peace with your body, the risk is that you will feel so scarred that you won't be able to hear or accept the genuine caring of people around you: "He doesn't really find me attractive; he's just feeling sorry for me." Perhaps your partner is trying to tell you that he loves you and not your breast, but you feel so disfigured that you cannot believe it. You may find yourself pushing him away, unable to believe that he could still want to be close, as if to save him the trouble of avoiding you. In this act, you may create the very response you fear. This can leave your partner feeling hurt and rejected ("She doesn't really love or need me" or "She thinks I only love her for her body"). You both then avoid physical intimacy, which isn't good for either of you.

It is true that some spouses, lovers, or friends will be frightened or rejecting, and this can be very hurtful. At some point in a close relationship you both have to face it, hopefully together. A time will come, preferably when you are feeling well physically and emotionally, when you have to say to your partner, "Well, here I am. Can you accept me and love me as I am?" Bear in mind that a certain amount of discomfort in your partner is normal and does not mean rejection —he or she, too, is getting used to a new situation. Your ability to accept your changed body will help your partner accept it as well. Let him touch the scar, talk about how it feels. Rather than avoid it, face it together and move on.

Some partners simply cannot or will not deal with it, and it is best to make your peace with their limitations. If they cannot face what has happened to your body, remember that that says more about their own anxieties and inability to see you beyond the effects of the cancer than it does about your appearance. This can also be an occasion when longstanding resentments may surface, with the illness merely a catalyst. The main point is that you will be feeling very vulnerable. A loving partner can help you see the damage for what it is and nothing more. Some will let you down, others can make you feel worse for it. Give your partner a chance; it is hard on him or her as well. Many of us don't like to have to admit that we are so powerfully affected—perhaps even repelled—by the changes in our loved one's body. Perhaps we feel petty or shallow or selfish for having such feelings. But it's important to own up to them and deal with them. The effects that a life-threatening illness has on couples are complex and can bring out both the best and the worst in people.

My experience is that the mutilation involved in some cancer surgery, such as mastectomy, is far more disturbing to the women who undergo it than to their husbands. On the one hand, this is understandable—it is, after all, their bodies. By the time a relationship has matured, love should be for the person, not just the body. Yet those men and women whose bodies have changed have trouble believing that. Pam joked about a time after she had undergone a hysterectomy and bilateral mastectomies and was beginning to feel "neutered." She and a friend dressed up in short skirts and went to a local firemen's ball. "Lots of men asked me to dance, and it made me feel much more like a woman again." As we discussed in the chapter on dealing with fears about dying, there are *two* components here—the loss of a part of the body, and the feelings about that loss. The feelings are as real as the scar and need attention as well.

SEXUAL FEELINGS

There is no doubt that sexuality, one of the most sensitive and intimate aspects of a relationship, is vulnerable to the ravages of serious illness and its treatment. Many women and men feel like "damaged goods" after treatment. Some have lost many external attributes of sexual attractiveness: a breast or hair, the ability to become aroused. They have scars. There are internal losses as well: They feel weak, tired, nauseated, frightened. Add to that possible stresses and strains in the relationship caused by the disease. You may each be losing sleep, worrying in secret so as not to "trouble" your partner. Even if you were both in the best of health this would interfere with your sexual intimacy.

For some couples, sexual interest simply diminishes with serious illness, and neither partner is particularly worried about it. For others, tentativeness about how to treat the bodily changes mushrooms into a permanent reticence about being physically close, which is an unnecessary loss:

Karen is a slender, attractive woman with an iron will and a master's in business administration. She was diagnosed four years ago with breast cancer and underwent a mastectomy with little emotion.

However, her first physical encounter with her boyfriend after the surgery had lasting consequences. "I could see the look on his face—he seemed shocked, then looked away. I could tell he was repelled by it." She recalled some earlier conflict in their relationship. They had become close when he was dating a mutual friend. When the friend rejected him, he came to Karen for consolation, which later bloomed into a passionate romance. However, when Karen returned from a trip to visit a dying family member, she learned that her boyfriend had been on the phone with his old girlfriend. She was furious. She felt the same sense of betrayal over his immediate reaction to her mastectomy scar, and vowed that she would not be so vulnerable to being hurt again.

This meant that their sex life ended. She did not want to be touched, although she worked out to the point of obsession to keep her body fit. She was as hard on herself as she was on him.

Karen's partner's initial reaction may indeed have been less than ideal. On the other hand, what could prepare a boyfriend for the sight of his beloved with a scar in place of a breast? Should he have feigned nonchalance? Karen had refused him the opportunity to become accustomed to her changed body and to love her in a physical sense again—a high price to pay. If you are to adjust sexually, you cannot ignore body changes. Let your partner know what will make you feel comfortable again. May he or she touch the scar? Does it hurt? Will you tell him or her if it does? While such discussions are uncomfortable, they can help you both admit that something has changed and needs to be put in context. It may even be a reminder of your adolescent awkwardness with sexuality when you didn't know what to do or say. If you want to resume your sexual relationship, you will have some negotiating to do. Remember that it is difficult for both parties, the one whose body is hurt and the one who has to witness that hurt intimately and fears causing more hurt.

Sexual problems can develop from a variety of sources, both emotional and physical.

(1) The damage caused by an illness may limit sexual abilities. Some men may become impotent after surgery for prostate cancer or as a result of the nerve damage that may occur in diabetes. Hormone-blocking treatments for breast cancer may cause vaginal dryness, making intercourse painful and difficult. These problems can be humiliating, so embarrassing that it is hard to discuss them even with a loving sexual partner. They are often misinterpreted as a failure of will

or desire rather than of the body, as "my fault" rather than "my body's limitation."

If you have a physical limitation on sexual activity, discuss it openly with your partner. Choose a time and place in which you have privacy, and are not overtired or worried about something else. Talk about what the limitation is and how you both feel about it. One of you may say, "It doesn't matter." But that doesn't address the issue sufficiently. It *does* matter. An expression of sadness or disappointment from a loving partner is also an affirmation of how much the sexual relationship means. This can lay the foundation for working around the limitation by emphasizing other forms of sexual contact, using lubricants or other aids, or exploring nonsexual kinds of physical intimacy (hugging is great all by itself!)

One of the more effective treatments for sexual problems is learning to separate intimate contact from the pressure of sexual performance. If you are trying some new form of physical contact, do it one step at a time. Agree together that you will just try touching in a different way, without going on to anything more serious. This reduces the kind of anxiety that puts a sure damper on passion.

(2) Sexual difficulties may result from the general loss of energy that comes with being sick. Sexuality flourishes when general health is good, and is often the first casualty of a loss of well-being. It is no accident that "having a headache" is the standard means of begging off sexual intimacy. It helps to feel good in general when you want to feel good in a sexual way. Lack of interest may be the result of feeling sick, tired, or frightened.

First, recognize that this is the case. It helps a partner to know that it is not that you aren't interested in him or her, but rather that you just feel lousy and are frustrated yourself at the loss of sexual drive. Second, the kind of close communication that enhances any sexual relationship is especially important when you do not feel well. Let your partner know what feels good, and even more important, what does not. He or she may be worried about hurting you, touching a sore spot, damaging a body weakened by illness. Let your partner know. If you don't, and he or she does hurt you, the consequence is avoidance and resentment, which is far worse. You may be reluctant to be so direct about how your body is feeling because of your own frustration about it, but try to help your partner be more sensitive to your body's current state.

(3) Disfigurement, weight loss, or weakness may leave you feeling undesirable, even if you experience desire. So much of our sense of attractiveness is based upon physical appearance that any imperfections make it hard for us to believe that someone else could find us appealing. If you have an understanding partner, talk about it. Give your partner time to adjust to the changes in your body. He or she may find them upsetting at first, but then, so did you. Find a way to move beyond it together—by talking about it, then allowing your partner to touch that part of your body. Rather than pretend the change is not there, face it directly, then move beyond it.

A loving partner may indeed be anxious that sexual activity will cause you harm. This is a common problem among those who have recovered from a heart attack. It is crucial to talk with your doctor about what kinds of physical activity are safe. However, even after such talks, many couples are unnecessarily reticent to reactivate their sex lives. Stanford cardiologist Robert DeBusk performed an interesting experiment. He was examining ways to teach couples about cardiac rehabilitation. He had spouses observe their partners taking a stress test—working out on a treadmill with an electrocardiogram recording heart function. He could show worried wives that their husbands could exercise quite vigorously with no adverse consequences for heart function. Despite the demonstration, they were not much reassured. However, when he had the *spouses* take the stress test, they got the message. They could *feel* how much exercise their spouses could tolerate. Similarly, building up to the kind of sexual contact you are both comfortable with can be both pleasurable and reassuring.

COPING WITH FEELINGS OF DESPAIR

Some of the women with breast cancer in our group found that their husbands' emotional reaction was too strong, not too weak.

Gwen's cancer was progressing, and she had recently decided against further surgery. She was mainly concerned about her husband's emotional reaction to her illness. She said, ruefully: "I just want to be able to tell him how sick I am without his breaking down and crying." Since this response seemed unusual, I asked about her husband, and she told me that he suffered from recurrent depression, had tried to commit suicide two years earlier, and was currently receiving antidepressant medication from a psychiatrist. He had been involved in a failed business venture, and was blamed (unjustly, she believed) by his friends for the failure. However, as a result of his depression, he was inclined to believe them, and on top of that, he was unemployed.

Gwen saw herself as always being the strength of the family. She thus saw his tears as being for himself, not for her. She was both worried about him and irritated with him that she had to worry. We pointed out to her that his tears might be for her *as well as* for himself, and she seemed relieved to have the opportunity to vent her fears and concerns.

Not surprisingly, serious illness will bring out preexisting problems in relationships, like water freezing and expanding in a crack. It can make them worse, but at the same time it can be an important occasion to reexamine relationships. There is a tendency, as in Gwen's case, to slip into believing that you are facing nothing but the "same old problems." This almost seems like a relief, as though you could re-create your old life before illness. On the other hand, old difficulties do not simply evaporate. Rather, they must be taken into account in the light of the new stressor. Gwen was both angry and relieved that her husband depended on her. She might well have felt useless and dispensable had he "snapped out of it." At the same time, she understandably wanted to feel that the concern in the family was a two-way street.

Four rules can help family and friends talk about these emotionally trying problems:

1. *Choose the right time and place for a talk.* Discuss difficult problems when you are rested, when you are not likely to be constantly interrupted, and do it when you do not have an audience. The same comment will have a very different effect if children or in-laws are listening to it.

2. *State feelings, not conclusions.* Talk about what you *feel*, not what you think your spouse is doing. You and only you know what you feel. Talking about how you feel tends to make your partner less defensive than lecturing about what he or she is "doing." "When you looked away and said nothing, I felt lonely" invites a very different response than "You were shutting me out again."

Some people find it difficult to recognize or state a feeling they are having. John, a successful businessman, responded to his wife's distress about his preoccupation with work with a ringing defense of his success: "Can't you see that what I'm doing is right and necessary? You love to have the things I provide for you." "But," Carol countered, "I feel alone. I have to turn to others for support. I did some 'retail therapy' (spent too much money shopping) because I was lonely." Carol in fact had rejected some of John's awkward attempts to be more sensitive to her, but he could not express any sense of failure or rejection. Rather, he thought that she was being "irrational." When he finally admitted to feeling a sense of failure as a husband, they began to repair their marriage.

3. **Listen and restate what you heard.** This will force you to actually think about what your partner is saying, and will reassure him or her that you are listening. You don't have to yell it even louder if you know you have gotten the message across.

4. **Admit when you have had enough.** You and your partner should feel free to end discussions that are in fact too painful or over-whelming. Try saying, "Thank you for being willing to discuss this with me. I just don't feel up to dealing with it right now. Let's find a time tomorrow."

FIELDING FEELINGS

Feelings are important signals to us. They help us attach appropriate importance to parts of the overwhelming volume of information we process daily. They are best handled out in the open, on the playing field of life, not in the dugout. The best way for you, your family, and your friends to cope with illness is to do the hard emotional work of recognizing and feeling what those losses might mean. All of this is said with the understanding that you are receiving the best possible medical treatment. But the social and emotional side of treatment should involve realistic and passionate acceptance of the realities, not indulgence in fantasies at the expense of those realities. A good cry together can do wonders and is far more therapeutic than avoiding unspoken fears. Being together emotionally and physically makes us feel alive. This source of vitality is an especially precious resource at a time of serious illness and it is far more likely to have its effect when family and friends face and put into perspective their own fears. This comes from seeing illness neither as the end of everything nor as nonexistent, but rather as the beginning of a new phase in life in which everything has changed, a phase that makes the important things from before more important.

When my friend Bryan was diagnosed with a brain tumor in

March we did not know if he would live to go to the football games we enjoyed every year in the fall. As we sat in the stands at the beginning of the last game of the season, we hugged each other, with tears in our eyes, because of how sweet it was that we were there together. Moments like that both acknowledge and transcend death. It was in fact the last game we enjoyed together.

DOING

My father, who enjoys a good fire more than most, likes to say, "Firewood warms you three ways: when you cut it, when you carry it, and when you burn it." Similarly, the concrete help you offer someone who is ill warms in two ways: it helps both the other person and you. Doing whatever you can for another offers concrete assistance, but it also gives you the sense of doing something that makes his or her life easier.

When your spouse, child, parent, or friend becomes ill, everything changes. He or she is frightened, sad, or perhaps in pain. Previously a pillar of strength in the family, he or she now requires support and can no longer cook and clean or go to work and come home and cheerfully (or grudgingly) make dinner and read with the children. Others must make up for the loss. As one otherwise serene and controlled minister said reluctantly about his wife who had cancer, "I really resent it. My wife gives every ounce of energy she has at work and when she comes home she is totally depleted—there is nothing left for us."

One obvious thing family and friends can do is take on tasks. Divide up the chores and see that they get done. Get some advice from the family member who is ill about how to do what he or she did, what is most important to do first, and what he or she still wants to do. If you cannot do it all, mobilize help from outside. Swallow your pride and ask for help fixing things, running errands, shopping. If the family is facing big problems, at least you do not have to be buried in the little ones.

On the other hand, you need to strike a delicate balance. You can make the ill person feel more incapable than he or she is:

> When a woman in one of our groups talked about how hard it was for her to let her family do things for her, another member said: "If you do everything for yourself, you are depriving your family of the opportunity to feel that they have been of help to you."

LIVING YOUR DYING

One of the tragedies of the current "cult" of death and dying is the mistaken notion that someone who is dying is instantly relieved of all responsibilities and concerns for others in order to turn inward and "do" the best possible death. This is unfair from two perspectives. It deprives the family of the benefit of that person's help, wisdom, and love; and it deprives the dying person of the opportunity to carry out a real and important role. This makes that person feel as though he or she were already dead, unneeded by the rest of the family.

> A Chinese patriarch was dying of lung cancer and had tried to commit suicide by lunging at a second-story window. His wife and daughters, in tears, brought him to the hospital. He was emaciated, looked sad, and felt both depressed and useless, as though he were nothing but a burden to his distraught family. He saw no role for himself. I expressed my sympathy to him and his family over the seriousness of his medical situation, but pointed out to him that he still had an important role as head of his family: "Your wife and children will all become sick and die sooner or later, and they look to you as a role model of how to handle this inevitable part of life. The way you deal with this now will affect how they deal with both your death and theirs. You cannot let them down in this way." Within a few minutes, he was giving orders, pointing out to his son-in-law that his bedroom was too warm, and that they should install

an air conditioner. He had begun to resume his neglected role as head of the family.

It is easy but unfortunate to overlook what dying people have to offer to their families, in which case both lose. I learned this lesson in an odd way when I was consulting with an Episcopal priest who was counseling a dying woman:

"I met with Ann weekly while I was in seminary. She was dying of cancer, and I kept trying to discuss her life, to give her some peace about it. Yet each week we ended up discussing *my* life. She would give me advice about the parishes I had been offered and actually helped me decide to accept the one I did. I still feel guilty about it, yet I really enjoyed talking with her, and I believe she relished the time spent with me."

I pointed out to the priest that he was probably the one person in her waning life who treated her like a normal person who could give as well as receive. His taking advice from her made her feel alive, rather than giving her the sense that her life was over while his was beginning. She became a part of his developing life, thereby staying alive in a metaphorical way. This was his gift to her.

I can recall watching, with increasing discomfort, a PBS special some years ago in which a woman who was purportedly dying of breast cancer allowed her death to be filmed. I was at first inclined to admire her courage and openness, but what I observed troubled me. She became totally absorbed in herself and "her" process of dying, which eventually took five years, rather than the few months they had expected. Her husband, a college professor who had married her knowing she had breast cancer, felt increasingly burdened, ignored by his wife, and isolated. I remember him breaking down in the kitchen late one evening, tearfully telling the camera crew: "I just don't know how much longer I can take it." Watching what was happening, I marveled that he had taken it that long already. He left for Europe some months before his wife died, and none could have reproached him. He had given but not gotten, which was a disservice both to him and to his dying wife.

Lena, a woman with breast cancer, had initially tried to get her family to be independent of her, to make their plans and do what they needed to do. She found herself feeling more and more isolated as they did exactly that. Ellen commented, "I know exactly how you feel. I had that 'invalid' feeling [perhaps in the two meanings of that word], like things were out of control—not needed, not being needed. It was the worst feeling I ever had to contend with. I felt so sick I couldn't do anything, and then I felt so helpless because I couldn't be part of the family."

Renee then added: "My husband told my children, 'When you're in trouble or have any problem, don't go to your mother.' This bothered me. I confronted my family and said: 'Look, I don't want to be left out. What I'm going through is difficult, but there is almost nothing that can happen in this family that I can't handle or that's greater than what I'm going through myself.' "

There are times when being "protected" means being left out. It is not good for either the living or the dying to relieve someone of responsibilities simply because he or she is "ill." That person may not be able to do the dishes, take out the garbage, repair the roof, or pay the bills, but he or she can convey a tremendous amount of knowledge and caring to the family. The fact that you are dying does not mean that you can or should stop living.

HOW YOU CAN HELP ONE ANOTHER

Networks of family and friends can be enormously important in helping people cope with serious illness. My colleagues and I have found that several principles can enhance such support:

1. *Banish secrets.* Direct and open communication with important family and friends reduces the strain that comes with maintaining secrets, increases intimacy and empathic understanding of what the ill person is going through, and improves cooperative problem solving. There is always a desire on the part of patients and family members to protect one another from bad news. However, you cannot protect loved ones from the effects of serious illness. You can enhance mutual caring and coping by sharing information. This means sharing the discomfort of facing the serious consequences of illness. But it also helps family members to feel part of a common mission to help the person who is ill to know what is going on.

2. *Choose your support network carefully.* As I've said before, serious illness changes most relationships. They either improve or get worse. Decide who you want to include in your supportive network and keep them informed. Save your energy and use the illness as an excuse to disengage from unwanted social obligations. Simplify the relationships that are necessary but unrewarding, and eliminate the ones that are unnecessary *and* unrewarding.

3. *Make it clear to family and friends how they can help.* One cancer patient wrote a newsletter listing tasks friends could perform that would be helpful: bringing a meal once a month; calling friends with information; driving to medical appointments. It helps friends to teach them how to help. Often people are embarrassed or shy about asking for or offering help. Developing executive skill at organizing friends helps the helpers provide support.

4. *Feeling included is often more important than doing something concrete, even for children.* While there are limits to what they can understand, if children sense they are being left out, they will feel that they have done something wrong to merit exclusion. Find something even young children can do to be of help. If they are told that straightening up their rooms or making their beds will help Mommy because she is not feeling well, it will: (a) make

it more likely that they will do it; (b) give them a feeling of doing something about her illness; and (c) make them feel a part of the family effort to help.

Confronting and Comforting Children

Even young children need to be made aware of and feel involved in the problems facing their families. It is quite important to discuss such matters carefully with a young child. Very young children have little concept of death, but may understand it as something like sleep, reversible when you wake up. Younger children primarily need comfort and closeness, lots of attention, and physical contact from parents and other family members. As children grow (between five and ten), they develop a more abstract idea of death and may witness it in pets or family. They think of death in terms of space, someone going far away —they are not likely to return, but they could. These children benefit from a "grown-up" talk about what is happening. The thought of losing a loved one is frightening, but figuring that out on your own is even more frightening. Children feel important and respected if they are included in the family crisis. It is better to err on the side of telling too much rather than too little. Children have very sensitive antennae for feelings. They will first sense that the grown-ups are preoccupied with something, seem worried, and have less time and energy for them. They usually interpret this to mean that the parents are avoiding them, probably because of some real or imagined misbehavior.

Pam's seven-year-old son, Johnny, who had been somewhat troubled before, was now deeply disturbed by her illness. His behavior was becoming worse and the teacher at school reported that he had difficulty paying attention in class. We reviewed how she had explained illness to him. She had said, "The disease I have is very serious and may end my life. I want you to know that I will love you *wherever* I am." I pointed out that this use of words, while well intended, could make it seem to her son that it was a matter of his mother *choosing* to be with him or somewhere else. Young children cannot comprehend that things happen that have nothing to do with them. They are the center of their world and so they find some way to explain each event in terms of what they did to make it happen. Children often misbehave at times of stress because that provides a way of explaining to themselves why a parent would go away from them. Johnny had convinced himself that he would drive his mother away through his bad behavior: She would leave because he was bad. Although this way of explaining his mother's impending withdrawal from him was painful, at least it was understandable.

I observed that what Pam was telling her son reinforced that view. I encouraged her to say instead, "Mommy loves you very much, but the time may come when I cannot be with you. I'll always want to be with you as long as I can." They cried together, and Pam and her son began to feel differently about the sadness they were facing. His misbehavior in school markedly decreased, as suddenly as it had started. Pam did something else that was quite moving. She sat down one day and wrote her son a series of birthday cards, to be given to him every year until his twenty-first birthday, expressing what she hoped for him and how she felt about him. This was an act of enormous courage. It required her to face the likelihood that she would not be with her son as he grew. In doing so she gave him an enormous gift, an ongoing message into the future of extraordinary value. By facing her death now, she found a way to help her son beyond the time of her death.

Since children cannot understand that things happen independently of them (adults have plenty of difficulty with this concept as well), if they lose a parent, they tend to blame themselves for it. Thus, as mentioned, they view a parent's illness as punishment for something they did or imagined they did wrong. The child feels more in control of what is wrong at the price of feeling and acting bad. Being included in the problem, to the extent they can understand it, is crucial. Simply telling a very young child "Something is wrong" or "Mommy is not feeling well" will help the child feel more a part of what is going on in the family. Secrets are corrosive. They put an unnecessary strain on the keepers of the secrets as well as those kept from the secrets. One of my professors in medical school, who was not keen on keeping things from patients, commented: "If you are going to lie to patients, you had better have a darned good memory. Keeping the stories straight is not easy."

Billy, an eight-year-old boy, was diagnosed with acute myelogenous leukemia, a progressive and frequently fatal cancer of the white blood cells. The medical staff met and planned to discuss the diagnosis and prognosis with Billy's parents. They decided that it would be unwise to discuss the illness with the patient himself. Billy's parents were devastated but resolute, telling the doctors: "We can handle it; just don't tell Billy." However, one member of the medical team missed the instruction and went to talk with him. When Billy was told what his illness meant, he said: "I can take it, but it will upset my parents. Just don't tell them." Fortunately, everybody found out what had happened, and they dealt with the illness together.

It is a good idea to ask children after you have told them something this important, "What did I just explain to you? Can you tell me what you heard?" This allows you to clarify any misunderstandings and gives them an opportunity to say what they have learned and perhaps how they feel about it as well. Obviously, this is not a one-shot procedure. You are opening a channel of communication and telling children that whatever is happening, it is not so terrible that it cannot be discussed. The late psychologist Bruno Bettelheim, in *The Uses of Enchantment,* pointed out that children have fertile imaginations, full of demons as well as angels. What they hear in fairy tales, the bloody ones included, helps them understand and modulate their own inner frightening thoughts and fantasies. What you tell children, bad as it might be, is probably no worse and may well be better than what their own imaginations have provided for them. Giving children clear explanations and allowing them to help in some way can reduce their anxiety and guilt a great deal.

Marilyn is a bright, intellectual, emotional woman with an intense voice and a tendency to look you right in the eye and take over a conversation. Having divorced several years ago, she is essentially the single parent of a nine-year-old boy. As I mentioned in the opening chapter, when she first entered the group, she was extremely sensitive about the possibility that any information about her or her cancer might get out. She had been careful to limit the information that friends, relatives, and especially her son had about her illness, feeling that she did not want to "burden" them with it.

I reassured Marilyn that we would release no information about her to anyone, but I wondered about her apparently rigid insistence that her "secret" be kept. "Whom are you really protecting?" I wondered aloud. Marilyn cried easily and often, and did not appear to be avoiding a confrontation with herself over the cancer. Her very real suffering had earned her the right to our solicitude. And yet she had erected this elaborate wall of secrecy around her. I found myself becoming bolder, confronting more directly her "secret": "Are you not really just conveying to your son that you and he cannot talk about your illness?"

"No," she said, "it is just too much for a child his age." Meanwhile, the child's wisdom seemed to percolate through nonetheless. "The other night I was just too exhausted from chemotherapy and cooking dinner to read him his story at bedtime. You know what he did? He came marching into my bedroom with his sleeping bag, and *he* read *me* a story." I commented on how nice it was that he wanted to comfort her, and that she let him.

I continued to pressure Marilyn to tell her son more and gradually the demands for absolute secrecy became fewer and farther between. They did not, however, disappear. "Michael has been asking me whether the metastases in my lungs mean that I will stop breathing and die. He wants to know what my doctor says after each visit," said Marilyn. "I told him I would ask. After I came back from the doctor, he asked again."

"What did you say?" I asked, eager to pursue this promising sign.

"That I could live a long time," she replied.

"So your son knows that you have cancer and could die from it," I summarized. Marilyn was not about to give me the satisfaction of her complete agreement, but admitted that she and her son could talk more openly about her illness now. She seemed increasingly willing to talk about it, and appeared to be getting more from her son as well as giving more to him.

Children are especially sensitive to subtle emotional cues. A mother's reticence to discuss her illness is experienced by the child as distancing. If, as mentioned before, the child feels pushed away he or she may react by misbehaving. This, in turn, gets the mother upset and distracts her from her illness at the same time. She may be relieved to be in the familiar and comfortable role of dissatisfied mother, instead of the frightened woman dealing with a serious illness. But the price is high, because mother and child lose a precious opportunity to comfort one another.

Preparing children is hard from many points of view, not the least of which is your own understandable ambivalence. You love them and want them to do well, but not *too* well.

Arlene brought up her illness at dinner, just after a neighbor died of cancer, leaving two children of similar age to hers. "They took it very well—almost too well. It is hard for me to think of them doing well without me, although I very much want them to."

Sharing information with your family makes the problem real but manageable. It means admitting the need for help, but increases the help you get. It widens the circle of concern, and makes both you and your loved ones feel less isolated. It is hard but necessary.

CONSTRUCTING SOCIAL SUPPORT

Our discussion of how much family members can do for one another only highlights how alone people with little or no family support can feel when they are ill. The loneliness they may have felt before is multiplied by the need for help and closeness occasioned by illness. Yet making new relationships becomes even more complex. There seems to be no "right time" to tell someone new about your illness. Many group members talk ruefully about seeing a potentially interesting partner back away as soon as the word *cancer* is mentioned. Others commented that they want a "normal" part of their lives, devoid of discussion about illness, yet they could not avoid dealing with the illness at some point in a developing relationship.

> Laura talked often about her desire to meet a man she could become involved with. Yet as her illness progressed, she gradually gave up that hope. Instead, she befriended another woman with advanced breast cancer, and they moved in together. She felt an instant rapport with her because of their common problem (and oncologist). They offered great comfort to each other and laughed and cried about the effect of the illness on their lives.

Support groups can be helpful to anyone, but they are especially useful for those who lack family support. The intense sense of belonging engendered in many groups is especially welcome to those who feel alone.

If you and your family are already surrounded by a helpful network of friends, do you all need the help of a more structured support group? Extra support may well be necessary for two reasons:

1. Even people who have good friends and family in normal times may find that the persons in these support networks have much to learn about coping with the crisis that comes from a serious illness such as heart disease or cancer.

2. There is something special about meeting with people who are "all in the same boat." The customary reluctance to discuss fears and sadness can be overcome more quickly when everyone in the room is nursing the same problems and reticence.

Support groups for family members as well as those who are ill can be very helpful in accomplishing some of these goals. For one thing, they help people accept and normalize their own mixed-up feelings. When the minister I mentioned earlier said how much he resented his wife's giving what energy she had to her job, there were heads nodding all around the room. It becomes acceptable to resent spouses' and parents' loss of energy and their need to set priorities, even though it may seem unfair on your part and lacking in nobility. Acceptance of the expression of these feelings in a support group can quickly lead to acceptance within.

My colleagues and I established a family support group program that complemented the Supportive/Expressive groups for women with metastatic breast cancer. We invited husbands, children above the age of fourteen, parents, close friends, and partners to attend monthly meetings held in the late afternoon/early evenings for one and a half hours. These meetings were coled by leaders who ran the groups their loved ones attended. However, these meetings did not, as a rule, include the cancer patients themselves. We felt it would be important for family and friends to have their own time and place to talk, to be "the patients" themselves, to express their own fears, concerns, needs, and problems.

We found these groups interesting from a number of perspectives. First of all, the women wanted their families to attend, and would often use methods just this side of coercion to get them there: "If you care about me . . ." Usually such pressure was necessary for only a time or two.

Since our Supportive/Expressive groups were composed only of women, we wondered how men would do in such a setting. After all, men are thought to sit on their feelings, acting as though they have mastered them when in fact they have not. Would they be willing or able to talk to one another? My general prejudice is that men have a higher threshold for getting involved in such emotional support, but that they need it more because they so rarely avail themselves of emotional support on their own.

Jerry, Jane's husband, said that despite his determination to handle these difficulties, he found himself needing to talk. He would pour out his feelings, surprising even himself, to a friend over lunch, and would find himself looking forward to the monthly family group meetings. He had noticed how he resisted making changes in his relationship with Jane, because to do so somehow meant acknowledging and accepting her illness and imminent death. He put it concretely: "She doesn't like her car, and I caught myself thinking: If I buy a new one, would she have time to drive it? So not buying the car would in a way be giving in to death. And yet, getting the new car would be yielding to it as well." He found himself torn between feeling that he should do everything and anything for Jane, since the illness was so terrible, and feeling overwhelmed, that nothing would be enough.

He found himself saying to Jane, "Now, describe our pain. Tell us exactly what it is like." In one sense, he was losing himself, merging her pain with his experience. In another sense, this was not a mistake—it was indeed their pain, not just hers.

We found that these family members valued the group time and made excellent use of it. One of the themes that arose quickly was having their own needs met. Just because their loved one had cancer did not mean that their needs were always subsidiary. Indeed, they helped one another realize and accept the fact that they still needed things and had a right to them. Perhaps their wife/mother/daughter could not do what she used to do physically, but she could help organize and direct those who were doing the work. She could express appreciation for the help she got. She could let them know how much they were helping her.

I became convinced as I listened to family members talk about their loved ones that they needed a place to share their concerns, that they said things in groups with one another that they kept inside elsewhere.

We worked toward a sense of interdependence, counting on and appreciating one another. It is not helpful for the person with the illness to fly off in a separate direction, in a quest for independence, leaving family members behind. Likewise, a rigid role of dependence, where you cast yourself as the "sick one" who depends on everyone else, demeans yourself and deprives everyone else of the help you can give. What seems to work best is for everyone to recognize and admit what he or she needs. Futhermore, when the help comes, it must be acknowledged and appreciated. When you do this, problems do not dissolve, but you feel drawn together in working at them.

Havdalah Candle

My life with you is like a braided candle
we've slept entwined for thirty years
you're the hand upon me in the night
the breath upon me at break of day.
Our thoughts cross, intersect, curve around
each other like our bodies in bed.
Three years ago my cancer diagnosis came
I endured the knife, the chemo
gave my breast, but still
I had to wrestle midnight panic.
Uncertainty grew familiar like an old slipper.
And just when I nearly tamed it
just when I breathed easier and began to trust
Your diagnosis was hurled down too.
The sleeping terror wakes up

fear pounces back
breathing short and quick again
the challenge returns: quiet the breath.
Who takes care of whom now?
The truth blinks on and off
we're each headed toward the end
only the timing is unclear.
Let's light the braided candle
let's light the twisted strands
May the wicks burn down together,
leave a glow in Sabbath dusk.

—ANN DAVIDSON, NOVEMBER 1, 1991

9. Suicide: The False Escape

When an illness is hurtling you toward the end of your life at a terrifying speed, it is not uncommon for you to ponder ending it yourself. Many ill people contemplate suicide. Perhaps the thought crosses your mind as merely a shapeless abstraction. Perhaps it seizes you with utter clarity in moments of great despair or fear. Perhaps you have wittingly or unwittingly entertained the option because you see it as a way of wresting back the reins of your life; by choosing to end it yourself rather than leaving it to fate, you may feel that you're back in charge of a life run amok.

The notion of suicide may be your own private devil to wrestle with, or it may have become a family affair—an issue laid out on the table for family and friends to deal with. In either case, the thought of suicide is pernicious and needs to be confronted.

"RATIONAL" SUICIDE

The idea that suicide is the rational conclusion to a period of thoughtful, logical debate has been promulgated by a stream of best-selling books, talk-show hosts, and workshop leaders. There is almost what could be called a "death movement" afoot these days. The increasing acceptance of suicide as a viable option for ending a less-than-perfect life has led many people with terminal illness to plan their deaths.

Ellen, the outdoors woman with a love of hiking, talked with some satisfaction about her determination to take her life "when things got too bad." She assured us that she had the full "support" of her family and that this gave her a sense of "control" over the progression of the disease. I had serious reservations about this "plan," which I expressed with some vigor: "Isn't this a false sense of control? Once you have instructed your physicians about how you want your terminal care managed, shouldn't you let nature take its course? Why deprive yourself and your family of any time you have remaining, especially when pain can be so effectively treated?"

The group jumped into the discussion. Sheila, who is quite devout, pointed out that family members may be afraid to say what they really think, so they just go along. "I believe that there is God's time for you to die, and your time. I think you should wait for God's time."

I determined to take this up with Ellen's husband in the family group. He agreed that they had discussed it and said he had wanted to "be supportive" of her. I asked him to consider how he would feel two weeks afterward. He admitted he might feel rather bad, and this unleashed a torrent of comments from other group members.

Frank said: "I would be furious if Mary chose not to be with me for one week, one day, one minute that she could be. The cancer is taking her from me, and that is bad enough. I don't want her to take herself from me even sooner."

Steve said: "There really can be no such thing as a rational moment to commit suicide. You have to do it before you need to. By the time you get to the point where you really are either overwhelmed with pain, or are insensible, you can't make a rational decision to commit suicide. If you have a clear mind, you still have some good time left, even if it is only a minute or an hour. Then suicide always means not living that extra week, day, hour, or min-

ute that you could have. So there *can be* no 'right time' to do it."
Ellen's husband said he would rethink his position about helping his
wife end her life.

I spoke with Bob four days after Ellen died. He said: "It is a
terrible thing. We were so suited to one another, we knew what each
other wanted, and I am feeling very lonely. At the same time," he
said, "for this kind of a thing, it went as well as it could go. I am
really glad we had her at home, it was the right decision. We had
some good times together. We had a round-the-clock nurse at the
end. She woke me at about four-ten A.M. because she was having
trouble breathing and she died at four-thirty." I asked him about the
discussion we had about hastening her death. He said: "We didn't
do it and I am glad. She had no pain. She was really worried about
that but she didn't have any pain at all. It was the right way for her
to die."

So much for "rational suicide." The final weeks, days, and moments are so important that I have become increasingly concerned
about the requests from my patients for help with the oxymoron
known as "rational suicide." Everyone may indeed have moments
when they just want to die and get it over with. Derek Humphrey's
miserable book *Final Exit* has sold an enormous number of copies,
and patients in my groups from time to time express the odd idea
that having the power to end their life puts them "in control." I well
understand the desire to be in control, and nobody should live in
fear of abandonment, untreated pain, or helplessness. Nonetheless,
choosing to kill yourself is hardly a transcendence of death. It gives
you a little control over when, but none over whether you will die.
Furthermore, asking someone else to kill you places a terrible burden
on them.

When Ellen and others raised the issue of asking someone to help
them die, there was really a covert as well as an overt question. The
overt one was: "Will you help me to do what I want to do?" The
covert question was: "Are you fed up with me and would you just as

soon be rid of me?" Thus, a "yes" to the overt question could stir up considerable anxiety, even though it might seem like the supportive thing to do. We have a fantasy in the West that we can and should control all situations. In fact, there are some events that just happen to us, and pretending to control them only makes them worse. To die, leaving a husband, wife, or child with an endless sense of guilt for having helped to kill you, is hardly a gift to them. How you die affects them profoundly, and any suffering you may have is not in vain. Rather, your perseverance in the face of adversity sets an example for them and tells them how much you want to be with them.

Even when death is very near, our fundamental moral responsibilities do not change. Facing death does not mean hastening it. It takes courage and patience to let nature take its course, but that allows for the very important work of emotional sharing that should occur at such a time. A dying person can give an enormous amount to his or her family.

Every so often we would arrange joint group meetings for both patients and their family members to talk about just this issue.

Betty's husband told the group about the day he came home from work and found her in tears. She had washed her hair, but lacked the strength to dry it. As her physical stamina waned, she focused more on the memories of herself she would leave with her husband and children. Betty was a soft-spoken, warm woman. She sat with her husband and daughters, who were in their late teens. We had been discussing fears of dying, and Betty turned to her husband and said: "I want you to mourn me for a decent period of time, but you are not the kind of man who should be without a wife, and I want you to remarry."

This statement almost took my breath away. Betty was not only confronting her own death and the idea of being "replaced," but was trying to reach beyond her grave and help him and her family get on with their lives after she had died. It was extraordinarily touching, and they responded. She died several months later, and her husband and daughter came to the next meeting of her support group. They described her last days, saying that the lingering and deterioration were very difficult for her, but they took pride in the fact that there were always family members with her. We grieved together, but were comforted by feeling the presence of Betty's warmth in her daughter, and in how loved she was.

> Her daughter said: "I am doing as well as can be expected. It's just that there is a great big hole in my life." Betty's husband read a note she had written a year earlier, in which she had acknowledged her anger and frustration at having cancer, and her tremendous sense of warmth and caring for her family. She had written: "I have a hog's appetite for life."

I have become increasingly worried that our justifiable concern with the rapidly rising costs of health care will lead us to push seriously ill patients toward suicide. Such a plan has recently been enacted in the Netherlands: Patients and their doctors may agree not merely to cease active treatment but to actively end life. The concerns are real: On average, individuals lavish more than half of their total lifetime health care expenditures during the last year of their life, often with little real medical benefit. Increasing reliance on so-called capitation health plans such as health maintenance organizations is intended to provide economic incentive to cut health care costs. Seriously ill individuals will cost more to care for. However, pressure to commit suicide as a solution to these or other problems at the end of life raises serious ethical questions. Even if doctors cannot cure, we may not kill. As former Surgeon General C. Everett Koop said, "If doctors become killers as well as healers, you'll never know which one it is who approaches your bedside."

It is one thing to decide to discontinue active treatment, to abandon efforts to prolong life. It is another to hasten death. We must do everything we can to make seriously ill people as comfortable as possible. This includes vigorous control of pain and attention to the anxiety and sadness that may accompany the end of life. But there is a kind of *hubris,* a fatal and flawed pride, in thinking that we must take control of the course of life and death. Treating serious illness is a humbling experience. It reminds you of your limits, whatever role you play in it: as doctor, nurse, family member, or dying person. Our respect for life is inseparable from our respect for death. It comes soon enough for all of us. When you cannot cure, care.

10. Dealing with Doctors

Doctors, nurses, and other health professionals have a tough job. They confront tragedy with regularity, face their own limitations, struggle with long hours, complex health care, reimbursement, and legal systems, and have to learn constantly evolving treatments. They can perform these complex tasks better with the help of an informed, assertive, and collaborative patient.

There are certain doctors who earn the most striking affection, respect, and loyalty from their patients. One in particular was a man who by all accounts from his patients had three attributes: He was always available and welcomed their calls; he was caring, making his patients feel he both knew and liked them; and he was direct: He told them what he knew and what they needed to know. They could take hearing anything from him, because they knew he was concerned about them. This was especially noteworthy because he worked in a large health maintenance organization. He managed to make the people who came to him feel that they were his personal patients, and they loved him for it.

What is it that patients are seeking in their doctors and nurses? In most non-Western cultures, healing ceremonies take an interesting form. The patient goes to the healer in a state of distress. The healer (and often the patient along with him) enters an altered mental state, usually trancelike, and does battle with the illness. Frequently the healer symbolically takes the illness into his body and struggles with it. Then, the battle over, both return to a more or less normal mental state, and the sick person leaves with an altered perspective on his illness and its treatment. Symbolically, these ceremonies tell us that a necessary (but not sufficient) condition for being a healer is an emotional ability to confront disease, to tolerate the reality of another human being's *dis-ease,* an ability to take it upon oneself, which is a deep form of empathy. In order to get to the point where it is possible to apply modern diagnostic techniques and treatments, it is necessary to get to know patients, to be close to them, to understand and even feel their discomfort. Yet this crucial aspect of medicine is often overlooked by doctors and patients.

This lesson was brought home to me in an unexpected way. My family and I were walking along a beautiful stretch of San Diego beach on a holiday, taking in the ocean, gulls, and vacationers. We strolled past a volleyball game, and I saw someone sink to the ground, obviously in severe pain. I remember a very long moment (it seemed like a minute, but was probably seconds) in which I thought "Should I get involved in this? Is he really hurt?" I ran over to him and saw that he had dislocated his shoulder. I knew all too well how to reduce dislocations, since my shoulder had suffered the same fate on several occasions. I knew how painful it was, and that if you do not get the shoulder back in place within the first few minutes, the muscles go into spasm and treatment becomes much more difficult and painful. Within a minute I managed to get his shoulder back into place. Then I helped him immobilize the arm, and instructed him about the follow-up care he would need. The players thanked us, and we left.

I was shaken, and at first could not figure out why. It was an occasion to feel good—in contrast to the ambiguous problems and outcomes that are the day-to-day fare of psychiatry, I had done something almost surgical—fixed a problem instantly and obviously. Furthermore, I had seen far worse human distress and physical damage in emergency rooms. Why was I upset? The missing ingredient was the mental preparation to confront and share misery. I had to gear myself up to realize how much this young man was suffering in order to get to the point at which I could do something about it. I could see how different this "doctoring" state of mind was because of the contrast from my previous state of lazy reverie. As doctors we do this every day at work, and therefore do not realize what it takes.

It used to be that the ability to confront illness and death was the main prerequisite for being a physician. Curing disease was a distant hope, so comfort and relief of suffering was the main expectation.

REDEFINING MEDICINE

A strange thing has happened to medicine in this century: It has become focused almost entirely on curing disease. The oldest adage of medicine, its guiding standard for millennia, has been: "To cure, rarely; to relieve suffering, often; to comfort, always." Throughout most of the history of medicine, doctors have reassured the well, comforted and relieved the sick, and cured only occasionally. Indeed, doctors have, at times, done more harm than good when attempting an impossible cure—witness centuries of bloodletting and cathartics for the bowels, symbolized in the tragic and unnecessary operation performed by Emma Bovary's struggling physician/husband in Flaubert's *Madame Bovary*. As an antidote to this danger, medicine's other guiding doctrine has been "*Primum non nocere*" (First, do no harm). A constant confrontation with serious illness is taxing: If as a physician you feel helpless, you want to *do* something to make the suffering person feel better. If comforting the ill is considered an honorable art (and it was for many centuries), then providing comfort fulfills the wish to do something. If cure is everything, then harm will be done when cure is impossible.

In the early part of the twentieth century, physicians rewrote their job descriptions. Alexander Fleming discovered penicillin, and suddenly physicians were able to cure a substantial number of previously fatal diseases. Bacterial infections, such as pneumonia, were no longer widespread killers, and the ability to cure such diseases was understandably exciting. This established a new model for medical practice. More effective and aseptic surgical techniques accompanied by anesthesia were developed, and modern medicine charted a new course: to cure often.

However, even with the stunning growth in modern medical technology allowing for far more sensitive and safer diagnostic techniques, a wider range of effective medications, and advanced and less destructive surgical procedures, an odd thing happened. As we cured acute bacterial illnesses and proved expert at repairing injured bodies, people lived longer and died in increasing numbers from chronic diseases: cancer, heart disease, and stroke. Many people with these illnesses can be treated but not cured. Yet doctors, trained in aggressive, high-technology medicine to cure illness, have relegated to others the less prestigious task of comforting the sick. Even relieving suffering, clearly a medical task, is often given short shrift. Cancer patients, for example, are frequently undermedicated for pain. This is not to say that there are not many superb physicians and other health care practitioners who comfort constantly. Also, allied medical specialties such as nursing and social work have developed special skills in doing just that. Nonetheless, medicine as a whole has overemphasized the dream of cure at the expense of the reality of providing comfort. After all, no matter how advanced medical care becomes, at some point everybody will need help in dying with dignity, rather than waiting for a cure. This is not to say that I advocate that doctors give up easily, or that they medically help people die. I do not. Rather, physicians need a more balanced view of their task. Cure when you can; comfort always and view it as part of your job, not a sign of failure.

If doctors feel like failures for lack of a cure, they will tend to retreat from seriously ill patients. Indeed, this sense that anything less than cure is a failure makes doctors vulnerable to patients' anger and disappointment. If, on the other hand, doctors know that they are providing the best possible help to their patients in managing their illness, the relationship is not damaged by the disease. It is helped even more by a spirit of collaboration with the patient.

THE IMPATIENT PATIENT

Patients expect everything from their doctors. They depend upon them for their lives. One comment from a doctor can transform their lives: Was the test positive or negative? Did the bone scan show anything? Patients are often frightened to ask their doctors even very important questions, let alone insist on getting them answered. They hesitate to negotiate about how and when treatment is given. In our groups we provide examples of how patients can learn to become partners with their doctors in their care.

> Jean had a recurrent nightmare: She saw herself lying on a slab surrounded by people in white coats who were trying to pass a wire over her head. She struggled desperately, grabbing the wire, feeling certain that if it passed over her head she would die. She would awaken fighting the wire and once found herself pounding on her husband's arm as he tried to comfort her.
>
> Sometimes when you understand a dream, it is a simple visual pun, a translation of words into images. I knew that the dream must have something to do with her doctors—the white coats were a dead giveaway. I also knew that the group of people in the dream might have something to do with her discussing that dream in our group.
>
> I asked Jean to talk more about the thoughts stirred up by the dream. She told us how helpless she felt during each visit to her oncologist, never knowing whether she would get a new dose of chemotherapy and end up nauseated and vomiting for the next few days. She also told us: "My doctor is very efficient."
>
> This worried me. "What do you mean by 'efficient?' " I asked.

"She sits behind her desk and types while she is talking to me, so her notes will be all done when the interview is over." I did not take this as a good sign. "Also," Jean added, "sometimes when I talk to her I start to cry. She asks me to leave the office." I then understood her dream—she felt as though her doctor was trying to put something over on her.

I advised Jean to work out a deal with her oncologist. "First," I said, "tell her: 'I'm going to start to cry, but I will also stop crying, so please don't ask me to leave your office. Second, on any given week I decide whether or not I take the chemotherapy at that time. You decide how much I need; I decide whether I take it now.'" The nightmares disappeared as she felt more in control of her medical care.

For a doctor to be empathic need not necessarily take a great deal of time. It just requires attention to the right issues with the right words.

In turn, patients are eternally grateful for meaningful signs of caring. What they want to hear is that their doctor will be there, no matter what happens. They sense immediately whether or not their doctor is with them emotionally.

Marianne recalled lying in a hospital bed, awaiting the results of a biopsy of her rib cage, which would determine whether her breast cancer had spread, causing the pain in her chest wall. Her doctor stood *at the door* (she said with emphasis) and told her that it was indeed a recurrence of the malignancy.

"I could see that he wanted out of the room as fast as possible. That bothered me as much as the news—he didn't want to be near me." She added: "I would have one rule for any doctor. *No matter what you are telling them, hold your patient's hand.* I know doctors are busy. They can't sit with you all day. But they must be in contact with you when they tell you bad news.

Say the same thing, but don't be halfway out the door when you do it!"

Doreen was a talented dancer and teacher who was particularly bitter about her cancer. Her mother had died of breast cancer, and Doreen had an especially aggressive form of it. We had noticed in the group that it was difficult for us to console her. We could spend an hour sympathizing, helping her express her frustration that she got no respite from the disease, and yet we felt little reward in the way of appreciation from Doreen or even a sense that we had somehow been of help to her. It was thus all the more striking when she commented on her surgeon:

> "It meant so much to me that my doctor was on the verge of tears when he talked to me. He knew me from my dance class, and he said he was sorry that I had gotten an illness that was so terrible."

Professionalism does not mean a lack of emotion, although most doctors struggle to contain their emotional responses in front of patients. Hard as it was for her to admit, it meant a great deal to Doreen that her doctor wept for and with her. On the other hand, some cancer patients get upset when their doctors show evidence of emotion.

> Jean discovered that her doctor asked her to leave when she started to cry because her doctor would begin to cry as well. While on the one hand she felt closer and more in control, it worried her to see her doctor so upset: "Things must be bad if she is crying too."

It is easy to become angry with your physicians. Serious illness often highlights their limitations, and patients do not like them any more than doctors do. You will inevitably have other irrational feelings about your doctor. There were times in our groups when participants resented me for being healthy. They wondered aloud how I could understand what they were going through:

Jean said: "I just made my thirty-seventh birthday, but I don't know if I'll make the next one. The disease is lousy. I don't know if I'll feel good enough to live my life the way I would really like to." Then (to me): "You don't express feelings. You don't think you have to because you are healthy. What do *you* get from this group, anyway?"

I told them that I had come to appreciate how precious time is in the group and had become more aware of the fact that, while I was likely to live longer, none of us knew who would be there next week. On the other hand, I told them I understood their resentment of people like me without a diagnosis of cancer.

This meeting was not a comfortable one for me, but it was an important one, a reminder that just as the commonalities among cancer patients help them help one another, their differentness can evoke divisiveness. The difference between health and sickness can also divide patients from doctors, who seem to be on the other side of some imaginary wall of invulnerability.

CULTURE AND MEDICINE

Bad as the problem of discussing illness openly can be in the United States, a woman reporter visiting the national Y-Me conference from Japan astonished us by telling us that in Japan women patients are simply not told what their diagnosis is. Even when the emperor of Japan died of cancer, no mention of his true illness was made in the press, and he himself was apparently not told what was killing him.

When I lectured in Tokyo, I was informed that the doctor will often spend only two or three minutes with a breast cancer patient and may inform the family rather than the patient of the diagnosis, on the premise that a woman is not capable of receiving the news and being involved in treatment decisions, especially if it is bad news. Only recently have support groups for cancer patients, such as Ake Bono Kai, been formed in Japan, and there is growing interest among oncologists and other doctors there about how to better inform cancer patients and help them face their disease more directly.

Whatever the reason, cancer seems to carry with it a unique fear and dread, accompanied by a reticence on the part of physicians to discuss it with patients, and on the part of patients to ask troubling questions of their doctors.

COLLABORATING IN TREATMENT

There is a tremendous sense of helplessness engendered by having your body suddenly subjected to an illness that you don't want, followed by treatments that you don't like. Life-threatening illness puts a rude end to the myth of invulnerability that we all live by. It is a daily reminder that things may not always proceed as we wish them to. That is why becoming a partner with your doctor in the treatment of your illness is terribly important. The process of treating the disease should help you feel you're regaining control of your body, yet medical treatment often has the opposite effect. Many people with cancer, for example, feel as victimized by the treatment as they do by the disease, just as many rape victims feel raped all over again when the police interrogate them insensitively about it. Simply being told that your body will be put through a series of indignities, an inevitable series of physical traumas over which you have no control, can feel as dreadful as the disease itself.

Mary was a warm, energetic nurse who was beloved by her patients. She suddenly felt a "pop" in her chest one day when she took a deep breath and was soon diagnosed with lung cancer. She recalled being seen in the examination room by a group of doctors who talked among themselves, occasionally listening to her chest with their stethoscopes and examining other parts of her body. "You know what I felt like?" she told me later. "I felt like an old truck in a garage with a bunch of mechanics standing around it talking about what to do. Every once in a while one would stick in a wrench and fiddle with something. I felt like that truck."

That doctors and patients do not always communicate perfectly is no surprise, yet it is a two-way street. Doctors could clearly learn more about how to help patients feel at ease, how to inquire about their reaction to the illness and its treatment, and could do better at making time for such discussions. But patients are also more than a little reticent about asking. In addition to normal shyness, there is tremendous fear of the answers. Patients often have (even without being aware of it) magical fantasies about their physicians, seeing them as all-powerful rescuers. They do not want to challenge them in any way or burst the bubble of hope that the doctor can make everything better, by asking tough questions. That might yield tough answers. But when you don't ask, you don't get the answers you need, and your doctor may not know what he needs to know to help you most effectively. Screw up your courage and ask, even if you are afraid of the answer.

On the other hand, you have to be prepared to hear things you really do not want to hear.

An extremely intelligent and accomplished woman with rather advanced breast cancer came to consult with me because of anxiety and difficulties in communicating with her oncologist. He was a leading authority in the field and had a reputation for bluntness. Nonetheless, she felt that he was withholding information from her. Indeed, she insisted that he was refusing to tell her what was in store for her. I asked for a typical interaction. As she recounted it, it was clear that when he got to the point of describing what was likely to happen, she changed the subject. She wanted the truth, as long as it was good news. When I reflected on that with her, she smiled sadly and agreed. Finally, she let him convey the truth she needed to hear, rather than what she (understandably) wanted to hear.

There is good evidence that participating in medical decisions is helpful. A study of the responses of breast cancer patients who elect to have breast-conserving lumpectomy plus radiation rather than modified radical mastectomy, conducted by Dr. Lesley Fallowfield and colleagues in England, revealed two surprising things. First, about a third of women who underwent mastectomy and breast-conserving procedures suffered significant anxiety and depression a year later. Their primary worry was the possibility of a recurrence of the cancer, although damage to the body was also an important concern. Interestingly, many of the women over age sixty-five elected the breast-sparing intervention, putting to rest the myth that as women get older their body image and appearance is less important. While it is excellent to have breast conservation as an option, it does not guarantee an easier adjustment to the diagnosis and early treatment of breast cancer.

The second finding was quite interesting. Some physicians in the study only recommended mastectomies, others clearly preferred lumpectomy plus radiation, and a third group of doctors had a more balanced view and would discuss with patients the pros and cons of both alternatives. Patients who had the kind of surgeon who would discuss either option and let them choose were *less* anxious and depressed in the ensuing year, *regardless of which procedure* they chose. These findings suggest that having a sense of influence and control over the structure of their treatment had a positive emotional effect on them, independent of what the treatment was. It also puts to rest the myth that it is a bad idea to involve patients in treatment decisions because if the outcome is poor they will feel guilty. Rather, patients benefit from the opportunity to involve themselves in the choices that affect their bodies and their lives.

CULTIVATING CONTROL

The importance of feeling in control is crucial in developing a collaborative relationship with your doctors. Think of yourself as your own advocate, there to make sure that the tests are done right, questions are answered, alternatives considered, treatments delivered as promised.

The women in our support groups have developed a checklist for getting the most out of your health care:

1. *Humanize your relationship with your physician.* You are both people. Do not be overawed by the professional aspects of the relationship to the point that you ignore one another's humanness. A good physician should help with this, but half of the responsibility is yours. Go out of your way to form a relationship with your physician in the same way you would to form a working relationship with anyone else important to you. As was mentioned earlier, some do this by asking for a hug, others by making sure their questions or special concerns are addressed, or by letting their doctor know what particular needs they have: to postpone chemotherapy until after a vacation; to bring their family into the office for a discussion of the diagnosis and prognosis; or to ask the doctor about his or her special knowledge or interest in the disease and its treatment.

2. *Write down your questions.* Think through in advance what information you want from your physician and write down your questions. You will spend very little time with him or her, and will probably be anxious. You are likely to forget the most important question and think of it only after the door has closed. Plan ahead to learn what you want to know.

3. *Announce at the beginning of the interview that you have questions.* Often people wait until the interview is over to ask questions. As I've said before, if you let your doctor know at the beginning that you have questions, she or he can plan the time accordingly and will have more time to provide answers.

4. *Bring a friend or family member.* Medical visits are often emotionally taxing and require considerable waiting as well. Bring someone to keep you company, keep your courage up, go over with you what you have learned, provide distraction, and take you to lunch afterward.

5. *Negotiate.* Ask your doctor what your options are, the consequences of differences in treatment (for example, lumpectomy and radiation versus mastectomy; radiation before or after chemotherapy; hormone treatment versus chemotherapy; surgery versus medication). Ask about flexibility in the timing of the treatments. Can you take that long-planned vacation before starting a new round of chemotherapy? If you do not tell your doctor that you have other plans, he or she will not take them into account in planning your treatment.

   Lucy told her oncologist: "My quality of life is worth something. I am all in favor of more chemotherapy, but taking it every two weeks just ruins my life." She told us with pride: "You know what? My doctor is giving it to me every three weeks. I don't mind taking it that often, and he says it will not make much of a difference."

   Cancer treatment, like other medical treatment, involves trade-offs, risks versus benefits. One of the considerations in choosing treatment is your ability to tolerate side effects, such as nausea and vomiting, weakness, low white blood cell counts, and hair loss. You can and should discuss with your doctor which of the side effects bothers you most, and make him or her aware of your willingness to treat the disease aggressively even if the risk of side effects is high. You may be far more willing to tolerate side effects if your doctor is going for a cure than if the chemotherapy and radiation therapy is designed to alleviate symptoms. Your doctor has to make such decisions, but your desires should be part of those decisions.

6. *Do not hide symptoms.* In the book *The Doctor* (called *A Taste of My Own Medicine* before Hollywood made a movie of it), Dr. Edward Rosenbaum, who developed cancer of the larynx, admitted how long he hid his radiation burns from his own doctors before finally pointing them out to them. If you notice something, make sure your doctors notice it too. Let them worry about it—that's their job.

Ellie admitted to the group that she had been wheezing all week and felt she could hardly breathe. However, when she saw her doctor, she just said to him: "I'm having trouble breathing." She was aware that she had not given him a clear impression of the depth of fear and anxiety she had suffered: "I did this because I didn't want any kind of medicine and I didn't want him to find anything."

Your anxiety about your doctor finding something may lead you to hide the information your doctor needs to help you.

7. **Don't wait if you don't have to.**

Jane felt a new pain in her neck and was worried that it meant her cancer had spread: "It's not fair—I just finished chemotherapy and was visiting my family in the mountains when this happened."

"When is your next bone scan?" asked Sandy.

"In three weeks—I guess I'll wait," said Jane.

"Oh no you won't," replied Sandy. "Call up your doctor and get it scheduled this week."

Sandy was right—three weeks of anxious waiting create an unnecessary drain on your resources. If you are worried, do something about it. Similarly, the days between a scan and a result inflict considerable emotional wear and tear on you and your family. See if you can negotiate quicker results. Jane is the woman I talked about in Chapter 3 who learned to pick up her scan as soon as it came out, take it to the radiologist on duty and ask for her reading on the spot. Sometimes a quick reading like this can be misleading—the doctor may not have previous scans for comparison. But, Jane felt that, good or bad, she had an answer. All the more remarkable, she got her care from the huge Kaiser Health Maintenance Organization. She received this kind of responsive and personal care because she insisted on it.

8. **Express appreciation when the health care team does something right.** Doctors, nurses, and social workers are human. They like

to hear it when they have been helpful. Think of it as shaping their behavior by providing positive reinforcement for doing what makes you feel good. If you make them feel good for it, they are more likely to do it again.

9. *Take charge of your health care.* As the practice of medicine becomes increasingly complex and bureaucratic, it becomes more and more necessary that you take control of your care. You need an advocate in the system, and who better to be it than you? You know yourself and your medical situation well and you are highly motivated. Ask questions about treatments, costs, experimental trials. Since serious illness makes you feel helpless, take every opportunity to feel as much in control of your treatment as possible. This will counter your sense of helplessness and assure that you get the best possible care. You deserve it.

10. *Love them or leave them.* Your doctors are important to you. Inevitably situations will arise in which you and your doctor cannot get along. You may well have tried to ask questions, state your needs, negotiate, and you still feel not cared about or misunderstood. You want a doctor who is competent and compassionate, who knows about treating the disease, and who cares about you as a person. If you feel things are not going well, try the following:

(a) First, ask for an appointment at an unhurried time of the day. Prepare your thoughts, and let your doctor know exactly what he or she could do that would make you feel better about the treatment. Be specific about what is happening. Discuss what he or she did ("When I started crying you just walked out of the room and I felt rejected") rather than present a conclusion that leads only to defensiveness ("You don't care about me"). Suggest solutions: "It would help if you gave me a week's warning before the next round of chemotherapy so I could plan child care." If you have contributed to the problem, admit it as well: "I know I sometimes don't let you know how bad I feel until things have gone pretty far." Ask for your doctor's suggestions about improving things: "Please let me know if you start to feel I am not paying enough attention."

(b) You may find it easier to write your doctor a brief letter describing your concerns and asking what he or she could do that would help to remedy the situation. Writing a letter has the advantage of giving you time to reflect on your comments and modify them.

Marianne had an oncologist who was competent but brusque. With tears in her eyes she described a recent encounter: "I just wish she would sit down. She breezes into the room and doesn't make eye contact. She writes down in the chart things I am supposed to do without looking at me or discussing them with me. I have been worried about my increasing pain, and thought about Jane's recent death—she died in pain. I don't want to do that, and the articles I have been reading indicate that I don't have to. When I asked her about it, she said: 'You're not at that point yet. Don't worry about it. When it is time to die, you just close your eyes and go to sleep.' She didn't hear me."

Marianne decided to compose a letter to her doctor, asking for what would help her feel more comfortable:

1. *Sit down with me.*
2. *Look at me.*
3. *Discuss your thinking about my treatment with me.*
4. *Acknowledge that you have heard my concerns.*

(c) If this does not work, tell your doctor that you would like to get a second opinion from another physician about your care. Your doctor should readily agree, and should be glad to provide names. This is a standard part of medical practice, and any good professional should welcome such an outside opinion. Don't worry that your doctor will resent your request and "turn the other doctors against you." This is not an "us versus them" proposition. You may learn that you are receiving excellent care. The second doctor may have some other suggestions to give you or your doctor and, like the first, may be right or wrong. You may decide to seek treatment elsewhere, but don't start out with that assumption.

(d) If you are uncomfortable with your doctor for professional or personal reasons and cannot resolve them, find another with whom you are more comfortable. Some doctors are better at handling early or late stages of the disease. You may want a very aggressive if impersonal physician early on, but a more compassionate and less active one later. Changing doctors will not alter the disease, but you need someone whom you can trust, rely on for the best treatment decisions, feel comfortable with, and count on for support and advice. Most of us would not change doctors lightly, and should not. But there is enough discomfort associated with illness as it is; a doctor should reduce that discomfort, not increase it. Find someone who works with, not against you. Feeling like a partner in your health care will give you a greater sense of control over your treatment, your illness, and your life.

11. Controlling Pain

The strain in pain lies mainly in the brain.

Most of this book concerns the psychological issues of serious illness and how to confront them. But for many with serious illness, the physical threat of pain—present or anticipated—is also a powerful force that should be confronted and dealt with. Just as physical pleasures, be it a gorgeous vista, a tasty meal, or sexual intimacy, can highlight the best of the relationship between mind and body, pain underscores the worst. It conveys a physical and mental discomfort that often seems inescapable. Even worse, pain and fear reinforce one another. Pain tends to saturate your attention, diverting it from other more pleasant activities. Over time, your stamina is eroded, leaving little mental energy for attention to anything other than physical discomfort. Pain consists of both a physical signal and a mental message: Something is wrong with my body, and I cannot think of anything else. Not only do I feel bad, I cannot think, sleep, or relate well. I am worried about what this pain means: Is it a signal that my cancer is spreading, that I have broken a bone, that I will no longer be able to pick up my child, hike, or walk? When you feel that something is wrong with your body, it can cause both anxiety and depression. These, in turn, complicate pain by reducing your ability to put it in its place.

Pain is a common and distressing problem. For people with cancer it represents the spread of their disease into bone, causing fracture or irritation of the sensitive membrane around bones; into hollow organs, causing obstruction; or into other soft tissues, where it may stretch nerve endings. While most cancerous invasions of the body are painless, and cancer pain is not inevitable, it is common enough that it causes alarm when it happens. About one third of people experience pain when they first have cancer, and two thirds of people with cancer that has spread to other parts of their body experience pain.

However, the very attention that can amplify pain also provides an opportunity to control it. If fretting about the meaning of pain can amplify it, learning to handle such fears in other ways and attending to something else can diminish it. Pain is not a solid, indivisible quantity, but rather an interaction between a signal generator (the body) and an amplifier (the brain), which either increases or diminishes it.

Simple techniques using self-hypnosis can be quite effective in controlling pain. You can learn quickly, either individually or in groups, how to produce a combination of physical relaxation and control over attention to substantially reduce the amount of pain you experience. As you sit reading this page, you are hopefully unaware of the sensations of your back, bottom, and legs touching the chair—at least until I remind you of them. Then, suddenly, they enter your awareness, only to depart almost as quickly as you ponder the next line. We focus attention toward and away from sensations constantly, and you can learn to do the same even with pain—the most compelling sensation of all.

Indeed, most people with chronic pain come to realize that there are certain times when the pain seems to be worse—usually during evenings and weekends, when there is less going on in the way of natural distraction from the pain sensations. Absorption in work or play is a natural analgesic. Diving into a project may seem such a

HERMAN
By Unger

The way we treat a headache here is to divert your attention to something else.

© 1977 by Jim Unger

welcome relief that we do it naturally, without crediting this redirection of our attention with its pain-relieving properties. In part this is because the minute we think about pain, we tend to feel it. Just being aware of pain tends to exacerbate it.

TENSION AND PAIN

There are some simple exercises you can do to better understand and control your pain.

First, make a tight fist, tensing all the muscles in your forearm and upper arm. Now make it twice as tight—as hard as you can. You should by now be feeling some discomfort in the normal muscles of your arm and hand. Now let go.

Lesson number one: Muscle tension causes pain. You can produce painful sensations in an uninjured part of your body simply by tensing up your muscles. And yet, what do most people with chronic pain do? They splint the part of the body that hurts, thereby producing tension in normal muscles and pulling on the part that already hurts. This causes a natural but unwelcome increase in pain sensation.

ATTENTION AND PAIN

Second, squeeze the webbing between the thumb and index finger of one hand with the thumb and index finger of the other hard enough that it hurts. See how much it does hurt. Now, while continuing to apply the same pressure, think of the name of your second grade schoolteacher. Now, let go.

You have just done a little experiment. You had the same physical discomfort in two situations: first when you were paying full attention to it, and then while you were thinking about something else. If you are like most people, you felt more pain in the first situation, when you were paying attention to it. Occasionally, someone feels more pain in the second condition, especially if they had a particularly bad second grade schoolteacher.

Lesson number two: You have to pay attention to pain for it to hurt. All pain is a product of the physical discomfort that triggers signals from the body and the amount of conscious attention you pay to those signals. Note how you can alter the amount of pain you feel by shifting your attention toward or away from the physical signals. Many athletes suffer serious injuries that they become aware of only after the game is over. They are so absorbed in the competition that they ignore important signals from their bodies. Ignoring pain can be dangerous, but this example underscores the fact that it is also possible to control, reduce, and even eliminate serious physical pain. The physical side is only one half of the equation.

These exercises suggest that you can do several things to control pain simply: (1) reduce the amount of muscle tension that can increase the physical component of pain; and (2) increase control over your attention so that you focus away from pain sensations.

The success of these techniques does not mean that your pain is not real. None would seriously claim that childbirth is not painful. Nonetheless, women have, for millennia, learned to bear children while modulating their physical discomfort, most recently with techniques such as Lamaze. There is no doubt that they experience real physical pain, but they can learn, by focusing on their breathing, looking at a spot, and staying in touch with their partner/coach, to reduce the discomfort that the stretching and contraction of their muscles causes in the process of giving birth. Using such techniques does not imply that the pain is not real. Rather, it indicates that you want the pain to interfere minimally with your life.

DEPRESSION, MEANING, AND PAIN

There are other factors besides muscle tension and attention that affect pain: emotion and meaning.

It has been known for some time that depression and pain interact: People in pain seem more depressed, and depressed people complain more of pain. Indeed, the medical community used to think that people with various emotional disorders complained more in general, and about pain in particular, because they were anxious and depressed. These individuals made more of a fuss about pain, thereby amplifying it. More recently, an alternative point of view has emerged, suggesting that the experience of having chronic pain may itself make someone depressed.

Depression is more than mere sadness, the feeling you have in the face of a disappointment, loss, or regret. It involves both mental and physical problems. Mentally, depressed people tend to be excessively guilty and self-critical. They ruminate endlessly about past failures, blame themselves inappropriately for real or imagined shortcomings, and ignore positive aspects of themselves. They feel "hopeless, helpless, and worthless." They believe that there is little hope for improvement in the future, that there is little they can do to change their lot, and that they are worth very little. They may even contemplate or attempt suicide. Physically, they have little energy, often sleep poorly, typically waking early in the morning unable to get back to sleep, and report little appetite or sexual energy. Such serious or major depression is not uncommon, affecting some 4 percent of the United States population at any one time.

My colleagues and I became suspicious that the experience of chronic pain could indeed induce depression. We looked for factors that were associated with reports of pain among the breast cancer patients involved in our support group study. We found three key factors in the intensity of their pain:

1. *Mood disturbance.* We found that those breast cancer patients who rated themselves as being more anxious and depressed also had more pain. As other research has shown, anxiety and depression amplify pain. In a more recent study we sought to better understand this relationship between depression and cancer pain. We recruited and intensely assessed two samples of cancer patients, one with substantial pain, one with very little pain. We found, as you might expect, differences in the frequency of depression in the two samples. Twenty-eight percent of those with substantial pain met criteria for major depression, the most serious kind, versus only 6 percent of the low-pain patient group. But of even more interest is the fact that a previous history of major depression was far more common in the *low-pain* group. Thus, by history alone, they were the ones who should have been more vulnerable to depression. Yet, it was the high-pain patients who had it, leading us to the conclusion that *pain produces depression.* Rather than finding that depressed people exaggerate pain, this study suggests that pain makes people depressed, and this, in turn, makes it harder for them to tolerate the pain they have. Thus, a downhill cycle is produced in which, as pain makes people more depressed, they tolerate the pain more poorly, which causes them to become even more depressed, and so on.

There are good treatments available for depression, both antidepressant medications and psychotherapies aimed at correcting depressive thought patterns and managing the emotional and interpersonal problems associated with depression. These treatments can, in turn, reduce pain. If you find that you or a loved one is depressed, you may want to see a psychiatrist, who can assess you, prescribe medication, and offer psychotherapy, or a psychologist, who can assess you and offer psychotherapy. If you have any suicidal thoughts or have attempted to take your life, you should seek professional help.

2. *Meaning.* The way our cancer patients interpreted their pain—that is, its meaning—affected its intensity. To the extent that our breast cancer patients thought the pain signaled a worsening of the disease, they were more likely to report that the pain was more intense. A new pain grabs your attention and feels all the more terrible because you are afraid that it indicates that the cancer is spreading to a new part of your body. How you yearn for the good old-fashioned aches and pains that indicate nothing more than overexertion!

Anesthesiologist Henry Beecher returned puzzled from his World War II combat experience on the Anzio beachhead in Italy. His main job in combat had been to stop the bleeding and administer morphine for pain to wounded soldiers. He stopped a lot of bleeding, but noted that he had very few requests for morphine, even from very seriously injured soldiers. After the war he tried an experiment. He went to a group of civilian surgical patients at the Massachusetts General Hospital who were equally or *less* seriously injured than his soldiers and asked if they wanted morphine for their pain. They insisted on medication. Thus, despite less serious injury, they reported substantially more pain. Beecher concluded, correctly, that the *meaning* of pain influences its *intensity*. To a combat soldier, being alert after you had been wounded meant you were likely to get out of the war alive, and you wanted to remain alert to make sure you got off the battlefield in one piece. To a civilian, the surgery and associated pain was a threat to life and therefore less tolerable and more painful.

Of even more interest in our study was the fact that the site of metastasis—that is, where the cancer had spread in these women's bodies—did not significantly predict the amount of pain. It has been reported that cancer that has spread to bones or organs produces more pain than cancer that has spread to soft tissue. Yet this was not the case in our study, and others have shown that the majority of identifiable metastatic lesions do not produce pain. Indeed, contrary to popular belief, cancer is not uniformly associated with pain.

3. *Underuse of pain medications.* These patients, like many cancer patients, were *undermedicated* for their pain. What seems to happen is that doctors prescribe too little medicine for pain because they are afraid that their patients will abuse analgesics or develop tolerance to them. Tolerance means that the same amount of pain medication produces less of an analgesic effect, leading to increased doses and possible habituation or addiction. At the same time, many patients are wary of taking such medications, seeing them as an indication that the end is at hand, fearful of addiction, or wary of more common side effects such as sedation, loss of energy, or constipation. "I prefer to think in torment than not to be able to think at all," wrote Sigmund Freud, who suffered during the last years of his life with cancer of the mouth and who disliked pain medication.

Yet, as a group, people with cancer do not become drug abusers, and concerns about this are seriously exaggerated. The main problem is that, effective as modern analgesic medications are, they are not a panacea. They do not always work, and they do have significant side effects, often making people tired, sleepy, or confused. They cannot replace psychological pain-control techniques, which can allow patients to cut their dosages of analgesics.

It is clear that pain is always a combination of physical

and mental distress. Factors such as muscle tension, attention, emotion, and meaning all contribute to the pain experience. And to the extent that we can control these factors, we can alleviate pain.

HYPNOSIS: MIND AND BRAIN

I started in medicine with an interest in learning more about how the mind and body influence one another. My clinical experience had made me mildly optimistic about the power of the mind to influence the body. Some "pathways" by which the mind can affect the body seem quite obvious. As I mentioned in the preface, I had been able to use hypnosis to help a young girl control a severe asthma attack. This makes sense. When an asthma attack begins, due perhaps to inhaling an allergen, you become anxious. Anxiety causes your brain to secrete certain neurotransmitters, which cause the bronchi (tubes in the lungs) to constrict even more, the asthma worsens, you become more anxious, and so on—a vicious circle. Hypnosis can help you control your mental state, thereby reducing the anxiety and its damaging effects.

Similarly, I had had good luck using hypnosis to help cancer patients and others with chronic pain control their discomfort. Clearly, and not too surprisingly, altering your mental state could influence what you felt in your body.

Over the years I have spent considerable time in the laboratory examining how hypnosis might affect the way the brain processes information. It seemed to me that if a hypnotized person could reduce pain perception so substantially, or breathe more easily during an asthma attack, there must be a way of measuring the effect of these hypnotic changes in the brain. In an attempt to do this, we used a technique called event-related potentials (ERP). In this method, electrodes are placed on the scalp. They record minute amounts of electrical activity from the brain in response to stimuli: flashes of light on a television monitor, small electrical shocks to the wrist, or tones in headphones.

We studied highly hypnotizable Stanford undergraduates who were instructed during hypnosis to imagine a cardboard box blocking their view of a television monitor. They saw this imaginary box quite vividly, and it did indeed obstruct their view of the television screen. At those times, the amount of electrical activity generated by the standard flashes of light was very low. In other words, their brains acted as though they had been presented with less light, even though the computer was providing an identical amount of light on the television monitor. When Stanford students who were not at all hypnotizable tried the same experiment, there was no difference in their brains' responses to the stimuli under these different conditions. Thus, there seemed to be something special about the response in hypnosis. This shows that when hypnosis is used to help people alter their perception, they change the way their brains process what they see.

We then tried a similar experiment using a mild shock administered to the wrist, which feels something like snapping your fingernail against your skin. We thought this might offer advantages over studying the visual system. It is easier, after all, to look away from something than not to feel a tapping on your wrist (although we had monitored the direction of the students' gaze in the first experiment). We also thought that since hypnosis is so effective in helping people control pain, we should examine the effects of hypnosis on that kind of stimulation. Again, we selected students who had either a very high or a very low ability to experience hypnosis.

We asked these students to imagine while under hypnosis that their hand had been immersed in ice water, making it cool and numb. The highly hypnotizable ones responded well, reporting tingling, numbness, and decreased sensation in that hand. We administered the same series of electric shocks with and without hypnosis. Their brains responded as though the stimulus had been reduced when they imagined that their hands were numb. We then told them (also while they were under hypnosis) that the stimulus would feel extremely pleasant and interesting and that they should pay full attention to it. This time, they responded as though the stimulus had been stronger, even though in fact it was the same. We found that hypnotizable individuals could either increase or decrease the electrical response in their brains to stimuli within a tenth of a second of perceiving them. Usually only differences in the actual strength of a signal are detectable that soon after a stimulus is given. In other words, their brains were reacting as though the hypnotically imagined conditions of stimulus reduction or amplification were real.

We then tested whether patients with pain caused by chronic illness—not just students with minor pain—could either increase or decrease electrical activity over the portion of their brain that processes physical sensation in response to hypnotic instruction. Using a more sophisticated measuring technique called brain electrical activity mapping (BEAM), we found that when these patients used the hypnotic pain reduction technique, they showed less electrical activity over the part of the brain that registers physical sensation. When they found the sensation enjoyable, as instructed in hypnosis, they had a bigger electrical response than usual over the same part of the brain. In short, hypnosis acted as effectively on the brains of patients as it had among the college students we tested.

THE NATURE OF HYPNOSIS

Before we turn to hypnotic strategies for pain management, let me dispel some common myths about hypnosis. The French anthropologist Lévi-Strauss once said that "myths are things that never were true and always will be." Many people have fixed "mythunderstandings" about what hypnosis is that tend either to exaggerate its power or dismiss its utility.

1. *Hypnosis is focused attention, not sleep.* You are not asleep when you are hypnotized, but rather in a state that combines physical relaxation with alert and focused attention. This means that you can enter a hypnotic state in seconds. Long, boring inductions involving counting up and down stairs, dangling watches, etc. are

unnecessary. When you enter a hypnotic state, you do not go to sleep—you wake up.

2. *Hypnosis involves mobilizing your inner resources, not submitting to the will of others.* When you concentrate fully, attending to one idea, perception, or feeling, you are drawing on your inner resources for focused attention. You tend to *do* rather than judge *what you are doing.* You are employing your concentration optimally in the service of attending to a mental or physical task, regardless of whether you or someone else has assigned the task. You *still choose* whether or not to do it.

3. *Hypnosis is a sign of mental ability, not weak-mindedness.* The capacity to focus attention in this way is an important and useful mental skill, not a sign of weakness or inability. While not everyone is hypnotizable, in general those with good mental health and intellectual skills are more likely to be able to experience hypnosis.

4. *Hypnosis occurs spontaneously, not just when a doctor decides to use it.* Since hypnosis is a simple state of focused concentration, it may occur at times when you concentrate fully, for example during athletic performance, while watching a good movie, or in response to sudden trauma.

   A Stanford student who was both highly hypnotizable and an excellent wide receiver for the football team observed that when he was playing well, he was aware of only two things: the ball and the defender. The other twenty players and the sixty-five thousand screaming fans in the stadium were not part of his awareness. This is an example of a spontaneous use of hypnotic ability.

5. *Hypnosis is a helpful state, not a dangerous one.* There is nothing inherently dangerous about hypnosis. No one has ever been lost in a hypnotic state, never to return. Rather, it is a natural and relaxing state of mind and body that can be mobilized to help control anxiety, pain, and a variety of other problems.

HYPNOSIS IS A SIMPLE and natural form of focused attention that most people can use to filter out awareness of many kinds of pain and other discomfort. Hypnosis has three main components: *absorption, dissociation, and suggestibility.*

Absorption is a state of completely involving and self-altering attention, such as being so caught up in a good movie, novel, or play that you lose awareness of your surroundings and focus entirely on the activity. Playwrights consider the "suspension of disbelief" to be a necessary prerequisite for good theater. You may have had the experience of emerging from a movie theater and needing a few moments to reorient yourself to the real world. Similarly, you may find yourself so absorbed in a sunset or an idea that you ignore someone calling you. Research shows that individuals who frequently have such absorbing experiences are more highly hypnotizable on formal testing.

Dissociation is an ability to separate or compartmentalize aspects of memory, identity, or consciousness that would ordinarily be processed together. The example given at the beginning of this chapter of ignoring the sensation of your body touching the chair until it is called to your attention is typical of everyday dissociation. Other examples include the experience of discovering that you have injured your body —finding a cut or a bruise—and yet having no memory of how it happened. There must have been sensations at the time, yet you cannot recall them.

Indeed, there is growing evidence that people frequently respond to physical trauma with dissociation. They spontaneously use it as a way to distance themselves emotionally from physical discomfort.

A young woman who suffered from Hodgkin's disease proved to be very hypnotizable, and learned quickly to control her persistent nausea and vomiting from chemotherapy with self-hypnosis. She simply imagined that she was on vacation, enjoying the beach rather than being in the chemotherapy infusion room.

I was interviewing her about her successful use of this technique in front of some psychiatric residents, and by way of taking a "routine" history, I asked her if she had ever been hospitalized before.

"Yes," she replied. "I broke my pelvic bone when I fell off of a third-story balcony."

My God, she was suicidal and must have jumped, and I missed it, I thought. "Did you jump?" I asked.

"No," she answered, "I was pushed."

By this point I had concluded that she was paranoid. "What do you mean?" I asked.

"I was standing on a balcony next to this huge, beefy guy with a beer in his hand. He turned around suddenly and just knocked me over the edge of the balcony. It was a stupid accident." Feeling upset just thinking about this sudden fall, I summoned my most empathic tone, and said "That must have been terrifying."

"No," she replied, "it was quite pleasant." By this time I knew she must be psychotic. "Let me tell you how I experienced it. I felt as if I were standing on another balcony watching a pink cloud float down to the ground. I felt no pain at all and even tried to walk back upstairs."

She had spontaneously used this remarkable dissociative ability to distance herself from the fear and pain that would normally go hand-in-hand with such an injury.

Dissociation is a natural complement to the absorption that typifies the hypnotic state. The more engrossed you are in one object of attention, the more likely you are to ignore others. Thus the price paid for intensity of attentional focus is putting out of conscious awareness —dissociating—portions of conscious experience.

Suggestibility is the third main component of hypnosis. There is a common fear that, once hypnotized, a person is deprived of will and choice and can be made to do anything. My father, Herbert Spiegel, a psychiatrist at Columbia University who has pioneered the medical use of hypnosis since World War II, likes to respond to the fearful question "If you hypnotize me, can you make me do anything you want me to?" with the response "If I had the power to do that, do you think I would be sitting here with you? I would be on Wall Street, at the United Nations, or in the White House."

It is certainly not the case that a hypnotized person is unable to make choices, or to refuse to do something. On the other hand, there is something to hypnotic suggestibility in that in a hypnotic state people are *less likely* to break with a suggestion because they are less likely to think it over. When you are in a state of mind in which you are focusing on the content of an idea, you are less likely to evaluate it or the person who suggested it. We have all had the experience of wondering how on earth we went along with doing something that in retrospect seemed unwise. "It seemed like a good idea at the time," is what we usually tell ourselves. Another price of hypnotic absorption is a suspension of critical judgment, a willingness to immerse yourself in the "what" rather than the "why" of a situation. This lets you *do* more but *reflect* on it less.

All this means is that it is a good idea to choose your goals carefully, and if you have the need, find a well-trained and licensed doctor, psychologist, or therapist who can induce hypnosis. You will tend to focus intently on the content of the experience rather than on the reasons for or against it. Hypnosis has been used with thousands of people, and the worst that usually happens is they may receive little benefit. Many others profit substantially. Think of the use of hypnosis like planning a vacation trip. Choose the journey with care. Once on it, you will be following a given course and not others, but you are always free to stop. Most of the time you will enjoy it.

HYPNOSIS AND MIND/BODY CONTROL

There are at least three ways in which allowing yourself to enter such an altered mental state as hypnosis may be helpful in controlling mind/body interactions.

First, there is the state itself. It may be that there is something inherently useful about being in a trancelike state from time to time. It is a kind of relaxed attention, allowing for comfortable alertness. Such a state may help you examine problems without the usual associated physical tension, making it possible to deal with them without being overwhelmed by them.

Barbara came to see me not primarily because of her breast cancer, but rather because her husband had just been diagnosed with Alzheimer's disease (a relentlessly progressive dementia that leads to loss of memory, other cognitive disabilities, decreasing physical control, and eventually to death). She was overwhelmed with misery. She had just come to terms with her own cancer, which was a worry but had not spread, and had been planning a happy period of retirement and freedom to pursue creative activities. She felt imprisoned by her life, unable to escape the endless worries that beset her.

Her concerns were real and understandable, but I tried to help her see them from a different point of view. In hypnosis, I told her to picture one of her concerns on an imaginary screen, as though she were watching a home video, with the rule that no matter what she saw on the screen, she would maintain a physical sense of floating relaxation in her body. She cried as she saw an image of her beloved husband deteriorating. I then asked her to divide the screen in half, and picture on the other side something she might do about the problem.

We also tried another technique. I helped her use the hypnosis as though she were looking through a camera with a telephoto and a wide-angle lens. She could thus make what she was looking at bigger or smaller, either focusing on it intensely or placing it in a broader context. She was intrigued by this, finding a sense of emotional relief in being able to "play" with the size of the problem. She emerged from the hypnosis with a tear-stained face, but noticed that she did not feel quite as overwhelmed by her problems: "I realize that my illness and my husband's illness are just part of my life—there's more to my life than that."

As she wrote later about the experience: "Under hypnosis, I pictured my husband and me 'goin' down,' which was extremely frightening and upsetting. Then you asked me what I wanted, and I saw so clearly that what I wanted was to 'go down with love.' This image was very powerful and has remained with me. Another hypnosis technique which helped was putting a 'problem' up on the screen (which in my case became my computer screen) and then subdividing the problem into smaller chunks (files). Then you asked me to move one small section over to the right side of the screen and 'work on it,'—brainstorm possible actions or solutions for that bit of the problem—then close it up when I wanted to rest. Another was picturing a 'difficult family member' and imagining moving toward that person in some way.... These techniques, along with many others, remain extraordinarily useful and comforting to me, even still."

A second benefit of hypnosis is that there may be something healthful about the alternation among mental states. We know, for example, that it is not only refreshing but necessary to alternate between sleep and wakefulness each day. Restorative processes occur in sleep that help the brain function better during wakefulness. Sleep researcher Allan Hobson at Harvard has shown that there is a shift in the dominance of neurotransmitter activity in sleep toward the neurons that secrete acetylcholine, with a relative shutdown of the nerves that produce the alerting neurotransmitters epinephrine and norepinephrine (commonly referred to as adrenaline), which are secreted in large amounts during fight-or-flight reactions. Thus sleep provides for restoration of depleted arousal neurotransmitters as others take over.

It may well be that the cyclic alternation between normal and trancelike states in consciousness serves a similar restorative function, allowing not only for a change in cognitive or emotional appraisal of a difficult situation, but for restoration of mental energy.

There is evidence that people in hypnotic states have unusually good control over physical processes, a third benefit of hypnosis. It has been clearly demonstrated, for example, that hypnosis can be used as part of an effective treatment for warts. Patients given a hypnotic suggestion that their warts will go away will lose them at a much faster rate than control subjects who have not been given such hypnotic suggestions. Similarly, hypnosis has been used effectively to induce or eliminate allergic skin reactions, treat other skin conditions such as psoriasis, and control skin blood flow and temperature. Highly hypnotizable individuals can produce a difference in the temperature of their hands of as much as 4 degrees Centigrade in just a few minutes, simply by imagining in hypnosis that one is warm (in the sun, in a warm bath) and the other is cold (in snow or ice).

Hypnosis has also been used to facilitate treatment of disorders of the digestive system, such as irritable bowel syndrome, in which people suffer chronic abdominal distention, discomfort, and diarrhea. It has also been effectively used to help people with asthma, who are subject to sudden attacks of wheezing because of constriction of the bronchioles, air passages in the lungs, as I had witnessed early in my medical training. Asthmatics can learn to shift quickly into a simple state of self-hypnosis and reduce the anxiety-related physical tension that increases constriction in the lungs. There is evidence that those who are more highly hypnotizable are more likely to respond well to such treatments.

Given this evidence that hypnosis provides an opportunity for enhanced control over physical processes, the reader may well be wondering why we don't simply hypnotically suggest that the cancer cells recede or be consumed by eager white blood cells acting like sharks and devouring them, as some have advised. (This process is sometimes called visualization or imaging.) The reason is that there is simply no evidence that this works. Just because your ability to control physical processes may be increased in hypnosis does not mean that you have infinite power to fix things in your body, having "fixed" them in your mind. While you may find that imagining that your body is fighting off the cancer effectively is emotionally reassuring in some way, my concern is that you may wind up blaming yourself if the cancer progresses, feeling that you have not done a good enough job of visualizing.

Research on trauma has shown that people tend to blame themselves for anything that happens to them. Rape and accident victims berate themselves for not having "foreseen" the danger, even though they could not have known it was coming. Cancer is in its own way a trauma, and some individuals may blame themselves for it even though they were in no way responsible. Nonetheless, coming to believe that the right mental attitude can control your illness can add to the burden of guilt or even create one if your illness worsens.

This is an important issue, since the popular press is full of accounts of wishing away cancer. In their book *Getting Well Again,* Carl and Stephanie Matthews-Simonton claim that individuals who utilize their imagery technique, picturing white blood cells killing cancer cells, live longer than cancer patients with similar disease. The problem, as I mentioned earlier, is that they have never conducted a randomized, controlled trial. Rather, they have compared those who have the health, time, money, and energy to go to their programs with "national norms." It is not hard to divine that those who attend their programs are not typical of all of those with a given type of cancer and are likely to be far healthier to begin with.

USING HYPNOSIS TO CONTROL PAIN

At the same time, there is every reason to use whatever techniques we have at hand to help people with cancer and other illnesses control symptoms such as pain, anxiety, and nausea and vomiting. In our support groups, professionals formally induce hypnosis to carry out these techniques. However, you may receive some benefit simply by closing your eyes and imagining the same type of mental and physical experience. (I'll explain how shortly.) Should you find yourself feeling a bit disoriented afterward, give yourself a few moments to talk yourself back to normal awareness. Sometimes it helps to have a personal ritual for entering and leaving the hypnotic state—for example, counting to yourself from one to three to enter it and counting backwards from three to one to exit. Such transitions from intense concentration to ordinary awareness are normal. We all need to "get our bearings" at times after immersion in a task. You can always bring yourself out of such a state of focused concentration. The goal here is to help you use such states to enable your body to feel more comfortable.

In the unlikely event that you continue to feel confused or disoriented, contact your physician, psychiatrist, psychologist, or therapeutically trained social worker or nurse. Should you wish to obtain professional help using hypnosis, it is essential to contact a state-licensed and well-trained professional in one of these disciplines who also has special experience with hypnosis. Seek a referral from your doctor or psychotherapist, or from one of the two national professional hypnosis societies: the Society for Clinical and Experimental Hypnosis in Liverpool, New York (315-652-7299), or the American Society of Clinical Hypnosis in Des Plaines, Illinois (708-297-3317). It is most important that this person be competent in his or her primary professional discipline; that is why state licensing is an absolute essential. Many people who are trained as "hypnotherapists" and listed in the yellow pages often have little or no professional training or licensing and are to be avoided.

Some find it helpful to establish a baseline for evaluating their pain, so they can assess how effective these exercises are in reducing that pain. Right now, take a moment to rate your pain on a zero-to-ten scale, with ten being unbearable pain, the worst ever, and zero being none at all. While occasionally techniques such as self-hypnosis can help you eliminate pain completely, more often you will be able to reduce it some 10 to 40 percent. While this may not seem like much, most individuals with recurrent pain receive great comfort from the knowledge that they can modulate it to a point where it is manageable. Furthermore, keeping track of the intensity of pain in this way can help you recognize the extent to which the technique is of help, and which methods are most effective.

The following are principles for using your inner psychological capacity to better manage pain.

First, find some quiet surroundings where you will not likely be disturbed for a few minutes. Put yourself into a quiet state of reverie. Some find it useful to look upwards at a point on the ceiling or sky and then close their eyes, counting "one, two, three" to themselves. Others may wish to simply sit quietly with eyes open. The main point is to get physically comfortable and concentrate.

1. *Float.* Imagine your body floating somewhere safe and comfortable, just floating down through the chair or bed on which you are resting. You might find yourself floating in a lake, a bath, in the ocean, in a hot tub, or just floating in space. Feel that pleasant sense of your weightless body, and perhaps a sense of warmth or coolness, whichever is more comfortable. As you breathe, make each breath deeper and easier as you let the tension flow out of your body. Feeling your body floating is the first step in pain control, since it naturally reduces the physical tension that increases pain.

    Some individuals, especially those who are less naturally hypnotizable, find it reinforcing to actually be in a situation in which they are floating, such as a warm bath, when doing such an exercise.

2. *Filter.* Next, establish a psychological filter between yourself and the pain signals. You can learn to *filter the hurt out of the pain.* You do this not by insisting that the pain (or the cancer) will go away, but rather by altering the sensation of the pain, and learning to separate that sensation from the suffering, or amount of discomfort, it causes you. You focus instead on a positive, comforting image of tingling numbness.

    First, remember what physical remedies give you relief from the pain. Some get real relief by taking a warm bath, others by putting ice or cold water on the part of their body that hurts. Whatever works for you, try it now in your imagination. Picture yourself taking a luxurious warm bath or, alternatively, surrounding the part of your body that hurts with ice or snow. Feel a sense of warmth or cool tingling numbness penetrate deeper and deeper into that part of your body. This becomes a psychological filter that filters the hurt out of the pain. In place of your pain or discomfort, learn to focus on the warm or cool tingling numbness.

Take a moment now to examine how much this imagination exercise has helped you to reduce your pain. Rate your discomfort on that same zero-to-ten scale.

3. *Focus.* For some people, modulating sensations other than temperature works better. Try imagining lightness and heaviness, or tingling and numbness. Others find that they are capable of more dramatic leaps of the imagination. Picture yourself simply going somewhere else, where the pain isn't. Take an imaginary vacation to a place you enjoy or have always wanted to see.

Marc is a world-class swimmer who collapsed one evening and was brought to the Stanford Hospital Emergency Department. It turned out that he had a lymphoma (a cancer of the lymph system) the size of a grapefruit in his abdomen, and it had begun to bleed. He very nearly died that first evening, but was stabilized and admitted to the hospital, where he began chemotherapy.

He was suffering considerable pain, to the point that he would literally bang on the walls, and the nurses were reluctant to care for him because they found it so emotionally stressful. His parents were afraid that he was becoming a drug addict. At that point, I was asked to see him.

I first reassured his parents that drug addiction was the least of his problems. When I saw Marc, he was lying in bed, groaning. "I bet you don't want to be here," I commented.

"You spent years in medical school to figure that out?" he replied.

I assessed his hypnotizability, and finding him a good candidate, taught him to enter a state of self-hypnosis. I then asked him, as he continued to groan and writhe, where he would rather be.

"I'm a great swimmer, but I've never surfed," he replied.

"Good," I said, "we're going to Hawaii." He continued groaning, but soon there was a slightly different tone to his groans. "What happened?" I asked.

"I fell off the surfboard," he replied.

"Good. This time, get on it and do it right," I insisted. I had him practice this self-hypnosis "surfing" exercise every one to two hours, and any time the pain got bad.

Within forty-eight hours, he was off of all of his pain medications and was joking with the nurses, chasing them up and down the halls in his bear-claw slippers. One of the oncologists concluded that this could be explained only by regression of his tumor, rather than by Marc's newly learned skill of hypnotic pain control.

Marc was especially good at carrying out the hypnosis on his own. Others, especially younger patients, benefit more from structured exercises:

Julie was a bright-eyed twelve-year-old with pigtails who suffered from two serious diseases: juvenile rheumatoid arthritis and sickle-cell anemia. She and her doctors had to walk a tight-rope, since the very antiinflammatory drugs that reduced her joint pain tended to make her anemia worse, causing her round red blood cells to contract into the unhealthy sickle shape. I had been asked to teach her about hypnosis and happened into her room shortly after her morphine intravenous line had failed. She had an intern on each arm trying to start a new IV. She was crying. The girl in the next bed was crying. Her mother was crying. My initial temptation was to return when things were calmer, but instead I worked my way up to the head of her bed, asked her to close her eyes, and told her that when I lifted her left index finger I would be turning on an imaginary television set in her mind's eye. I first had her imagining she was playing with her pet cat.

She did not find that very absorbing. Next, I had her imagine she was watching *Sesame Street*. Suddenly she started describing with great animation the adventures of Big Bird and Oscar the Grouch. She winced occasionally when the interns made an unsuccessful attempt to hit her vein, but she stopped crying, as did the girl in the next bed and her mother. She shifted her attention from her pain and fear, both of which were real, to this far more pleasant imagined world. After a few minutes, her mother said: "I didn't know you were such a good story teller!"

4. *Forget.* For others, distraction works better. Simply concentrate on sensations in other, nonpainful parts of your body. Notice, for example, the delicate sensations in your fingertips as you rub them together. Notice how pleasant and interesting those sensations can feel, and concentrate on them when you are tempted to pay attention to the pain.

Then bring yourself out of this state of concentration using any simple technique, such as counting backwards to yourself from three to one and opening your eyes. Take note of how you and your body feel.

Once again, take a moment to rate your current discomfort on the zero-to-ten scale. This is an exercise you can practice every one to two hours, and any time the pain seems to be worsening. Your body deserves a few minutes of this kind of attention to help it feel more comfortable every few hours.

Dealing with the pain early is an important principle in pain management. It is far easier to interrupt an attack of pain before it becomes established than to reduce severe pain that has been troubling you for some time. This is true of pharmacologic as well as psychological interventions. It seems that a kind of feedback pathway gets set up as pain intensifies that makes it more difficult, though not impossible, to interrupt. You need not simply be a victim of pain. You can employ straightforward techniques to reduce associated physical tension and to modulate your attention in such a way that you can reduce the strain in pain.

USING HYPNOSIS TO CONTROL ANXIETY

A certain amount of anxiety is normal and adaptive. We need to worry at times. There is an old French saying that "He who is laughing hasn't heard the bad news yet." The problem is not *that* we worry, but rather *how* we worry. We sometimes tend to set up a feedback cycle of mental and physical tension that makes it harder rather than easier to deal with the things we worry about. When worries make us feel passive and helpless—victims of our own anxieties—they multiply. On the other hand, when we worry in such a way that we can sort out possible solutions to problems, worry leads to change and adaptive activity, reducing the initial anxiety. One trick is to learn to convert anxiety into fear. As I explained in an earlier chapter, anxiety is a general sense of dread, a sense that something—though we don't know what—is wrong. Fear is a dread of something in particular, and knowing what you are afraid of already begins to suggest possible remedies. Looking directly at the object of fear reduces, rather than increases its power.

Anxiety tends to proliferate not only because it does not suggest a possible resolution, but also because it stimulates physical reactions that intensify the associated state of physical discomfort. I often tell my patients with rampant anxieties, "Just because *you* are uptight about a problem doesn't mean that your body has to be uptight as well. I want to teach you how to worry in such a way that you leave your body out of it." Here is the basic technique.

First, close your eyes and feel your body float—in a bath, a lake, a hot tub, or just in space. Learn to enjoy that pleasant sense of floating relaxation.

Now as you continue to float, picture in your mind's eye an imaginary screen. It could be a movie screen, a television screen, a computer screen, or a piece of clear blue sky. Picture on it a pleasant scene, a place you enjoy being. Take a good look at it, and then notice how your memories and fantasies of this place help you and your body feel more comfortable.

Now, if you are worried about something, don't fight it—admit it—but picture some aspect of what you are worried about on that imaginary screen. Do so with the rule that no matter what you see on the screen, you will allow your body to float. Just because you are worried about it, don't let your body get caught up in *your* tension. If you notice yourself starting to fidget and becoming more tense, stop the image on the screen and reestablish the sensation of floating. If you need to, return to a pleasant image to get the sense of floating back. Keep practicing this until you are able to maintain the physical sense of floating while you picture the image of what worries you on your screen.

Then try to divide the screen in half, and put the image of what worries you on the left side of the screen. We'll call that your "worry" screen. Now use the right side of the screen—the "problem-solving" screen—to brainstorm solutions to the problem. At first, don't try to judge or perfect the ideas; just be more open to your own thoughts and feelings. After reviewing some possible solutions, you can begin to select strategies for dealing with what worries you. Keep the floating sense in your body, but use this technique to face your fears.

We use a technique like this to conclude each group session, first focusing on physical comfort and pain control, and then using the screen technique to reflect upon the major theme of the group. For example, after a session in which we grieved Donna's recent death, we did the following exercise:

"On one side of the screen," I told the group members, "picture Donna, and allow yourself to feel her absence, the fact that she will not be back with us. On the other side of the screen, remember something Donna gave to you that remains with you, even though she is gone."

Members of the group had an image of her face and of their deep sadness. At the same time, we recalled a comment she had made to Rachel, who had said: "I really don't deserve to be here with you —you are all so young, and I have lived my life already." Donna had replied: "A minute of your life is worth as much as a minute of ours." We were able to feel our loss, and at the same time feel that part of her was still very much with us.

At another group meeting in which the members voiced their frustrations over not receiving what they wanted from their families, we concentrated on the idea that the best way to get what you want from someone might be to give it to them. On the left side of the screen I suggested they picture "something I want from someone I love." On the right side I suggested they picture giving that very same thing (words of concern, a statement of affection, an offer of help) to that very same person.

We have also used the screen to consolidate our feelings about having to give up abilities. I asked participants to picture on the left screen some attribute that was no longer available to them, but on the right side something new they desired to become. These exercises served to place whatever the problem was in a new perspective. The participants neither avoided the problem nor allowed it to become overwhelming. The problem was changed, not in itself, but rather by placing it in a new and broader context.

USING HYPNOSIS TO REDUCE SITUATIONAL ANXIETY

This self-hypnosis technique can easily be adapted to other situations that tend to provoke anxiety, such as undergoing medical diagnostic and therapeutic procedures. Modern diagnostic scanners such as CAT (Computerized Axial Tomography) and MRI (Magnetic Resonance Imaging) are noninvasive techniques that provide elegant and detailed images of the inside of the body. They are a remarkable advance over simple X ray and invasive angiography (injecting radio-opaque dyes into blood vessels coupled with X ray) used only a few years ago. Nonetheless, the techniques, although now physically quite safe, can be emotionally stressful. You are often required to lie in a tightly enclosed space for an hour or more. MRI scanners have a loud clanking sound. On top of that you are naturally worried about what the scans will show: Has the disease progressed or not? Is the treatment working?

As you prepare for these tests, just allow your body to float, and picture in your mind's eye an imaginary screen—a movie screen, a TV screen, or a piece of clear blue sky. As you let your body float here, just imagine that you are somewhere you enjoy being.

One woman had been so afraid of her MRI scan that she had been refusing it. It was absolutely necessary, since she had a brain tumor that threatened to impinge on her spinal cord and might at some time require surgery to prevent paralysis. She made creative use of the self-hypnosis exercise, imagining that the clanking of the MRI scanner was the noise of a motor boat engine. She loved water skiing and pictured herself being pulled along by a motor boat while the scan was being done. She found it surprisingly easy to undergo the test in this way.

A young man had consistently refused or failed to appear for surgery for a tumor that was beginning to encroach on his spinal cord. Once he showed up so drunk they had to send him home. He had been told that the surgery was risky—there was about a one-in-four chance that he would lose the use of his legs afterward. However, it was virtually certain that he would become paraplegic within a year without surgery. He said that he simply "panicked" at the very thought of the operation. He was taught the self-hypnosis exercise described here, and managed to maintain a sense of floating in his body, even while visualizing the operation on an imaginary screen. He was then told to divide the screen and on the problem-solving side he reviewed all the things he had done to assure that he had the best possible surgeon and the least likelihood of a poor outcome. He was amazed afterward that he felt so calm, despite having been thinking about the operation for almost half an hour.

These techniques can be applied in almost any medical situation: waiting for lab test results, undergoing an X ray, having an IV started. You can use this mental state to "escape" and go somewhere you would rather be, or to face and manage your fears while maintaining physical comfort.

USING HYPNOSIS TO REDUCE NAUSEA AND VOMITING

Unfortunately, modern chemotherapies have some uncomfortable side effects. Prominent among them is nausea and vomiting. While newer drugs are more effective in suppressing the adverse effects of chemotherapy on the gastrointestinal tract, it still remains a troublesome problem for many people with cancer. A strange kind of association may be set up between the sights, smells, and sounds of the treatment environment and the feelings associated with treatment, known as classical conditioning. If you become sick to your stomach after receiving chemotherapy, you learn to associate the place of treatment with the feelings of discomfort. Some patients find themselves feeling ill *before* receiving chemotherapy rather than after. At times just the sight, or smell, or even the thought of the treatment room may be enough to provoke an attack of nausea. The side effects of the medication are bad enough without psychological amplification.

It's often helpful to try to distance yourself emotionally from the treatment environment. I tell my patients to do the following:

You have to deliver your body for treatment, but *you* do not have to be there. Ask the nurse or technician to let you rest quietly, then lie down, close your eyes, and let your body float. After you have established that floating sensation, use your imaginary screen to picture yourself where you would rather be. It might be a safe and comfortable room at home, a beautiful place in the mountains or by the sea, or some vacation spot you enjoy. Try picturing parts of the world you would like to see. You can play a little trick on the treatment team—leave your body here for them to treat and you go somewhere else.

Using this technique, you may be able to disrupt the associations between the setting and your physical response to it by imagining that you are somewhere else. In this way, you can stop treating your body as though it were an emotional battleground.

One woman found that she tired of simply enjoying the view at her imaginary getaway and needed to involve herself in a productive task. She loved interior decorating, so she imagined that she had acquired an old castle on the Rhine, with some forty rooms. She spent her chemotherapy time decorating these imaginary rooms, one by one.

This exercise can be used in anticipation of the treatment sessions as well.

I HAVE EMPHASIZED the use of self-hypnosis in managing pain, anxiety, and the physical side effects of treatment because it is simple, often effective, and easy to learn. This does not make it the only approach. Yoga, meditation, and other relaxation techniques often tap the same kind of mental function coupled with physical relaxation; they simply use different methods to help you enter the desired state. Some, such as progressive muscle relaxation, emphasize step-by-step alteration in tension in various parts of the body. Others, such as yoga and some forms of meditation, couple physical exercises involving stretching and maintaining various body positions with an altered mental state that seeks to obtain clarity and simplicity of attentional focus. Each has its appeal for certain people. None is the answer for everyone, nor are any of these techniques a cure-all. Rather, they can help you increase the leverage you have over the natural discomfort in your mind and body that is associated with serious illness and its treatment. Investigate these options with a qualified professional and find out what works best for you.

Simple changes in your mental approach to some of the physical problems associated with cancer—pain, anxiety, and nausea and vomiting—can make a big difference in how much trouble they cause you. Like the rocks in the Salmon River I mentioned in the preface, they are still there, but the comfort and enjoyment with which you make the trip can be powerfully influenced by how you mentally steer your way down the river.

Conclusion

O ur romance with technological treatment of disease must not come at the expense of caring for the people attached to the bodies we treat. There is now better reason than ever to put the *care* back into health care. The evidence in this book makes it clear that the human side of coping with disease is not merely an add-on, something to do after the "real" treatment is done, or an unnecessary luxury. Rather, it is as important as any other medical intervention, in that it can affect the course of the disease.

What people with life-threatening illness need and deserve is the best of both worlds: accurate and effective physical treatment coupled with support in expressing the feelings associated with being ill and dealing with a new life. "There are no diseases," said one professor of medicine, "only people with diseases." There are no treatments, I might add, only people participating in treatment. The best medical care is a combination of sophisticated, high-tech intervention with "low-tech" compassionate human support.

Let me summarize what we know so far about psychosocial support and cancer.

1. Support groups can improve the quality of life. Numerous studies in a variety of settings with people with many different types of

cancer have shown that those who participate in support groups are less anxious and depressed, have better coping skills, and are less beset by symptoms such as pain and nausea.

2. A thorough understanding of illness requires not only knowledge about the nature of the illness and its spread, but also of the person it affects and the physical and psychosocial factors that affect that person's response to treatment and resistance to the spread of the illness.

3. It is possible that as seriously ill people learn to better manage the inevitable stressors in their lives, they allow their bodies to devote their fullest resources to fighting the illness. In some, and perhaps many, cases this can affect the progression of the disease for the better.

4. This is different from denying the illness, wishing it away, visualizing it away, or maintaining a "positive attitude." None of these has been proven to be effective treatment.

5. The most effective psychological techniques involve facing the seriousness of the illness directly, and using that confrontation with limits to better manage your life, family relationships, interactions with physicians, and your own feelings about having the illness.

6. There is no evidence that such techniques are a cure for illness, but there *is* some evidence that such techniques may prolong life with cancer, heart disease, and other chronic diseases.

7. Should future research confirm these results, group support should become an integral part of routine care for people with life-threatening illness.

There clearly is a need for more studies about the interaction between mind and body, and we as well as other investigators are doing those studies. There is a growing awareness among people with cancer and their families, as well as in the public at large, that research on psychosocial aspects of cancer, including the effects of support groups, has lagged behind traditional biomedical cancer research. Why is this? First, we have difficulty conceptualizing the relationship between talking and physical change, an issue I have tried to address in this book. We tend to assume that only a physical treatment can have physical effects, despite the fact that our moment-to-moment experience of life rests upon constant translation of mental into physical processes.

Second, there is a pecking order within science, starting with the "hard" physical sciences examining the most minute phenomena, and working its way down, as the phenomena become larger, from atoms to molecules to organic compounds to small organisms to larger ones, and finally to those large, clumsy creatures with big brains and complex motives called "humans." Many hard scientists feel that the problems of people are simply too complex to be scientifically studied. I, of course, do not agree. If you frame your questions carefully and use systematic measures and techniques, you can ask clear, simple questions and get reasonably clear answers.

Third, we have been so dedicated to curing cancer and other life-threatening illnesses that we have almost considered it an admission of defeat to settle for helping people live with it. The sad fact is that cancer mortality is actually increasing in the United States and elsewhere in the world, largely because people, especially women, are smoking more, not less. This is producing an epidemic of lung cancer among women, which has now surpassed breast cancer as the leading cancer killer of women in the United States. While there have been some spectacular successes in curing certain cancers, they do not affect large numbers of patients. Until a general cure is found, which would be wonderful, we must direct more of our attention to preventing cancer before it starts and to helping those people who have it and must live and die with it.

Recently the Congress took special notice of the human side of cancer care, putting into its appropriation to the National Cancer Institute an instruction that $20 million of the money be spent on psychosocial research. This unusual instruction was meant to loosen the absolute lock on research funds for biological research and direct some small proportion toward helping people cope with the disease.

Some may wonder whether or not it is possible that mere talking and social support could have an effect on the course of cancer. The number-one question my patients have is "Will it help me live longer?" Our initial studies suggest this may be true, but few would doubt its effect on the *quality* of life, and I feel that it is essential to focus on that issue instead. Little in life prepares us to face and cope with a serious and progressive disease. A life-threatening illness by definition invades every nook and cranny of our bodies and our lives, and we need and benefit from help in dealing with it. Yet psychotherapeutic interventions are still often viewed in medicine as add-ons, interesting but fundamentally unimportant, the icing on the cake but not real sustenance. Perhaps it is time to change that outlook, to examine the possibility that supportive psychotherapy is not only humane but effective, a medical treatment as well as a psychological one. Mind and body are complex and interactive in output, why not in input as well? And why not mobilize our abilities to help one another live as well as we can with serious disease? This means "living beyond limits" in at least two senses. You are realistically facing the limits imposed by life in general, and illness in particular, and using that confrontation to live your life as fully as possible. And by doing that, you may indeed live beyond the limit your disease ordinarily imposes.

If you or someone you love is ill, use it as an occasion to reassess your life, strengthen the ties that matter, and eliminate the ones that don't. Look hard at what you and your body are facing, deal with the feelings of fear and sadness, and put it into perspective. Take charge of your treatment, allocate your time the way you want to, and savor every moment you have. "Have we lived longer yet?" asked Pam at the end of one of our group sessions. My answer is: By living better you are living longer. You are living beyond limits.

Readings and
References

Preface

Riessman, F. 1965. The "helper therapy" principle. *Social Work* 10:27–32.
This article describes an experiment in which children classified as poor readers improved their skills by becoming teachers to other students.

Yalom, I. D. 1980. *Existential psychotherapy.* New York: Basic Books.
Professor Yalom of Stanford, a noted authority on psychotherapy research, provides a lucid description of ways in which fundamental existential issues—freedom, death, meaning, and isolation—can become powerful psychotherapeutic tools.

1. Weathering the Diagnosis

Bukberg, J., D. Penman, and J. C. Holland. 1984. Depression in hospitalized cancer patients. *Psychosomatic Medicine* 46:199–212.
In this study, Dr. Holland and her excellent psychooncology group at Memorial Sloan Kettering Cancer Center demonstrate that many cancer patients become depressed but the depression is not recognized because symptoms of depression, such as sadness, fatigue, and loss of appetite, can be symptoms of cancer and its treatment as well.

Derogatis, L. R., et al. 1983. The prevalence of psychiatric disorders among cancer patients. *JAMA* 249:751–57.

In this study, Dr. Derogatis from Johns Hopkins and colleagues at several other medical centers found that some form of emotional disturbance (many of them transient) affected almost half of the cancer patients they studied.

Lazarus, R., and S. Folkman. 1984. *Stress, appraisal, and coping.* New York: Springer.
In this classic work, the authors describe fundamental principles and types of coping, which involve the style of gathering information, managing emotion, and solving stress-related problems.

Massie, M., and J. C. Holland. 1989. Overview of normal reactions and prevalence of psychiatric disorders. In *Handbook of psychooncology: Psychological care of the patient with cancer.* Ed. J. C. Holland and J. H. Rowland. New York: Oxford University Press.
This chapter provides an excellent overview of normal and abnormal emotional reactions to the diagnosis and treatment of cancer. It is part of an outstanding textbook on the psychological, psychiatric, and social issues which affect cancer patients.

———. 1990. Depression and the cancer patient. *Journal of Clinical Psychiatry* 51[7, suppl]: 12–17.
This study documents the frequency of clinical depression in cancer patients and the ease with which it is overlooked because of the similarity between the symptoms of depression and cancer.

2. The Lull After the Storm

Fobair, P., R. T. Hoppe, J. R. Bloom, R. Cox, A. Varghese, and D. Spiegel. 1986. Psychosocial problems among survivors of Hodgkin's Disease. *Journal of Clinical Oncology* 4:805–14.
———. 1989. Work patterns among long-term survivors of Hodgkin's Disease. In *Work and illness: The cancer patient.* Ed. I. Barofsky. New York: Praeger.
In these articles, Pat Fobair, Richard Hoppe, and colleagues at Stanford's Department of Radiation Oncology found that problems facing individuals with Hodgkin's Disease, a cancer of the lymphatic system, include loss of energy, which may last as long as a year after radiotherapy and

chemotherapy end. Furthermore, they found that one of the most stressful times for these individuals emotionally is when the active medical treatment ends.

Koocher, G. P., and J. L. O'Malley. 1981. *The Damocles syndrome: Psychosocial consequences of surviving childhood cancer.* New York: McGraw-Hill.

These Harvard researchers describe the stress associated with fears of cancer recurrence.

3. Illness, Personality, and Coping

Cassileth, B., E. J. Lusk, D. S. Miller, L. L. Brown, and C. Miller. 1985. Psychosocial correlates of survival in advanced malignant disease? *New England Journal of Medicine* 312:1551–55.

A major study showing no relationship between personality variables and cancer survival.

Fox, B. 1989. Depressive symptoms and the risk of cancer. *JAMA* 262:1231.

Professor Fox, a noted research methodologist from Boston University, reviews the evidence linking depression and cancer, and finds it wanting.

Friedman, M., and R. H. Rosenman. 1981. *Type A behavior and your heart.* New York: Fawcett.

———. 1984. *Treating Type A behavior and your heart.* New York: Knopf.

Drs. Friedman and Rosenman describe their discovery of the relationship between the hard-driving Type A personality style and heart disease, and how to treat it.

Greer, S., and T. Morris. 1975. Psychological attributes of women who develop breast cancer: A controlled study. *Journal of Psychosomatic Research* 19:147–53.

These British researchers found that women who came to have a biopsy of a breast lump, and who ultimately had a malignancy, were less likely to report having expressed anger openly than those whose biopsy revealed a benign lump.

Greer, S., and M. Watson. 1985. Toward a psychobiological model of cancer: psychological considerations. *Social Science in Medicine* 20:773–77.

British psychologists Steven Greer and Maggie Watson review evidence suggesting that psychological factors may influence the course of cancer.

Greer, S., T. Morris, and K. W. Pettingale. 1979. Psychological response to breast cancer: Effect on outcome. *Lancet* 2:785–87.
This is the original article in which the British research team showed an effect of "fighting spirit" on outcome.

House, J. S., K. R. Landis, and D. Umberson. 1988. Social relationships and health. *Science* 241:540–44.
In this excellent review article in the noted journal *Science,* James House and his colleagues review the strong evidence that social support reduces the risk of dying. They note that the relationship between social isolation and mortality is as great as that between high-serum cholesterol or smoking and mortality.

Jamison, R. N., T. G. Burish, and K. A. Walston. 1987. Psychogenic factors in predicting survival of breast cancer patients. *Journal of Clinical Oncology* 5:768–72.
These researchers at Vanderbilt found no relationship between psychological factors and survival time of women with breast cancer.

Kneier, A. W., and L. Temoshok. 1984. Repressive coping reactions in patients with malignant melanoma as compared to cardiovascular disease patients. *Journal of Psychosomatic Research* 28:145–55.
Patients with this cancer of the skin showed more of a tendency to repress feelings than did a comparison sample of individuals with heart disease.

Morris, T. A. 1980. Type C for cancer: Low trait anxiety and the pathogenesis of breast cancer. *Cancer Detection and Prevention* 3:102.
Here a personality style of someone at increased risk for cancer, opposite to the Type A personality prone to heart disease, is proposed.

Morris, T., S. Greer, and K. Pettingale. 1981. Patterns of expression of anger and their psychological correlates in women with breast cancer. *Journal of Psychosomatic Research* 25:111–18.
These British researchers develop their notion that cancer patients are less likely than most others to express anger openly.

Multiple Risk Factor Intervention Trial Research Group. 1986. Relationship between baseline risk factors and coronary heart disease and total mortality in the Multiple Risk Factor Intervention Trial. *Preventive Medicine* 15:254–73.

This major study attempted to show that changing health habits leads to reduction in death from heart disease. Its ability to show that was limited by the fact that many individuals randomly assigned to the control condition also (and fortunately for them if not the study) improved their health habits.

Ornish, D., S. E. Brown, L. W. Scherwitz, J. H. Billings, et al. 1990. Can lifestyle changes reverse coronary heart disease? The Lifestyle Heart Trial. *Lancet* 336(8708):129–33.

Ornish, D. 1982 *Stress, diet, & your heart*. New York: Holt, Rinehart and Winston.

———. 1990. *Dr. Dean Ornish's program for reversing heart disease*. New York: Random House.

In this study and two books, Dr. Dean Ornish provides evidence that a combination of group support, meditation, exercising and a careful low-fat diet can reverse coronary artery disease. He provides much useful information on means to use the stress of heart disease to reorganize priorities and change lifestyle in a positive way.

Pettingale, K. W. 1985. Towards a psychobiological model of cancer: Biological considerations. *Social Science in Medicine* 20:779–87.

Dr. Pettingale reviews evidence that psychological factors may influence the course of cancer.

Ragland, D. R., R. J. Brand, and B. H. Fox. 1992. Type A/B behavior and cancer mortality: The confounding/mediating effect of covariates. *Psycho-Oncology* 1:25–34.

A thoughtful and cautionary review which indicates how relationships between personality and cancer mortality may be more apparent than real.

Ramirez, A. J., T. K. Craig, J. P. Watson, I. S. Fentiman, W. R. North, and R. D. Ruebons. 1989. Stress and relapse of breast cancer. *British Medical Journal* 298:291–93.

Dr. Ramirez showed that relapse of breast cancer was more likely among women experiencing serious stress.

Rodin, J. 1980. Managing the stress of aging: The role of control and coping. In *Coping and health*. Ed. S. Levine and H. Ursin. New York: Plenum.

Professor Rodin, a noted Yale health psychologist, reviews evidence that even older people who are quite ill and in nursing homes can improve their health when given control by performing active roles.

Shekelle, R. B., W. J. Raynor, A. M. Ostfeld, et al. 1981. Psychological depression in seventeen-year risk of death from cancer. *Psychosomatic Medicine* 43:117–25.

This study of a Western Electric factory showed that depressed individuals were at higher risk for developing cancer. However, a later, large-scale study by Zonderman and colleagues failed to confirm this one.

Siegel, B. 1986. *Love, medicine, and miracles*. New York: Harper & Row.

In this widely read book, Dr. Siegel, a surgeon, gives his prescriptions for maintaining a positive attitude about cancer and weeding out inner "needs" for cancer.

Simonton, O. C., S. Matthews-Simonton, and J. Creighton. *Getting well again: A step-by-step, self-help guide to overcoming cancer for patients and their families*. Los Angeles: J. P. Tarcher.

In this widely read book, attitude and visualization are presented as treatments for cancer.

Spiegel, D. 1990. Facilitating emotional coping during treatment. *Cancer* 66:1422–26.

I review means of helping people with their emotional reactions to cancer and other problems such as pain and treatment side effects.

Taylor, S. E. 1989. *Positive illusions: Creative self-deception and the healthy mind*. New York: Basic Books.

———. 1983. Adjustment to threatening events. *American Psychologist* 38:1161–78.

Professor Taylor, a psychologist at UCLA, presents her theory that positive illusions are an important means of adapting to a stressful world.

Temoshok, L. 1987. Personality, coping style, emotion and cancer: Towards an integrative model. *Cancer Surveys* 6:545–67.

———. 1985. Biopsychosocial studies on cutaneous malignant melanoma: Psychosocial factors associated with prognostic indicators, progression, psychophysiology and tumor-host response. *Social Science in Medicine* 20:833–40.

Temoshok, L., and H. Dreher. 1992. *The Type C connection: The behavioral links to cancer and your health.* New York: Random House.

Temoshok, L., B. W. Heller, R. W. Sagebiel, M. S. Blois, D. M. Sweet, R. J. DiClemente, and M. L. Gold. 1985. The relationship of psychosocial factors to prognostic indicators in cutaneous malignant melanoma. *Journal of Psychosomatic Research.* 29:139–53.
Lydia Temoshok, a research psychologist, presents evidence that suppression of emotion (Type C personality style) is related to more rapid cancer progression.

Thoresen, C. E., M. Friedman, L. Powell, et al. 1985. Altering the Type-A behavior pattern in postinfarction patients. *Journal of Cardiopulmonary Rehabilitation* 5:258–66.
Professor Thoresen, a noted Stanford psychologist, provides evidence that the Type-A behavior pattern can be changed, even among individuals who have already suffered a heart attack.

Trichopoulos, D., K. Katsouyanni, X. Zavitsanos, A. Tzonou, and P. Dalla-Vorgia. 1983. Psychological stress and fatal heart attack: The Athens (1981) earthquake natural experiment. *Lancet* 1:441–44.
This study shows that stress increases the risk of a serious heart attack.

Watson, M., S. Greer, J. Pruyn, and B. Van Den Borne. 1990. Locus of control and adjustment to cancer. *Psychological Reports* 66:39–48.
These well-known British researchers demonstrate that when cancer patients feel in control of the *course* of their illness, their emotional adjustment is better, but those who feel responsible for the *cause* of the illness feel worse.

Weinberger, D. A. 1989. The construct validity of the repressive coping style. In *Repression and dissociation: Defense mechanisms and personality style*. Ed. J. L. Singer. Chicago: University of Chicago Press.

Weinberger, D. A., G. E. Schwartz, and R. J. Davidson. 1979. Low-anxious, high-anxious, and repressive coping styles: Psychometric patterns and behavioral and physiological responses to stress. *Journal of Abnormal Psychology* 88:369–80.

Noted psychologist Daniel Weinberger describes individuals who repress awareness of negative feelings. There are psychological, social, and health correlates of their personality style.

Williams, R. 1989. *The trusting heart*. New York: Times Books.

——. 1990. The role of the brain in physical disease: Folklore, normal science, or paradigm shift? *JAMA* 263:1971–72.

Dr. Williams at Duke University demonstrates that hostility and impatience are the key risk-increasing components of the Type A personality style.

Zonderman, A. B., P. Costa and R. R. McCrae. 1989. Depression as a risk for cancer morbidity and mortality in a nationally representative sample. *JAMA* 262:1191–95.

In this study, no evidence was found in a large sample of individuals to support the theory that depression makes it more likely that one will develop cancer.

4. Does Living Better Mean Living Longer?

Ader, R., ed. 1981. *Psychoneuroimmunology*. New York: Academic Press.

Ader, R., D. L. Felten, and N. Cohen, eds. 1991. *Psychoneuroimmunology*, 2nd edition. New York: Academic Press.

These are classic overviews of the entire field of psychoneuroimmunology, providing the evidence that such factors as stress and social support, as well as conditioned learning, influence various measures of immune system functioning.

——. 1990. Interactions between the brain and the immune system. *Annual Review of Pharmacology and Toxicology* 30:561–602.

This is an excellent recent overview of new developments in psychoneuroimmunology. In particular, these authors, pioneers in this field, review evidence that there is extensive two-way communication between the brain and the immune system. Organs important to the immune system, such as the spleen, are heavily enervated. White blood cells have receptors on their surfaces for neurotransmitters, the substances by which nerve cells communicate with one another, and in turn these neurons have receptors for cytokines—substances such as interferon and interleuken—which are secreted by white blood cells and which stimulate the immune response.

Angell, M. 1985. Disease as a reflection of the psyche. *New England Journal of Medicine.* 312:1570–72.

This widely quoted editorial was highly critical of the idea that personality and emotion had any effect on the risk of getting cancer or the speed of its progression. While some of this criticism is valid, the editorial overlooked much solid research showing some relationship between the two.

Antoni, M. H., and K. Goodkin. 1989. Host moderator variables in the promotion of cervical neoplasia-II: Dimensions of life stress. *Journal of Psychosomatic Research* 33/4:457–67.

Antoni, M. H., N. Schneiderman, M. A. Fletcher, D. A. Goldstein, G. Ironson, and A. Lapierre. 1990. Psychoneuroimmunology and HIV-1. *Journal of Consulting and Clinical Psychology* 58:38–49.

In these articles, the excellent University of Miami research group reviews evidence that stress, social support, exercise, and other psychological and social factors influence immune functions in normal individuals, cancer patients, and, to a lesser extent, among individuals with the Human Immunodeficiency Virus.

Ben-Eliyahu, et al. 1991. Stress increases metastatic spread of mammary tumor in rats: Evidence for mediation by the immune system. *Brain, Behavior, and Immunity* 5:193–205.

This study shows that in animals, stress causes an increase in the spread of breast tumors, and this effect may be mediated by stress-induced immunosuppression.

Berkman, L. F., and S. L. Syme. 1979. Social networks, host resistance, and mortality: A nine-year follow-up study of Alameda County residents. *American Journal of Epidemiology* 109:186–204.

This is a classic study demonstrating that social isolation is associated with increased risk of dying.

Bonneterre, J., J. P. Peyrat, B. Vandewalle, R. Beuscart, M. C. Vie, and P. Cappelaere. 1982. Prolactin receptors in human breast cancer. *European Journal of Cancer and Clinical Oncology* 18:1157–62.
This study demonstrates that prolactin, a stress hormone, may be involved in the progression of breast cancer.

Bovard, E. W. 1985. Brain mechanisms in effects of social support on viability. *Perspectives on Behavioral Medicine* 2:103–29.
In this article, Bovard explains possible mechanisms by which means of coping with illness may influence how rapidly the illness progresses.

Bovbjerg, D. Psychoneuroimmunology and cancer. 1989. In *Handbook of Psychooncology*. Eds. J. C. Holland and J. H. Rowland. New York: Oxford University Press.
This is a good review chapter on the relationship between immune function and the psychological and social variables which may influence it in cancer.

Derogatis, L. R., M. D. Abeloff, and N. Melisartos. 1979. Psychological coping mechanisms and survival time in metastatic breast cancer. *JAMA* 242: 1504–08.
In this widely cited study, Dr. Derogatis and his colleagues at the Johns Hopkins Medical School divided women with breast cancer into two groups: those who survived more than a year and those who did not. He found that the long survivors were considered less cooperative by the medical staff, suggesting that being a bit feisty is good for you.

Fawzy, F., N. Cousins, N. Fawzy, M. Kemeny, R. Elashoff, and D. Morton. 1990. A structured psychiatric intervention for cancer patients. *Archives of General Psychiatry* 47:720–25.
———. 1990. A structured psychiatric intervention for cancer patients: II, Changes over time in immunological measures. *Archives of General Psychiatry* 47: 729–35.
Fawzy, I. F., N. W. Fawzy, C. S. Hyun, R. Elashoff, D. Guthrie, J. Fahey, and D. Morton. 1993. Malignant melanoma: Effects of early structured

psychiatric intervention, coping, and affective state on recurrence and survival six years later. *Archives of General Psychiatry* 50: September issue.

Dr. Fawzy and his colleagues at UCLA have worked on a randomized trial of short-term group therapy for patients with malignant melanoma, a form of skin cancer. The patients who received the group support did better emotionally and on certain measures of immune function showed stronger killing activity at six-month follow-up. More recently, Dr. Fawzy has reported longer time to recurrence and fewer deaths among the patients given the group therapy at six-year follow-up.

Goodwin, J. S., W. C. Hunt, C. R. Key, and J. M. Samet. 1987. The effect of marital status on stage, treatment, and survival of cancer patients. *JAMA* 258:3125–30.

This study of 27,779 cancer patients shows that unmarried cancer patients are diagnosed later, receive poorer treatment, and, even taking this into account, are also less likely to survive as long as married cancer patients.

Herberman, R. 1985. Natural killer (NK) cells: Characteristics and possible role in resistance against tumor growth. In *Immunity to Cancer*. Eds., A. E. Reif and M. S. Mitchell. San Diego: Academic Press.

Dr. Herberman, a noted immunologist, describes how natural killer cells, the function of which has been shown to be influenced by stress and social isolation, play a role in fighting tumor growth.

Hislop, T. G., N. E. Waxler, H. A. Coldman, J. N. Elwood, and L. Kan. 1987. The prognostic significance of psychosocial factors in women with breast cancer. *Journal of Chronic Disease* 40:729–35.

These authors review the relationship between psychosocial variables and the progression of breast cancer.

Horowitz, R. I., C. M. Viscoli, L. Berkman, R. M. Donaldson, S. M. Horwitz, C. F. Murray, D. F. Ransohoff, and J. Sindelar. 1990. Treatment adherence and risk of death after a myocardial infarction. *Lancet* 336:542–45.

This study demonstrated that taking pills as prescribed reduced mortality by a factor of two-and-a-half times in the year after a heart attack, regardless of whether the pill contained a heart rhythm regulator (beta blocker) or was a pharmacologically inactive placebo.

Institute of Medicine. 1989. *Behavioral influences on the endocrine and immune systems.* Washington, D.C.: National Academy Press.

This report from the prestigious Institute of Medicine reviewed the literature on the effects of social, psychological, and behavioral factors on the functioning of the endocrine and immune systems. They reached a cautiously positive conclusion about the relationship among these factors.

Irwin, M., M. Daniels, T. L. Smith, E. Bloom, and H. Weiner. 1987. Impaired natural killer cell activity during bereavement. *Brain, Behavior, and Immunity* 1:98–104.

Irwin, M., M. Daniels, S. C. Risch, E. Bloom, and H. Weiner. 1988. Plasma cortisol and natural killer cell activity during bereavement. *Biological Psychiatry* 24:173–78.

Irwin, M., M. Daniels, and H. Weiner. 1987. Immune and neuroendocrine changes during bereavement. *Psychiatric Clinics of North America* 10:449–65.

This leading psychoneuroimmunology research group found evidence of immunosuppression during bereavement.

Kennedy, S., J. K. Kiecolt-Glaser, and R. Glaser. 1988. Immunological consequences of acute and chronic stressors: Mediating role of interpersonal relationships. *British Journal of Medical Psychology* 61:77–85.

In this article, members of the Ohio State psychoneuroimmunology research group demonstrate that social support reduces the adverse effects of stress on the immune system.

Kiecolt-Glaser, J. K., R. Glaser, C. Dyer, E. C. Shuttleworth, P. Ogrocki, and C. E. Speicher. 1987. Chronic stress and immune function in family caregivers of Alzheimer's disease victims. *Psychosomatic Medicine* 49:523–35.

The Ohio State research team demonstrated reductions in measures of immune function among individuals suffering the distress of caring for a family member with Alzheimer's disease.

Kiecolt-Glaser, J. K., W. Garner, C. E. Speicher, G. M. Penn, J. Holliday, and R. Glaser. 1984. Psychosocial modifiers of immunocompetence in medical students. *Psychosomatic Medicine* 50:7–14.

Kiecolt-Glaser, J. K., R. Glaser, et al. 1986. Modulation of cellular immunity in medical students. *Journal of Behavioral Medicine* 9:5–21.

These studies show a decrease in natural killer cell activity during examinations among medical students. However, this stress-induced reduction in immune function did not occur among those students with good social support.

Kiecolt-Glaser, J. K., and R. Glaser. 1991. Stress and immune function in humans. In *Psychoneuroimmunology,* 2nd edition. Eds. R. Ader, D. L. Felten, and N. Cohen. New York: Academic Press.

In this article, the husband-and-wife team of Dr. Ronald Glaser, an immunologist, and Dr. Janice Kiecolt-Glaser, a psychologist, review evidence showing that stress is associated with reduction of certain aspects of immune function.

LaPierre, A. R., M. H. Antoni, N. Schneiderman, G. Ironson, N. Klimas, P. Caralis, and M. A. Fletcher. 1990. Exercise intervention attenuates emotional distress and natural killer cell decrements following notification of positive serologic status for HIV-1. *Biofeedback and Self-Regulation* 15:3, 229–42.

This team from the University of Miami demonstrated that simple exercise has both an emotional and a biological therapeutic effect on individuals who have been notified that they have contracted the virus that causes AIDS.

Levine, S., C. Coe, and S. G. Weiner. 1989. Psychoneuroendocrinology of stress: A psychobiological perspective. In *Psychoendocrinology.* Eds. F. R. Brush and S. Levine. New York: Academic Press.

This article by a noted Stanford authority on the endocrine effects of stress demonstrates that social support acts as a buffer against the physiological consequences of stress.

Levy, S. M., R. Herberman, M. Lippman, and T. d'Angelo. 1987. Correlation of stress factors with sustained depression of natural killer cell activity and predicted prognosis in patients with breast cancer. *Journal of Clinical Oncology* 5:348–53.

Levy, S. M., R. B. Herberman, T. Whiteside, K. Sanzo, J. Lee, and J. Kirkwood. 1990. Perceived social support and tumor estrogen/progesterone receptor status as predictors of natural killer cell activity in breast cancer patients. *Psychosomatic Medicine* 52:73–85.

These studies from the cancer immunology program at the University of Pittsburgh demonstrate associations among immune and endocrine function and the speed of progression of breast cancer.

Lorton, D., D. L. Bellinger, S. Y. Felten, and D. L. Felten. 1991. Substance P innervation of spleen in rats: Nerve fibers associate with lymphocytes and macrophages in specific compartments of the spleen. *Brain, Behavior, and Immunity* 5:29–40.

Madden, K. S., S. Y. Felten, D. L. Felten, P. R. Sundaresan, and S. Livnat. 1989. Sympathetic neural modulation of the immune system. I. Depression of T cell immunity *in vivo* and *vitro* following chemical sympathectomy. *Brain, Behavior, and Immunity* 3:72–89.

These studies demonstrate how the central nervous system connects to and can thereby influence the immune system.

Malarkey, W. B., M. Kennedy, L. E. Allred, and G. Milo. 1983. Physiological concentrations of prolactin can promote the growth of human breast tumor cells in culture. *Journal of Clinical Endocrinology & Metabolism* 56:673–77.

This study shows that prolactin, a stress hormone, can speed the rate of breast cancer growth.

Maxwell, R. M., G. A. Gellert, and B. S. Siegel. 1993. Survival of breast cancer patients receiving adjunctive psychosocial support therapy: A 10-year follow-up study. *Journal of Clinical Oncology* 11:66–69.

Morgenstern, H., G. A. Gellert, S. D. Walter, A. M. Ostfeld, and B. S. Siegel. 1984. The impact of a psychosocial support program on survival with breast cancer: The importance of selection bias in program evaluation. *Journal of Chronic Disease* 37:273–82.

In these articles, of which Dr. Bernie Siegel is a co-author, a follow-up study was conducted on a group of patients who participated in Dr. Siegel's Exceptional Cancer Patient program. Their survival rates were compared to that of a matched (but not random) comparison sample of cancer patients. No differences in survival were observed between the two groups.

Pennebaker, J. W., J. K. Kiecolt-Glaser, and R. Glaser. 1988. Disclosure of traumas and immune function: Health implications for psychotherapy. *Journal of Consulting and Clinical Psychology* 56:239–45.
This intriguing study demonstrated that simply keeping a journal in which memories of trauma were recorded had a positive effect on the functioning of the immune system.

Razavi, D., C. Farvacques, N. Delvaux, T. Beffort, M. Paesmans, G. Leclercq, P. van Houtte, and R. Paredaens. 1990. Psychosocial correlates of estrogen and progesterone receptors in breast cancer. *Lancet* 335:931–33.
This study showed that breast cancer patients who were less anxious and depressed had tumors which were more likely to contain estrogen and progesterone receptors, which carries with it a better prognosis.

Richardson, J. L., D. R. Shelton, M. Krailo, and A. M. Levine. 1990. The effect of compliance with treatment on survival among patients with hematologic malignancies. *Journal of Clinical Oncology* 8:356–64.
This important study from the University of Southern California demonstrates that patients with lymphoma or leukemia who received a counseling intervention complied better with treatment and, independent of that, lived longer than did control patients who received routine care.

Riley, V. 1981. Psychoneuroendocrine influences on immunocompetence and neoplasia. *Science* 212:1100–09.
———. 1975. Mouse mammary tumors: Alteration of incidence as apparent function of stress. *Science* 189:465–67.
These classic studies demonstrate that crowding and other forms of social stress speed the development of tumors in animals.

Rodin, J. 1986. Health, control, and aging. In *Aging and the psychology of control*. Eds. M. M. Baltes and P. B. Baltes. Hillsdale, NJ: Earlbaum.
In this article, Dr. Rodin, an outstanding investigator and professor of psychology at Yale, demonstrates that older people given control of

various activities in their environment do better both emotionally and physically.

Rogentine, G. N., D. P. van Kammen, B. H. Fox, J. P. Docherty, J. E. Rosenblatt, and S. C. Boyd. 1979. Psychological factors in the prognosis of malignant melanoma: A prospective study. *Psychosomatic Medicine* 41:647–58.

This is one of several studies that demonstrated that a fighting spirit is associated with better prognosis.

Rose, R. M. 1984. Overview of endocrinology of stress. In *Neuroendocrinology and psychiatric disorder*. Eds. G. M. Brown, et al. New York: Raven Press.

Dr. Rose, a noted expert on the endocrine effects of stress, reviews the literature on the relationship between stress and endocrine function, especially cortisol.

Schleifer, S. J., S. E. Keller, M. Camerino, J. C. Thornton, and M. Stein. 1983. Suppression of lymphocyte stimulation following bereavement. *Journal of the American Medical Association* 250:374–77.

Schleifer, S. J., S. E. Keller, R. N. Bond, et al. 1989. Major depressive disorder and immunity: Role of age, sex, severity, and hospitalization. *Archives of General Psychiatry* 46:81–87.

Schleifer, S. J., S. E. Keller, A. T. Meyerson, et al. 1984. Lymphocyte function in major depressive disorder. *Archives of General Psychiatry* 41:484–86.

These studies demonstrated that severe depression and bereavement are associated with poorer immune function.

Shafie, S., and S. C. Brooks. 1977. Effect of prolactin on growth and the estrogen receptor level of human breast cancer cells (MCF-7). *Cancer Research* 37:792–99.

This study shows that prolactin, a stress hormone, can stimulate tumor growth.

Sieber, W. J., J. Rodin, L. Larson, S. Ortega, N. Cummings, S. Levy, T. Whiteside, and R. Herberman. 1992. Modulation of human natural killer cell activity by exposure to uncontrollable stress. *Brain, Behavior, and Immunity* 2:141–56.

This inventive study shows that it is specifically the experienced controllability of a stressor that mediates the negative effect of stress on immune function. The same stressor (a noise) reduced natural killer cell activity when subjects knew they could not control it, but did not when they thought they could control it.

Sklar, L. S., and H. Anisman. 1979. Stress and coping factors influence tumor growth. *Science* 205:347–65.
A review of early literature showing that social and psychological factors can inhibit or speed up tumor growth.

Solomon, G. F., and L. Temoshok. 1987. A psychoneuroimmunologic perspective on AIDS research: Questions, preliminary findings and suggestions. *Journal of Applied Social Psychology* 17:286–308.
This article applies knowledge about psychoneuroimmunolgy and cancer to the development and progression of AIDS.

Spiegel, D. 1990. Editorial: Can psychotherapy prolong cancer survival? *Psychosomatics* 31:361–66.
———. 1991. Mind matters: Effects of group support on cancer patients. *Journal of NIH Research* 3:61–62.
———. 1991. A psychosocial intervention and survival time of patients with metastatic breast cancer. *Advances* 7:10–19.
———. 1991. Psychosocial treatment and cancer survival. *Harvard Mental Health Letter* 7:4–6.
———. 1993. Psychosocial intervention in cancer. *Journal of the National Cancer Institute* 85:1198–1205.

Spiegel, D., and S. Sands. 1989. Psychological influences on neoplastic disease progression. In *Metastasis/Dissemination*. Ed. E. L. Gorelik. Dordrecht, The Netherlands: Kluwer Academic Publishers.
In these articles I summarize our research on group therapy with breast cancer patients and explore its implications for the treatment of cancer.

Spiegel, D., J. R. Bloom, H. C. Kraemer, and E. Gottheil. 1989. Effect of psychosocial treatment on survival of patients with metastatic breast cancer. *Lancet* ii: 888–91.

This is the original study in which we reported that women who received Supportive/Expressive group therapy lived significantly longer than those who did not.

———. 1989. Psychological support for cancer patients. *Lancet* ii:1447.
In this letter we discuss responses to our original report, including several proposals that reducing secretion of stress hormones might slow tumor growth.

Stein, M., A. H. Miller, and R. L. Trestman. 1991. Depression, the immune system, and health and illness: Findings in search of meanings. *Archives of General Psychiatry* 48:171–77.
This is a thoughtful and conservative review of the research findings linking depression with suppression of immune function.

Visintainer, M. A., J. R. Volpicelli, and M. E. P. Seligman. 1982. Tumor rejection in rats after inescapable and escapable shocks. *Science* 216: 437–39.
This study showed that stressful shocks which could not be avoided reduced rates of tumor rejection.

Webber, M. M. 1986. Prolactin in the etiology and progression of human prostate carcinoma. *Proceedings of AACR* 27:222.
This study showed that prolactin, a stress hormone, speeds the progression of cancer of the prostate.

5. A Little Help from My Friends

Bloom, J. R., and D. Spiegel. 1984. The relationship of two dimensions of social support to the psychological well-being and social functioning of women with advanced breast cancer. *Social Science in Medicine* 19(8):831–37.
In this study, my colleague Dr. Bloom from the University of California at Berkeley and I observed an interaction between social support for patients with advanced breast cancer and their ability to function well and feel good about themselves. Loss of social support results in reduced social activities and self-esteem, which in turn leads to further loss of social support.

Caplan, G. 1964. *Principles of preventive psychiatry*. New York: Basic Books.

Caplan, G., and M. Killilea. 1976. *Support systems and mutual help: Multidisciplinary explorations*. New York: Grune & Stratton.

Classic descriptions by a pioneering community psychiatrist of the importance of community networks in helping people adapt to stress.

Ferlic, M., A. Goldman and B. J. Kennedy. 1979. Group counseling in adult patients with advanced cancer. *Cancer* 43:760–66.

In this article, the authors demonstrate that support groups are effective in reducing emotional disturbance among cancer patients.

Maguire, P., A. Tait, M. Brooke, C. Thomas, and R. Sellwood. 1980. Effect of counselling on the psychiatric morbidity associated with mastectomy. *British Medical Journal* 231:1454–56.

This study demonstrated that early detection and treatment of cancer patients prone to depression results in far more effective treatment.

Spiegel, D. 1993. Psychosocial intervention in cancer. *Journal of the National Cancer Institute* 85:1198–1205.

Spiegel, D., J. R. Bloom, and I. D. Yalom. 1981. Group support for patients with metastatic cancer: A randomized prospective outcome study. *Archives of General Psychiatry* 38:527–33.

Spiegel, D., and I. D. Yalom. 1984. A support group for dying patients. In *Coping with Physical Illness*, 2d edition. Ed. R. H. Moos. New York: Plenum.

Spira, J. L., and D. Spiegel. 1993. Group psychotherapy in the medically ill. 1993. In *Principles of Medical Psychiatry* 2d edition. Eds. B. Fogel and A. Stoudemire.

In these articles my colleagues and I describe the psychotherapeutic processes in our and similar support groups, and report on the effects of these groups on participants.

Turner, R. J. 1981. Social support as a contingency in psychological well-being. *Journal of Health and Social Behavior* 22:357–67.

A good review of data on the interplay between social and psychological adaptation.

Waxler-Morrison, N., T. G. Hislop, B. Mears, and L. Kan. 1991. Effects of social relationships on survival for women with breast cancer: A prospective study. *Social Science in Medicine* 33:177–83.

This research group from the University of British Columbia in Vancouver found that support from friends, relatives, and neighbors predicted lower mortality rates from breast cancer.

Wood, P. E., I. Milligan, D. Christ, and D. Liff. 1978. Group counseling for cancer patients in a community hospital. *Psychosomatics* 19:555–61.

A good description of how group therapy for cancer patients can work well in standard medical settings.

Yalom, I. D. 1985. *Theory and practice of group psychotherapy,* 3d edition. New York: Basic Books.

This is the classic textbook on group psychotherapy.

6. Detoxifying Dying

Bateson, G. *Steps to an ecology of mind.* New York: Ballantine, 1972.

A well-known anthropologist challenges our ideas of knowing, pointing out that many of our "explanations" for things we do not understand, such as gravity, merely "put to sleep the critical faculty."

Bugenthal, J. 1965. *The search for authenticity.* New York: Holt, Rinehart & Winston.

Dr. Bugenthal, a noted existentially oriented psychotherapist, describes means of helping people confront, acknowledge, and incorporate basic realities of life, including death, loss of abilities, and the transience of many of the roles we play in life.

Kierkegaard, S. K. 1954. *Fear and trembling* and *The sickness unto death.* Trans. W. Lowrie. New York: Doubleday.

Two of the Danish existential philosopher's most important works, examining values and roles in life, faith, and the ability to face death in the future as a means of living the present fully. These books are a profound existential philosophical examination of the threat of death and its effect on authentic living.

Kübler-Ross, E. *On death and dying.* New York: Macmillan, 1969.
The widely read book by a compassionate physician who took time to listen
   to and talk with dying patients. She described "stages" of coming to
   terms with dying, including denial, bargaining, anger, and acceptance.

Lindemann, E. 1944. Symptomatology and management of acute grief. *American Journal of Psychiatry* 101:141–48.
A classic article describing the normal and abnormal grieving processes ob-
   served in survivors of the tragic Coconut Grove nightclub fire in Boston.

Sartre, J. P. *Being and nothingness,* trans. Hazel Barnes. New York: Philosophical Library, 1956.
A major work by the well-known French existential philosopher. He contrasts
   authentic existence with the instrumental, "objective" view that others
   usually have of our existence.

Spiegel, D., and M. S. Glafkides. 1983. Effects of group confrontation with
   death and dying. *International Journal of Group Psychotherapy* 33:433–
   47.

Spiegel, D., and I. D. Yalom. 1978. A support group for dying patients.
   International Journal of Group Psychotherapy 28:233–45.
Descriptions of our experience in group therapy with dying patients, showing
   that direct confrontation with death is not demoralizing, but rather helps
   patients cope more effectively with their fears of dying and death.

Taylor, S. E. 1989. *Positive illusions: Creative self-deception and the healthy
   mind.* New York: Basic Books.
———. 1983. Adjustment to threatening events. *American Psychologist* 38:
   1161–78.
Professor Taylor, a psychologist at UCLA, presents her theory that positive
   illusions are an important means of adapting to a stressful world.

Weisman, A. D., and J. W. Worden. 1975. Psychosocial analysis of cancer
   deaths. *Omega* 6:61–75.
This psychiatrist/psychologist team from the Massachusetts General Hospital
   describe processes and stages of dying, including mitigation, accommodation, deterioration, and decline.

Yalom, I. D. 1980. *Existential psychotherapy*. New York: Basic Books.

Professor Yalom of Stanford, a noted authority on psychotherapy research, provides a lucid description of ways in which fundamental existential issues—freedom, death, meaning, and isolation—can become powerful psychotherapeutic tools.

Yalom, I. D., and C. Greaves. 1977. Group therapy with the terminally ill. *American Journal of Psychiatry* 134:396–400.

A clear description from Stanford of group therapeutic processes in our early breast cancer support groups.

7. Taking Time

Bugenthal, J. 1965. *The search for authenticity*. New York: Holt, Rinehart & Winston.

Dr. Bugenthal, a noted existentially oriented psychotherapist, describes means of helping people confront, acknowledge, and incorporate basic realities of life, including death, loss of abilities, and the transience of many of the roles we play in life.

Kübler-Ross, E. *On death and dying*. New York: Macmillan, 1969.

The widely read book by a compassionate physician who took time to listen to and talk with dying patients. She described "stages" of coming to terms with dying, including denial, bargaining, anger, and acceptance.

8. Fortifying Families

Benjamin, H. H., and R. Trubo. 1987. *From victim to victor*. Los Angeles: Jeremy P. Tarcher.

The founder of the Wellness Community provides advice on common reactions to a diagnosis of cancer and on discussing it with family and friends. He recommends "directed visualization" and support groups.

Bettelheim, B. 1977. *The uses of enchantment*. New York: Vintage.

A noted child psychoanalyst describes the important purposes fairy tales and fantasies serve in the emotional and cognitive development of children.

Dollinger, M., E. H. Rosenbaum, and G. Cable. 1991. *Everyone's guide to cancer therapy: How cancer is diagnosed, treated, and managed day to day.* New York: Somerville House Books.

A thorough, illustrated, clearly written guide to the latest in cancer diagnosis, treatment, and supportive care. This book covers not only technical but personal aspects of coping with cancer, including relaxation techniques, home care, exercise, and sexual activity.

Dreifuss-Kattan, E. 1990. *Cancer stories: Creativity and self-repair.* Hillsdale, NJ: The Analytic Press.

An examination of the literary, artistic, and psychoanalytic understandings of living and dying with cancer.

Fallowfield, L., M. Baum, and G. Maguire. 1986. Effects of breast conservation on psychological morbidity associated with diagnosis and treatment of early breast cancer. *British Medical Journal* 293:1331–34.

These investigators found that anxiety about recurrence and possible differences in the types of patients offered breast conservation led to some unexpected emotional difficulties after the breast-sparing procedure.

Fiore, N. A. 1990. *The road back to health: Coping with the emotional aspects of cancer.* Berkeley, CA: Celestial Arts.

A psychologist who had cancer himself and published in the *New England Journal of Medicine* an article about his experience as a patient uses this and his professional knowledge to provide guidance about becoming an "active patient"—communicating with family and friends, and coping with stress, depression, helplessness, and the process of dying.

Goleman, D., and J. Gurin, Eds. 1993. *Mind/body medicine: How to use your mind for better health.* Yonkers, NY: Consumer Reports Books.

A clearly written, up-to-date examination of the relationship between the mind and medicine. Mind/body mechanisms are examined, along with mental effects for good or ill in specific diseases. Techniques for improving health using hypnosis, meditation, imagery, support groups, and psychotherapy, among others, are well described. The book provides a good list of resources and references.

Horowitz, M. J. 1976. *Stress response syndromes*. New York: Jason Aronson.
In this book, Dr. Horowitz, a noted research psychoanalyst, demonstrates
how people who have been through traumatic situations often alternate
between feeling overwhelmed by memories of the trauma and avoiding
any thought of it.

Kabat-Zinn, J. 1990. *Full catastrophe living: Using the wisdom of your body
and mind to face stress, pain, and illness*. New York: Delacorte Press.
Eastern meditation techniques are expertly applied to Western medical problems. The practice of "mindfulness" is described, along with means of
negotiating illness, and managing pain, anxiety, and stress.

Levy, S. M., L. T. Haynes, R. B. Herberman, J. Lee, S. McFeeley, and
J. Kirkwood. 1992. Mastectomy versus breast conservation surgery:
Mental health effects at long-term follow-up. *Health Psychology* 11:349–
54.
These researchers found that mastectomy patients surprisingly had somewhat
less emotional disturbance later than did those who had breast-sparing
procedures, in part due to obtaining more subsequent support from their
families.

Love, S. 1990. *Dr. Susan Love's breast book*. Menlo Park, CA: Addison-
Wesley.
Written by the director of the UCLA Breast Center, this is an outstanding
guide to the care of and diseases of the breast.

Moyers, B. 1993. *Healing and the mind*. New York: Doubleday.
Highly regarded television journalist Bill Moyers talks with experts in the field
of mind/body medicine. In this beautifully illustrated book, the art of
healing, means of self-regulation, stress reduction, support groups, mind/
body mechanisms, and Eastern medicine are discussed during Moyers's
typically skillful and probing interviews.

Rosenbaum, E. H. 1982. *Living with cancer*. New York: Mosby.
Wise guidance from an experienced oncologist about coming to terms with
and living well with cancer and its treatment.

———. 1980. *Decision for life: Portraits of living*. Palo Alto, CA: Bull Pub-
lishing Co.

A touching set of stories by an outstanding oncologist about how several of his patients lived fully with cancer.

Schain, W., B. K. Edwards, and C. R. Gorrell. 1983. Psychosocial and physical outcomes of primary breast cancer therapy: Mastectomy vs. excisional biopsy and irradiation. *Breast Cancer Research and Treatment* 3:377–82.

This study provided important evidence that the then new breast-sparing technique of lumpectomy provided important emotional help to cancer patients.

Simon, N. 1984. *Brighton beach memoirs*. New York: Random House.

How a cancer patient's family avoided using the word "cancer" as if the word itself were contaminated.

Sontag, S. 1978. *Illness as metaphor*. New York: Farrar, Straus, Giroux.

A forceful argument by a writer who had cancer about the special mythology surrounding the disease. She points out that there was a similar mythology about tuberculosis—that it resulted from frustrated passion—which evaporated when the cause and treatment were discovered. She predicts the same for cancer, having little patience with the "myth" that cancer results from frustrated anger.

Spiegel, D. 1992. Conserving breasts and relationships. *Health Psychology* 11:347–48.

In this editorial I review the literature suggesting that social support may have more to do with emotional adjustment to cancer than the type of surgical treatment.

Spiegel, D., and T. Wissler. 1986. Family environment as a predictor of psychiatric rehospitalization. *American Journal of Psychiatry* 143:56–60.

Spiegel, D., J. R. Bloom, and E. Gottheil. 1983. Family environment of patients with metastatic carcinoma. *Journal of Psychosocial Oncology* 1:33–44.

Studies of families of patients with mental and physical illnesses in which we show that family support, especially expressiveness—open and shared problem solving—leads to better patient adjustment.

9. Suicide: The False Escape

Gonda, T. A., and J. E. Ruark. 1984. *Dying dignified: The health professional's guide to care.* Menlo Park, CA: Addison-Wesley.
A clearly written and sensitive guide to helping the terminally ill.

Humphrey, D. 1991. *Final exit.* New York: Hemlock Society.
This book was written as a how-to guide for people who wish to commit suicide. Humphrey conveys the false idea that ending your life puts you in control of death.

10. Dealing with Doctors

Fallowfield, L., A. Hall, G. Maguire, and M. Baum. 1991. Psychological outcomes of different treatment policies in women with early breast cancer outside a clinical trial. *British Medical Journal* 301:575–80.

Levy, S. R. Herberman, J. Lee, M. Lippman, and T. d'Angelo. 1989. Breast conservation versus mastectomy: Distress sequelae as a function of choice. *Journal of Clinical Oncology* 7:367–75.
These studies demonstrated that the type of treatment (lumpectomy versus mastectomy) was less important in determining psychological outcome than was the patient's ability to participate in the decision about the type of treatment. Those helped to choose by their doctor did better than those who were simply told what to do.

Love, S. 1990. *Dr. Susan Love's breast book.* Menlo Park, CA: Addison-Wesley.
Written by the director of the UCLA Breast Center, this is an outstanding guide to the care of and diseases of the breast.

Rosenbaum, Edward. 1988. *A taste of my own medicine.* New York: Random House.
A doctor movingly describes his difficult transition to patienthood after he was diagnosed with cancer. The story was made into the highly regarded movie *The Doctor.*

Slevin, M., L. Stubbs, H. Plant, P. Wilson, W. Gregory, P. Armes, and S. Downer. 1990. Attitudes of chemotherapy: Comparing views of patients with cancer with those of doctors, nurses, and general public. *British Medical Journal* 300:1458–60.

This study showed that doctors are even more unlikely to accept risks of treatment than are their patients.

Steptoe, A., I. Sutcliffe, B. Allen, and C. Coombes. 1991. Satisfaction with communication, medical knowledge, and coping style in patients with metastatic cancer. *Social Science in Medicine* 32:627–32.
A survey of the relationship between better communication of medical knowledge and better patient's coping with illness.

Ullrich, A., and P. Fitzgerald. 1990. Stress experienced by physicians and nurses in the cancer ward. *Social Science in Medicine* 31:1013–22.
A study of the significant stress experienced by health caregivers.

11. Controlling Pain

Ahles, T. A., E. B. Blanchard, and J. C. Ruckdeschel. 1983. Multidimensional nature of cancer-related pain. *Pain* 17:277–88.
This article points out that there are many components to cancer-related pain, some involving physical, and some emotional, factors.

Beecher, H. K. 1956. Relationship of significance of wound to pain experienced. *JAMA* 161:1609–16.
In this classic article, Dr. Beecher, an anaesthesiologist at the Massachusetts General Hospital, demonstrated that the meaning of pain influenced its severity more than the extent of the injury.

Bond, M. R. 1973. Personality studies in patients with pain secondary to organic disease. *Journal of Psychosomatic Research* 17:257–63.
Bond, M. R., and I. B. Pearson. 1969. Psychological aspects of pain in women with advanced cancer of the cervix. *Journal of Psychosomatic Research* 13:13–19.
These early studies demonstrated that there is a strong relationship between pain and emotional disturbance in medically ill individuals.

Bonica, J. 1990. Evolution and current status of pain programs. *Journal of Pain Symptom Management* 5:368–74.
In this article, Dr. Bonica, a noted authority on pain, reviews the factors that contribute to pain and points out that while pain is more common in cancer patients with advanced disease, it does not always occur.

Brose, W., and D. Spiegel. 1992. Neuropsychiatric aspects of pain management. 1992. In *The American Psychiatric Press textbook of neuropsychiatry*. Eds. S. C. Yudofsky and R. E. Hales. Washington: American Psychiatric Press.

A review of the pharmacological and psychological management of pain.

Esdaile, J. 1957. *Hypnosis in medicine and surgery*. New York: Julian Press, reprint.

In this classic book, Esdaile, a Scottish surgeon, reported on the successful use of hypnosis in controlling pain during major surgery in India.

Fordyce, W. E., and J. C. Steger. 1979. Chronic pain. In *Behavioral Medicine*. Eds. O. F. Pomerleau and J. P. Brady. Baltimore: Williams & Wilkins.

In this article, the authors describe how social contact can reinforce rather than reduce pain.

Hilgard, E. R., and J. R. Hilgard. 1975. *Hypnosis in the relief of pain*. Los Altos, CA: William Kaufmann, Inc.

In this book, the husband-and-wife team review clinical and laboratory evidence that hypnosis is effective in helping people reduce pain.

Klein, K. B., and D. Spiegel. 1989. Modulation of gastric acid secretion by hypnosis. *Gastroenterology* 96:1383–87.

In this study we found that hypnosis could be used to increase or decrease substantially the secretion of acid in the stomach, depending on the type of image (food versus relaxation) concentrated on in hypnosis.

Kuhn, C. C., and W. A. Bradnan. 1979. Pain as a substitute for fear of death. *Psychosomatics* 20:494–95.

A woman with advanced cancer suffered intractable pain until she was able to discuss her disease directly with her adolescent son.

LeBaron, S., and L. Zeltzer. 1982. Behavioral treatment for control of chemotherapy-related nausea and vomiting in children and adolescents with cancer. *Pediatric Research* 16:208.

A controlled trial showing that behavioral treatment results in significant reduction of nausea and vomiting secondary to chemotherapy in children.

Melzack, R. 1982. Recent concepts of pain. *Journal of Medicine* 13:147–60.

This review article by a noted pain expert and originator of the gate control theory of pain notes that the intensity of pain may be modified by inputs from higher centers in the brain, making it understandable how techniques such as hypnosis, which alter attention, could modify pain perception.

Morgan, A. H., and E. R. Hilgard. 1973. Age differences in susceptibility to hypnosis. *International Journal of Clinical and Experimental Hypnosis.* 21:78–85.
This study shows that children are, as a group, more hypnotizable than adults, and that hypnotic ability is a stable trait in adult life.

Morrow, G. R. 1984. Methodology in behavioral and psychosocial cancer research. The assessment of nausea and vomiting. Past problems, current issues, and suggestions for future research. *Cancer* 53 (10 Suppl):2267–80.
This article by a noted expert in the behavioral management of chemotherapy side-effects reviews the evaluation and treatment of nausea and vomiting.

Pilowski, I., C. R. Chapman, and J. J. Bonica. 1977. Pain, depression and illness behavior in a pain clinic population. *Pain* 4:183–92.
This study demonstrates a strong connection between pain and depression.

Spiegel, D. 1987. The healing trance. Mar./Apr., *The Sciences,* 35–41. Reprinted 1989 in *Psychology 89/90.* Eds. M. G. Walraven and H. E. Fitzgerald. Guilford, Conn.: Dushkin.
Spiegel, D. 1992. Hypnosis: brain basis. In *Neuroscience year: Supplement 2 to the encyclopedia of neuroscience.* Eds. B. Smith and G. Adelman. Boston: Birkhauser.
———. 1988. Hypnosis. In *American Psychiatric Press textbook of psychiatry.* Eds. R. E. Hales, S. C. Yudofsy, and J. A. Talbott. Washington, D.C.: American Psychiatric Press.
Spiegel, D., and H. Spiegel. 1985. Hypnosis. *Comprehensive textbook of psychiatry IV.* Eds. H. I. Kaplan and B. J. Sadock. New York: Williams & Wilkins.
———. 1984. Hypnosis in psychotherapy. In *The psychiatric therapies. Report of the American Psychiatric Association Commission on Psychiatric Therapies.* Washington, D.C.: American Psychiatric Association.

Spiegel, H., and D. Spiegel. 1978. *Trance and treatment: Clinical uses of hypnosis.* New York: Basic Books. Reprinted 1987. Washington, D.C.: American Psychiatric Press.
What hypnosis is and is not.

Spiegel, D. 1986. Oncological and pain syndromes. In *American Psychiatric Association annual review, vol V.* Eds. R. H. Hales and A. Francis. Washington, D.C.: American Psychiatric Association Press.

————. 1981. The role of self-hypnosis in the management of chronic pain. In *Pain control: Practical aspects of patient care.* Ed. L. C. Mark. New York: Masson.

————. 1985. The use of hypnosis in controlling cancer pain. *Ca-A cancer journal for clinicians* 35:221–31. Reprinted 1986 in *Australian Journal of Clinical Hypnotherapy and Hypnosis* 7:82–99.

Spiegel, D., and J. R. Bloom. 1983. Group therapy and hypnosis reduce metastatic breast carcinoma pain. *Psychosomatic Medicine* 45:333–39.

————. 1983. Pain in metastatic breast cancer. *Cancer* 52:341–45.

Spiegel, D., and S. Sands. 1988. Pain management in the cancer patient. *Journal of Psychosocial Oncology* 6:205–16.
Uses of hypnosis in managing pain.

Spiegel, D., P. Bierre, and J. Rootenberg. 1989. Hypnotic alteration of somatosensory perception. *American Journal of Psychiatry,* 146:749–54.

Spiegel, D., S. Cutcomb, C. Ren, and K. Pribram. 1985. Hypnotic hallucination alters evoked potentials. *Journal of Abnormal Psychology* 94:249–55.
Studies from our laboratory showing that hypnotic alteration of perception is accompanied by measurable changes in brain responses to stimuli.

Spiegel, D., and L. Albert. 1983. Naloxone fails to reverse hypnotic alleviation of chronic pain. *Psychopharmacology* 81:140–43.
In this study we found that endogenous opiates such as endorphins and enkephalins are not involved in hypnotic analgesia.

Woodforde, J. M., and J. R. Fielding. 1970. Pain and cancer. *Journal of Psychosomatic Research* 14:365–70.
An early study showing that mood disturbance complicates pain in cancer patients.

Zeltzer, L., and S. LeBaron. 1983. Hypnosis and nonhypnotic techniques for reduction of pain and anxiety during painful procedures in children and adolescents with cancer. *Journal of Pediatrics* 101:1032–35.

Zelter, L., S. LeBaron, and P. M. Zeltzer. 1984. The effectiveness of behavioral intervention for reduction of nausea and vomiting in children and adolescents receiving chemotherapy. *Journal of Clinical Oncology.* 2:683–90.

Two randomized trials showing the effectiveness of hypnosis in controlling cancer symptoms among children.

Index

Bonneterre, J., 286
Bovard, E. W., 286
Bovbjerg, D., 286
brain, 87–88
   see also mind/body connection
brain electrical activity mapping
   (BEAM), 252
breast cancer, metastatic, 12, 110–11
Brighton Beach Memoirs, 185, 301
Broder, Samuel, 97
Brose, W., 304
Bugenthal, James, 168, 296, 298
Bukberg, J., 277
Burish, Thomas, 56, 280

Cambridge Hospital, 71
cancer
   acknowledging, 8, 9, 117–18
   as chronic illness, 12, 46, 110–11
   coping resource list, 163–65
   curing vs. coping with, 97–98, 104–
      5, 227, 228–29, 275
   double taboo about, 185
   vs. heart disease, 48, 51–52
   in Japanese culture, 232
   learning about, 24–25, 181–85
   and life expectancy, 4–5
   metastatic, 12, 110–11
   mythology of, 185
   pain in, 143, 243, 249
   and "patient" label, 29–30, 117
   and personality styles, 51–52
   and psychosocial support
      (summary), 273–74
   and sexual feelings, 197–200
   Simonton statistics, 69–70
   speaking about, 185–86, 190
   statistics, 4, 10
   survival predictions, 24, 32–34
*Cancer Stories: Creativity and Self-
   Repair*, 299
Caplan, G., 295
careers, 175–76
caring
   in health care, 227–29, 273
   in relationships, 192
   in support groups, 119–20
Case Western Reserve, 52
Cassileth, Barrie, 56, 279

chemotherapy
   and support group participation,
      90–91
   using hypnosis in, 270–71
children, in families with illness, 189,
   209–13
chronic illness, cancer as, 46, 110–11,
   228
chronic pain, *see* pain
comforting vs. curing, 227–29
common bond, in support groups,
   110, 111, 115–20
communicating
   about body image, 194–97
   about sex, 197–200
   in families, 186–204
   styles of men vs. women, 192–93
   "the unspeakable," 185–86, 190
control
   aspects of, 6
   and collaborative doctor-patient
      relationship, 235–41
   degrees of, 61
   over cause of cancer, 60, 104
   over course of illness, 60
   over living, 8, 64, 86
coping styles, 38–40
corticosteroids, 94–95
corticotropin releasing factor (CRF),
   93
cortisol, 62, 92, 93, 94
couples, *see* spouses
Cummings (Nathan S.) Foundation, 12
curing vs. coping with illness, 104–5,
   227–29, 275
cytokines, 96
cytotoxicity, 85

The Damocles Syndrome, 279
Davidson, Ann, 218
death
   addressing head-on, 142–46
   anxiety about, 127–33, 148–54,
      189–92
   comprehending, 133–35
   denial of, 125–26, 186
   and detoxification of dying, 136–38
   discussion in other cultures, 185–86
   "doing," 205–7